# AT THE HEART OF ENGLISH CRICKET

## The life and memories of Geoffrey Howard

**Stephen Chalke**

**with illustrations by Susanna Kendall**

**and a foreword by Scyld Berry**

FAIRFIELD BOOKS

Fairfield Books
17 George's Road, Fairfield Park, Bath BA1 6EY
Tel 01225-335813



First published 2001

ISBN 0 9531196 4 5

Printed and bound in Great Britain by
Bookcraft Ltd, Midsomer Norton, Bath

in memory of

**Nora Howard**

without whom the story of this book
would not have been possible

*Anyone of any distinction at all should, on reaching a certain age,*
*be taken away for a weekend at the state's expense, formally*
*interviewed and stripped of all their recollections.*

Alan Bennett

## CONTENTS

## ILLUSTRATIONS

The line drawings in this book are by Susanna Kendall.

The photographs are mostly from Geoffrey Howard's own collection. Many of them are taken with his own camera; others have been given to him. If any photographic source believes that it owns a copyright on any of these, it should contact the publisher to rectify the matter.

# FOREWORD

## by Scyld Berry

*Cricket Correspondent of The Sunday Telegraph*

We are all too good at taking things for granted. Parisians are reputed never to go up the Eiffel Tower. English cricket takes its past – the richest-playing past of any country – for granted, too. We have no national archive, no museum outside Lord's, no university which studies our game. Only when one of our great cricketers dies, taking his recollections with him, do we appreciate the significance of the loss – and then momentarily. We take it for granted that English cricket has plenty more heroes still around and don't do enough to preserve our past.

This book makes a most welcome and wonderful exception to the rule. Geoffrey Howard was probably the most informed witness of English cricket over a generation, from post-war to pre-Packer. He managed – and in every sense 'managed' – England's 1951-52 tour of India, Pakistan and what is now Sri Lanka. He managed the 1954-55 tour of Australia and New Zealand, with a party which included perhaps the most remarkable array of characters ever assembled in England caps. He was the man at the centre of the Peshawar incident in 1956 when Britain and Pakistan came close to a diplomatic crisis. He was Lancashire's secretary at the time of Laker's Test at Old Trafford in 1956, and Surrey's secretary when county cricket realised that it had to innovate to survive. He talked to, or rather listened to, Jack Hobbs and Sydney Barnes, signed for 100 bottles of champagne on the night England won the Ashes in Adelaide in 1955, and devised coloured clothing for one-day cricket in the early 1970s.

"Do you know Geoffrey?" John Woodcock would say if there was some detail of English cricket which *The Times* could not recall. "You really ought to meet Geoffrey." And being young and careless I never got round to it until Mr Howard was pushing ninety. Only then did I realise that he has been a unique witness – not only that but such an unbiased and sensible one. One or two cricket administrators have been known as pompous, egocentric, aloof, disorganised, insensitive and bigoted – and Geoffrey is the complete opposite. There are not many people like him, in fact, in the cricket world.

This book therefore makes one of the most valuable documents in English cricket history. Australian cricket, ahead of us at almost every stage, is clever at using its past to inspire the present and promote the future. English cricket must learn to make the most of its past as well, if it is ever to be fulfilled. To this end, you really ought to meet Geoffrey.

# INTRODUCTION

I first encountered the name Geoffrey Howard when I was writing *Runs in the Memory*, a book about county cricket in the 1950s. Dennis Brookes shared with me his memories of captaining the Northamptonshire side at Old Trafford in 1953, with Frank Tyson at his fastest wanting to demonstrate what Lancashire had missed in rejecting him. Tyson's letter of rejection had been signed by the secretary, Geoffrey Howard, and the first wicket Tyson took in the match was that of the Lancashire captain Nigel Howard. I looked up Nigel in Bill Frindall's *England Test Cricketers*, and there it was: 'His father was the county secretary and the manager of M.C.C. tours.' Frank Tyson had got his revenge by bowling the secretary's son.

Alas he had not, and a reviewer was quick to point out my mistake. I had confused Geoffrey Howard with his predecessor Rupert and, though I was not the first to make this mistake, I was quietly relieved when the book sold out and I could remove my howler from the reprint.

Then at the start of this year I received a telephone call from Scyld Berry, cricket correspondent of the *Sunday Telegraph*, asking me if I would like to conduct a series of interviews with Geoffrey so that his memories could be stored on tape for posterity. I was about to embark on another project, but something about the idea intrigued me.

First, there was Geoffrey's great age, almost 92. Oral history is a kind of archaeology, and with his memory I would be digging further back in time than I had previously done. He had watched Jack Hobbs in 1919; he had played for Middlesex in 1930. Secondly, as an administrator and tour manager, he had been at the heart of so much of English cricket in the first thirty years after the war. He had been in Len Hutton's bedroom when the England captain would not get up for the Melbourne Test; he had received the phone call from the South African Prime Minister's office after Basil d'Oliveira's century at The Oval. Thirdly, and not least, there was Scyld's enthusiasm. Geoffrey was a special man, he kept telling me. He was the best administrator in the history of the game. His testimony should not be lost.

At the end of January Scyld drove me to Geoffrey's house in Nailsworth, and between the three of us we decided that the project should go ahead. Derek Newton, a past chairman of Surrey, would provide whatever support we needed, and Geoffrey impressed upon me his greatest concern: 'The clock is ticking, you know. I haven't got much time.'

Since then we have been meeting every week. I drive from my home in Bath, up the A46, and we sit down in his front room with a cup of coffee and see what we can draw out of his memory. It is an activity best undertaken in short sessions, and many times I have left him so tired that he has slept for the afternoon. "My brain has just been milked by my amanuensis," he told me one day, paraphrasing John Milton. But, as the weeks went by, I began to accumulate a cornucopia of stories, and I grew confident that my ambition to turn it all into a book could be realised.

The greatest joy came when we discovered in his back room a box of letters which he had written to his wife Nora during his three winters away managing M.C.C. tours. Almost every day he wrote to her, and that enabled me to understand the tours as a daily journey before hindsight turned them into a completed experience. The cricket was only a part of it, especially in India and Pakistan where he observed with fascination the newly independent countries.

When summer arrived, we decided to go out and meet some of the people who could provide additional memories. I drove Geoffrey to Radlett, where we met up with Donald Carr, who had been with him on both of the tours to the East, and to Edgbaston where we ate a picnic lunch in the committee room with two of his former employees at Old Trafford, Rose FitzGibbon and Sheila Delve. I drove him to Longparish, to share memories of Australia with John Woodcock of *The Times*, and to The Oval, where Derek Newton, Bernie Coleman and Micky Stewart talked about his later years there.

All the while, I read around the various episodes of his life, so that his own testimony would fit into a fuller narrative. The Australian tour has been extensively chronicled, with fourteen books appearing the following summer and only Bob Appleyard of the England side not yet the subject of a biography. The full stories of the other two tours, however, have never been told, and, particularly for the one in Pakistan, I wanted to place the events there in a proper historical context.

For Geoffrey's years of administration I have aimed to provide the flavour of his working life, the personalities he dealt with and the issues with which he had to contend. At times, as in all places of work, there were conflicts and difficulties, and I hope that I have reflected them fairly. It is all a long time ago now, and this is not a book that sets out to sell copies by creating scandal.

Geoffrey has been a delightful companion, giving me his trusting confidence at every stage, and it has not been hard for me to understand the tributes paid to him by people who had the privilege of working or touring with him. I hope that I have conveyed properly his breadth of vision, his sense of humour and – most of all – his humanity.

It is nine months since we embarked on this project, nine months which I have greatly enjoyed; now the task is complete. Happily Geoffrey's clock is still ticking.

Stephen Chalke
Bath, October 2001

NOTE
The narrative makes use of quotations from a range of sources. For clarity, in the tour chapters, I have used italics for the letters which Geoffrey wrote home. In the other chapters, I have used italics for quotations from contemporary newspapers and other publications.

## CECIL GEOFFREY HOWARD

| | |
|---|---|
| Date of birth | 14 February 1909 |
| Place of birth | 22 Asmuns Hill, Hampstead Garden Suburb, London |
| Wife | Nora Le Plastrier (1910-1995) |
| Marriage | May 1935 |
| Children | Frances (1939), Joy (1941), Ursula (1946), Rosalind (1948) |

| | |
|---|---|
| 1947-49 | Assistant Secretary, Surrey County Cricket Club |
| 1949-64 | Secretary, Lancashire County Cricket Club |
| 1965-74 | Secretary, Surrey County Cricket Club |

| | |
|---|---|
| 1951-52 | Manager, M.C.C. tour to India, Pakistan and Ceylon |
| 1954-55 | Manager, M.C.C. tour to Australia and New Zealand |
| 1955-56 | Manager, M.C.C. 'A' tour to Pakistan |

# CHAPTER ONE

# THE FIRST TEST

# BRISBANE

# NOVEMBER – DECEMBER 1954

What was Len Hutton thinking?

The 38-year-old builder's son from Fulneck, near Pudsey in Yorkshire, was the first professional cricketer to lead an M.C.C. side in Australia and, on an unusually cool morning at the Woolloongabba Ground in Brisbane, he won the toss and asked the Australians to bat.

Almost half a century later, Geoffrey Howard – the tour manager – looks back with bewilderment. "It's amazing that he worked it all out and put them in. I wonder how often, as a Yorkshire cricketer, he'd seen his captain win the toss and put the other side in. With uncertain bowling, too. He only had four bowlers, and he must have had doubts about Alec Bedser's fitness."

Jim Swanton was the cricket correspondent of the *Daily Telegraph*, and he was a traditionalist. He did not approve of Hutton as captain, did not approve of playing just four bowlers, not one of them a spinner. He certainly did not approve of asking Australia to bat. 'It was a sort of midsummer madness,' he thundered.

By the time the manager arrived by tram from Lennon's Hotel, the innings had started, and he took his seat to see Alec Bedser running in to bowl to the left-handed Arthur Morris. The England wicket-keeper was Keith Andrew, making his Test debut in place of a feverish Godfrey Evans. He stood up to the stumps, as Alec Bedser always demanded, keeping to him for only the second time in his life, and in Bedser's third over the ball caught the inside edge of Morris's bat and deflected sharply to Andrew's right. It was at best a quarter-chance, but it was not held. A day of misfortunes had begun.

Within the hour Denis Compton was chasing a ball to the boundary. He grabbed at the white picket fencing, lost his footing and slipped, his left hand becoming impaled on one of the rungs. With a broken finger, he was effectively out of the match, out of the next Test as well.

The day became scaldingly hot. Other catches were dropped, run-out chances were missed, and at close of play Australia were 208 for two. 'Upon Hutton will fall the odium of an unsuccessful gamble,' Jim Swanton wrote.

"At close of play on the first day," Geoffrey Howard remembers, "Len couldn't speak. He was so depressed. Alec Bedser happened to go by. 'What's the matter with you, Len?' he said. 'There's no bloody bombs dropping, you know.'"

*

What was Len Hutton thinking?

On the sea voyage out, he had avoided the deck tennis and the swimming pool, settling for a few quiet games of quoits and retiring frequently to his cabin. Geoffrey Howard saw his first task as manager to be to form a working relationship with the captain, and his letters home expressed his hopes and frustrations:

*27 September, Red Sea. We are all well and the party is beginning to knit together and look like a team. Len Hutton is still very reserved but is slowly opening out a bit. Unfortunately he is inclined to open out then shut again, and he is by no means an easy one to get to know. I doubt if he even knows himself.*

*6 October, between Aden and Fremantle. I hope I have made strides with Len. I think so. He is easy and difficult, chatty and reserved – a whole host of opposites. An Enigma in fact. I think he will do well. Swanton thinks he will not, but by golly I hope he is wrong. It is so important to us that he should get going quickly and on the right foot.*

The first challenge was the press conference when they landed.

Back in the Coronation Summer of 1953 England had regained the Ashes in a rain-affected series by holding on for four draws, then winning at The Oval. So this was the first M.C.C. side to arrive in Australia as holders of the Ashes since 1928.

"I can see the headline in Perth," Geoffrey Howard remembers. "HERE THEY COME – THE BLOKES WHO HAVE GOT 'EM."

*Left to right, standing: Harold Dalton, Colin Cowdrey, Johnny Wardle, Brian Statham, Tom Graveney, Bob Appleyard, Vic Wilson, Jim McConnon, Frank Tyson, Peter Loader, Keith Andrew, George Duckworth. Sitting: Reg Simpson, Godfrey Evans, Peter May, Len Hutton, Geoffrey Howard, Alec Bedser, Bill Edrich, Trevor Bailey.*

The Australian journalists, quick to resent British snobbery, liked the idea of Hutton the professional captain – "it got him off the mark with a boundary before he opened his mouth," Colin Cowdrey reckoned – and in his cabin Len had decided to play back their questioning with self-deprecating northern wit.

"Noo, we 'aven't got much boolin'. Got a chap called Tyson but you won't 'ave 'eard of 'im because 'e's 'ardly ever played. ... Ah, yes, Lock and Laker. Aye, good boolers, but we 'ad to leave them behind. ... Batsmen? Well, we 'aven't got any batsmen, really. We've got these youngsters, May and

Cowdrey, but we 'aven't really got any batsmen. ... What it comes to is that we're starting out all over again. We're 'ere to learn a lot from you."

*Perth, October 12. Len is doing splendidly and is going to be a great success, I am sure. The Aussies are all for him. I am convinced of the wisdom of his choice as captain, and M.C.C. are to be congratulated. Quite apart from his many qualities both on and off the field, his tremendous skill and knowledge of the game give him a great pull with the players.*

His pull with the players increased when he sold the right to photograph them for £500. "He collected the fee and distributed it among them," the manager recalls. "I thought it was a dreadfully commercial thing to do."

*

The second day of the Test was just as hot. In John Woodcock's report in *The Times*, 'Thirty thousand spectators packed themselves shirtsleeve to shirtsleeve upon the slopes which climb away to the few low and isolated stands.'

The Australian batsmen accumulated runs remorselessly. Arthur Morris – according to Denys Rowbotham in the *Manchester Guardian*, 'in defence, all deference and civilised good manners; in attack, a hunter butchering his breakfast' – went on to 153, while Neil Harvey – 'not violent but perky, mischievous, puckish, his feet moving like quicksilver' – made 162. By close of play, Australia were 503 for six.

At Hutton's disposal, on a slow and even-paced wicket, were four fast bowlers, toiling wearily in the oppressive heat. On his previous two tours he had batted valiantly but in vain against the pace of Lindwall and Miller, and now he had hoped to exact his revenge with the youthful Tyson and Statham. He had Alec Bedser, the leading wicket-taker in Test history, and Trevor Bailey, his trusty all-rounder. All he could do was to perm two from four and to slow down the rate at which they bowled: 114 eight-ball overs in two full days.

"Len was pretty adept at keeping the overs down," his manager recalls. "He spent a lot of time placing the field. I can remember Lindsay Hassett protesting to me in the press box. 'This isn't the clean potato.'"

Alec Bedser was not at his best, 36 years old and still recovering from a debilitating attack of shingles. Frank Tyson had played just one full summer of county cricket, and in the heat he became so exhausted that he took to coming in off a shortened run. Brian Statham kept going best of the four, and Trevor Bailey created some chances with his shrewd cricketing brain. But there was no swing, no great bounce, and the England catching and throwing squandered several more chances, listed with precision in the *Daily Telegraph*.

'Thus England might have saved themselves much labour,' Swanton concluded. 'But the general shape of things was probably foredoomed when the wicket turned out so different from Hutton's hopes. All England's eggs were in the treacherous one basket.'

*

What was Len Hutton thinking?

He had rested himself from the warm-up match here in Brisbane against Queensland. He had already scored 469 runs at an average of 117, and he wanted an opportunity to think through his strategy for the Test.

Colin Cowdrey recalled his presence during the warm-up match: "He took a chair out to the front of the pavilion and watched every ball bowled without uttering a single word. They even brought drinks out to him, left them by his chair and departed without daring to disturb his concentration. Like those fourteenth-century generals, he was absorbing every factor, planning every move in the battle for which he had come across the world."

The conclusion of all that planning was that England selected just four bowlers for the Test – Bedser, Tyson, Statham and Bailey – with not a spinner among them. It was only the second time in 314 Tests that England had taken the field without a spinner, and on the first occasion – the second Test of the Bodyline tour – they lost for the only time in that series.

But there was a logic in his thinking. None of the spinners in the tour party had made a strong claim to be picked, and the wicket for the Queensland match had pace and bounce. Statham and Tyson had both been bowling well, Bailey was a key batsman and, though he was still getting over his shingles, it was surely unthinkable not to pick Bedser. The lower order had contributed few runs so an extra batsman seemed a safer option than a fifth bowler.

"When it came to picking the team for the first Test," vice-captain Peter May wrote thirty years later, "I would like to be able to record the thinking behind the decisions of the tour selection committee but, to the best of my knowledge, we did not have one. I imagine that Len picked the team after consulting those of us whom he thought might help."

From his chair Len Hutton observed the Queensland captain inviting M.C.C. to bat first, saw the life that their bowlers got from the pitch on the first morning. He could have played Bob Appleyard, that was what Peter May suggested, but his mind was made up. He wanted to bowl first, and Australia would undoubtedly choose to bat. So the spinner was a dispensable luxury.

The strategy was fixed, and the team was announced two days before the match.

It was all wrong. He had shown too much confidence in Bedser's recovery, he did not take stock when Godfrey Evans went down sick, and he assumed that the Test wicket would play in the same way as the one for the Queensland game. John Woodcock thinks that the early announcement of the team influenced the pitch preparation, but "I think that's very doubtful," Geoffrey says.

Len Hutton's strategy was wrong, and by the afternoon of the first day he must have known it.

E.W. Swanton's views were clear: 'It is asking an inordinate amount of four bowlers who take as much out of themselves as Statham, Bedser, Bailey and Tyson do, to bear the burden in an atmosphere as hot and humid as Brisbane, let alone to do so on a wicket which, as the match progresses, is liable to be more friendly to spin than anything else.'

*Swanton is very pompous and opinionated*, the M.C.C. manager wrote to his wife. *He is also pretty often right.*

*

It was not just the choice of Hutton as captain that caused Jim Swanton misgivings. He was also 'unable either to comprehend or condone' the managerial structure. On the previous Australian tour, when the gregarious amateur Freddie Brown was captain, there were two county secretaries sharing the managerial duties. Now, in Swanton's view, they had a professional captain ill-equipped for his diplomatic responsibilities and an inexperienced manager who knew nothing of Australia and who was being asked to cope without an assistant. 'The omission of a former Test cricketer to take his place at Hutton's right hand and to share the managerial functions is lamentable.'

He had not reckoned, however, with the efficiency and charm of the new man.

In Perth, where they played their first two matches, the manager visited the bank, only to discover that M.C.C. had neglected to make the necessary financial arrangements. Eight thousand miles from home, with the international transfer of money restricted and slow, he deployed all the charm he could muster to negotiate a flexible personal overdraft, with no limit. For six months he ran the whole tour from this account. Before he started to pay in their share of the Test match takings, his debt had risen to £20,000. "I don't think M.C.C. knew till I got back that they hadn't made any provision."

There were social functions to attend, and his letters home recounted how his Home Counties English was wrestling with the local dialect. *"My oath it was a big partee!! How are yer, son? Good? I'm right, thenks. How are you? Right, too." You won't know me when I start twanging away.*

By the time they were airborne for Adelaide, a local journalist Ray Barber was sending word of him on to the South Australians:

> Adelaide will like manager Mr Geoffrey Howard when he brings the M.C.C. team early tomorrow morning.
>
> In Perth he has been voted by officials as the best-looking M.C.C. manager to tour Australia and the most co-operative by English and Australian cricket writers accompanying the team.
>
> Mr Howard looks more like an English film star than a cricket manager.
>
> After playing for Middlesex 25 years ago, he became Surrey Cricket Club assistant secretary to Mr Brian Castor at The Oval.
>
> Since 1949 Mr Howard has been secretary of the Lancashire Cricket Club.

In a quiet moment the manager cut out and sent the piece to his father. Now, almost half a century on, it lies among his own collection of mementoes. Against the sentence likening him to a film star, he had placed two crosses, adding in pen on the attached sheet, *This chap knows his stuff!!*

Then in Melbourne, where rain washed away most of the cricket, he lost his golden image with the journalists:

*8 November. We had such a storm in a teacup last night. With yesterday's play lost, the Victorian Cricket Association asked me if I would agree to play an extra day, and I readily agreed to do so. Did the popular press howl at me – and why? Because it meant an alteration in their travelling arrangements – though few would admit it! They were quite childish. Jim Swanton was very much on my side, and I was grateful. They all hate him of course, but then they all hate each other.*

"That was a bit of exaggeration," he now says.

Jim Swanton, like Geoffrey Howard, had played three times for Middlesex before the war, though Swanton's appearances were limited to minor matches against the universities. Certainly, in the London club cricket of the 1930s, the manager had scored more runs than the journalist. "Jim didn't get into the school team when he was at Cranleigh, but he made himself into a useful batsman. He tried to bowl leg-spinners, too, but he wasn't really a bowler. In Perth, when we landed, we had some net practice and Len said to him, 'I wonder if you'd like to come and have a bowl. Our chaps are not getting any practice against leg spin.' Jim didn't fall for it, though. He realised he was being asked to make an ass of himself."

At Adelaide, Denis Compton joined the party. He had stayed on in London for treatment on his knee, and his journey had been eventful. His car and all his kit had been stolen the day before departure, then his plane had crash-landed in Karachi.

*27 October. Denis has just walked in. Poor chap – he has been through it. He's only had eight hours' sleep in four days and looks it! He arrived with two bulging suit cases but having left the keys at home!!*

"When we did get the cases open, all the kit he had was a pair of dirty boots, two gloves that weren't a pair and a bat marked F.TITMUS."

The decision was made to play him against South Australia two days later, and once more the manager and *Daily Telegraph* correspondent were at loggerheads.

*Jim Swanton at his most pontifical had severely criticised the action in playing Denis because of his experience at Karachi and the fact that he had some sleep to catch up: in fact it was <u>madness</u> to play him, etc etc. When Denis got to 50, I could hardly hold myself back from going along to the Press Box to say what about it! I refrained however and left him to decide how he would get out of what he had already written!*

Denis Compton's final score was 113. 'One heard with misgiving that Compton was going to be played straight upon his arrival,' Swanton wrote. 'It seemed to be asking a lot. However, Compton is no ordinary games player and, as things have turned out, it is no mean thing that Australians should have seen at the first opportunity so timely an expression of his genius.'

*

The Test matches in this series were six days in length, and on the third day at Brisbane Australia declared at lunch on 601 for eight, with the four main bowlers each conceding more than 120 runs. After seven long sessions of managing a fielding side that had dropped twelve catches, Len Hutton had just forty minutes to compose his thoughts and to summon up the intense concentration that was the great cornerstone of his batting. 'It is no good hiding the fact,' John Woodcock wrote, 'that through luncheon one had awaited England's innings with a cold feeling in the pit of the stomach.'

Against his old adversary Ray Lindwall, Hutton chopped the first ball of the afternoon through gully for four. But, before the over was out, he had repeated the shot and found himself caught at the wicket. 'There, as Langley threw the ball aloft, was the whole Australian side doing jigs and prancing around like children.'

According to Alan Ross of *The Observer*, Hutton was 'a lonely figure struck down by as many disasters as any overworked hero in Greek mythology'. In Jim Swanton's account, 'Back came Hutton, a stooping, downcast figure, and before his pads were off Simpson had been yorked and May bowled off his pads.' England were 11 for three. When Edrich followed within the hour, they were 25 for four. With Compton's broken bone, only Trevor Bailey and the 21-year-old Colin Cowdrey, making his Test debut, remained of the batsmen.

*29 November. A few lines written on the ground as we struggle against awful odds. It looks a bit hopeless though none will admit it. Poor old Len Hutton – after his sad ordeal in the field he was out in Lindwall's first over as you know. It is odd to think as I write that the thing will be history before you get it. ... What a grand lad the young Colin Cowdrey is – in every way. So modest, shy and pleasantly spoken. And what a fine choice he has been: the most criticised choice of all too!!*

In the last over of the day Cowdrey was caught at slip for 40 – 'an innings of considerable stature,' John Woodcock called it – and England closed on 107 for five. The deficit was still 494 runs. 'Things have gone wrong for England in many Test matches since the war,' Jim Swanton wrote. 'But one cannot remember them going quite so wrong as they have done this time.'

*I feel so sorry for the English public who will be so disappointed. We all do, but there is no end of fight in us and we won't let you down! We will struggle through somehow.*

*

It was the beginning of December. The people of Great Britain were looking forward to their first Christmas without meat rationing since 1939. The old age pension had risen by seven shillings and sixpence to two pounds, and there were plans for motorway roads and an independent television channel. With Everest climbed, the Ashes regained and the mile run in under four minutes, the new Elizabethan Age had started full of hope. An 18-year-old called Lester Piggott had won the Derby, and this England tour party had left Tilbury with high expectations.

After three days of this one-sided Test, the only comfort had been the promise of the young Colin Cowdrey.

*

At Tilbury, as the press gathered round the England party and sought interviews with the captain, Len Hutton slipped away to speak to Colin Cowdrey's father. "He drew him aside," Colin wrote, "and talked to him earnestly for twenty minutes. The tone of it, I gathered later, was that there was no need to worry. 'I'll look after him,' he reassured him again and again."

*Left to right, standing: George Duckworth, Tom Graveney, Peter May, Harold Dalton, Len Hutton, Bill Edrich, Charles Cobham, Bob Appleyard, Harry Altham, Reg Simpson, Vic Wilson, Alec Bedser, Geoffrey Howard. Kneeling: Jim McConnon, Brian Statham, Johnny Wardle, Keith Andrew, Colin Cowdrey, Godfrey Evans.*

Sixteen years earlier, it had been Colin's father, home on leave from India, who had passed on to his five-year-old boy the wondrous news that an England batsman had broken the world record by scoring 364 runs against Australia in a Test match. Now that batsman was offering to take care of his boy as he, too, set out in search of cricketing glory.

Three weeks later, when they arrived at the Palace Hotel in Perth, the telegram was waiting to say that Mr Cowdrey had died. Len sat at dinner that night, working out how to commiserate. "After the meal," Colin wrote, "he came round the back of my chair, put his hand on my shoulder and said, 'I'm sorry.' There were tears in his eyes. Then he walked away. I knew then that it had taken him a long time to work out how to react. He never mentioned my father again but from that moment he made certain that I was occupied every minute of the day."

At a golf match on the first Sunday, Hutton and Cowdrey were partners.

They shared a partnership of 127 against Western Australia, another of 163 against New South Wales where the youngster scored a century in each innings. Already it was clear that the selection had been a good one.

"I think that Colin excited Len," their manager recalls. "He thought he'd got a real winner. Not only as a player but as a person. Colin was the only one who gained the full benefit of Len's experience. Len was reluctant to say to somebody, 'You do realise, you're not getting your left foot near enough to the ball.' He wouldn't do that, however obvious it was. But if the chap said, 'What am I doing wrong, skipper?', he'd get the full treatment. And Colin would always ask."

His first innings in Test cricket – 40 patient runs in a crisis – was, in the words of Alan Ross, 'a warming proof of temperament'.

*

The fourth day went a little better. Though the first innings deficit was 411, at least Trevor Bailey batted brightly for 88 and showed that shots could be played – including one over long-on that won him a £100 prize for the first six of the match.

All was tense as Len Hutton and Reg Simpson opened the second innings. After forty-five minutes they were looking increasingly secure. 'The overs crept by,' John Woodcock wrote, 'and in the Press box there was a dreadful, brittle silence.'

They were batting for the draw but somehow, when Hutton nudged a ball that ricocheted away from third slip, Simpson called an impossible single and was run out by a yard. 'It was stark tragedy and when, a run later, the unhappy Hutton was leg before wicket to a beautifully controlled slow ball from Miller, one was resigned to the worst.' It was 23 for two.

Only once since the war had England won a Test in Australia – and that was at Melbourne in 1950/51 when Reg Simpson had made a dashing 156, one of the great innings of Ashes history. "I can't see how he can ever not be an automatic choice for England," John Woodcock said at the time. But Simpson's star had fallen under Hutton's captaincy – "He used to sit out with the crowd in the sun, which annoyed Len," Peter May recalled. "Len wouldn't sit in the sun, would he?" – and his dismissal here at Brisbane, needlessly run out, marked the end of his involvement in the series. "Mind you, Reg had little time for Len," Geoffrey says. "'Miserable bloody Yorkshireman,' he'd have called him."

Woolloongabba is Aboriginal for the meeting place of the waters, and it seemed that only rain could now save England. At least in the final session Bill Edrich and Peter May took the score to 130 without further loss, and that was enough for the Press box to agree that it was a better day.

*30 November. Last night I got caught up with Len Hutton – at a time when we least wanted it – in a dreary dinner party of Australians. All trying to be sorry for us which we did not greatly relish. We will be lucky to get a draw, with Denis out of it. Why do these things have to happen to touring cricket teams? You will all be so horribly fed up and disappointed – I could weep for you all – all of England.*

The list of misfortunes was long: Evans too ill to play, Compton injured in the first hour, the pitch misread, catches spilled, run-outs missed. The old Australian cricketer Jack Fingleton knew that England had not had their share of the breaks: 'Australia had more luck than they are entitled to expect for a whole series,' he wrote.

Denys Rowbotham was less inclined to use fortune as an excuse: 'Luck, as so often, favoured the strong.'

*

Shortly after four o'clock on the fifth day it was all over, with Australia winning by an innings and 154 runs. The pitch, for which England had selected four pace bowlers, was now taking turn, and Richie Benaud and Ian Johnson took five of the last six wickets to fall. After four days of large crowds, the ground was almost empty, and it fell to the M.C.C. manager to visit the Australian dressing room and present his congratulations to their captain, Ian Johnson, victorious in his first Test in charge.

"'Well played,' I said. And he spoke to me as if to say, 'Well, you didn't expect to win, did you? You may hold the Ashes, but you must know we're the better side.' I remember coming back to the dressing room and saying to Len Hutton, 'I just hope I don't have to do that again.'"

At Lord's, before departure, the tourists had been addressed by Charles, Lord Cobham, the M.C.C. president. "I want you all to go out there," he told them in the Long Room, "not thinking that you're playing cricket *against* Australia but that you're playing *with* them."

They were not words that came back too readily to the England cricketers as they packed up and left Brisbane. They were heading north to the Tropic of Capricorn, with a fortnight to forget this first Test, and the greatest challenge confronted their captain. 'His place in the assembly of cricketing immortals is secure,' Alan Ross wrote. 'But the next month will test fully his ability to inspire confidence in others. He has led, hitherto, largely by the example of his own prowess: now he will need to demonstrate similar qualities of resource off the field.'

The airmail editions of the British papers arrived before they left the hotel, and several members of the tour party stood in the lobby and pored over Jim Swanton's summary in the *Daily Telegraph* as, from separate doors, Jim himself and Len Hutton walked in. Under Swanton's arm was folded the *Daily Telegraph*. Colin Cowdrey told the story:

"One of the senior England players chose this moment to call out, 'Oh, by the way, Len, have you seen what the *Telegraph* said?' No one moved and the silence was total until Hutton eventually said, 'No, I haven't.'

"Slowly he walked across the foyer and removed the paper from under Swanton's arm. Even more slowly he unfolded it and turned the pages until he found what he was looking for. He absorbed what he was reading in his own good time, then re-folded the paper and handed it back. 'Yes,' he said with a twinkle. 'Yes, I've seen the *Telegraph.*' The general opinion was that he had been consulting his share prices in the stock-market columns.

"Len was smiling again."

LONDON LAUGHS (No. 6,066) *By LEE*

" Be awake half the night now, I suppose. Shouldn't read those horror-comics just before going to bed."

*

What was Len Hutton thinking?

He invited three of the team to his room – Bill Edrich, Brian Statham and Frank Tyson – and they each sipped a glass of ice-cold Australian champagne.

"He was far from disheartened," Frank Tyson wrote. "Next time we should hold our catches, and the god of luck would smile more benignly upon our cause. Less injuries and better catching and we should extend and beat Australia. Even at this stage Len Hutton had confidence in his fast bowlers and, as Brian and I listened, we realised that the series was far from over. The struggle had only just begun!"

Even Jim Swanton knew that there was all still to play for: 'Australia will be very much harder to beat now than they were before the series began. However, the match had its better auspices from the English angle. This rubber was always going to be hard to win; it certainly is not yet half lost.'

England had been beaten by an innings and 154 runs, but they were not convinced that their opponents were as invincible as they had seemed a few years earlier. Lindwall and Miller were ageing, and the batting – apart from Morris and Harvey – had weaknesses.

*1 December. Whatever the eventual result of this series may prove to be, I will not fear to say now that this 'Aussie' side is* <u>*not*</u> *a great one by any means.*

*

"Good old Nora, for keeping these letters all these years."

Geoffrey Howard is 92 now, living alone since the death of his wife, in the little house in the Cotswolds that he converted himself from a farmer's barn. In a box in the back room he had found the airmail letters that he wrote every day to his wife and four daughters in Altrincham.

"They were lovely letters," his third daughter Ursula recalls, "so exciting to receive. Sometimes he wrote specially to Rosalind and me."

*Left to right: Joy, Nora, Frances, Ursula, Rosalind (in front)*

Ursula was eight, Rosalind six, and Ursula remembers how the tears flowed after his departure. "We all sat around wailing, saying the ship would sink, we'd never see him again – all except Rosalind. 'What are you all crying about?' she said. 'He'll be back.'"

Forty-seven years have passed, forty-seven years since those six months when he exchanged his wife and four daughters for eighteen cricketers. The enigmatic Len Hutton, the fresh-faced Colin Cowdrey and the thoughtful Peter May, the carefree Denis Compton and the uncomplaining Brian Statham – they were his boys, and now so many of them are dead.

Yet he is still in good health, reliving the memories and handing me the bundle of letters. "I hope they'll be of some use to you. What surprises me is that I wrote all this stuff myself."

*

*3 December. I am very glad to leave Brisbane. It just did not suit us at all, and I got so fed up with the hotel. I paid the bill this morning. £1400 for 21 persons for 16 days!! Awful isn't it: I don't know how we can expect to see a large profit out of the tour with expenses as high.*

One by one the players reported to the manager to settle the bills for their extras, and he still recalls how the hard-living Bill Edrich followed the dour Johnny Wardle.

Wardle was a Yorkshireman, saving every penny for his wife and children at home, while Bill Edrich was riotously passing through a sequence of short-lasting marriages. "He was always chasing the girls. On the boat he formed quite a close attachment, and he kept in touch with her throughout the tour. I was in his cabin one day, having a few drinks, and there was a photograph of his wife. And he suddenly said, 'I hate my wife' and threw it out of the porthole. That was Bill.

"John Wardle's total extras were under a pound, and he disputed every item. 'I didn't have this bottle of milk,' he said. 'Somebody must have forged my signature.' It took me twenty minutes to get rid of him and, whilst I was with him, Bill Edrich appeared and sat outside. 'I'm sorry for you, Geoffrey,' he said when he came in. 'I wouldn't like to have your job.' 'Bill, you'd better stop being sorry for me and start being sorry for yourself. Because your extras are £45.' They were mostly phone calls to this girl he'd met on the boat. 'Oh, if you say so,' he said. He signed W.J. Edrich and walked out."

*

I opened the letter with care, and I started to feel that I was with him in the DC3 as they flew from Brisbane across the Great Barrier Reef.

*4 December. It was so fascinating. One reads of coral islands and there they were below us. Tiny islands – atolls mostly – standing in the middle of a lagoon with the most lovely shades of blue one couldn't imagine. White surf curling over in a ring all round it – they all seem to be circular – and outside the coral the deep, deep almost navy blue Pacific. We could not see the coral – over 2000 varieties – but I did see a great turtle roll over and over. There was even a wreck or two to fill in the picture a little. No words of mine can describe it.*

In a fortnight the second Test would start at Sydney. Only once in their history, in 1911/12, had England been to Australia, fallen a match behind and won the series. They had never come back from two matches down.

'They must do or die in this match,' Jim Swanton wrote.

The Ashes were at stake.

The success of the whole six-month venture hinged on the outcome of the Sydney Test – and what a Test it would turn out to be.

'Few Tests can have followed a more winding course,' John Woodcock declared in *The Times*, 'nor reached so great a climax.'

Or, as Frank Tyson put it at the end of his career, "It was the best game of cricket in which I ever played."

# AUSTRALIA v ENGLAND – FIRST TEST

Brisbane. 26, 27, 29 & 30 November, 1 December 1954

AUSTRALIA WON BY AN INNINGS AND 154 RUNS

## AUSTRALIA

| | | |
|---|---|---|
| L.E. Favell | c Cowdrey b Statham | 23 |
| A.R. Morris | c Cowdrey b Bailey | 153 |
| K.R. Miller | b Bailey | 49 |
| R.N. Harvey | c Bailey b Bedser | 162 |
| G.B. Hole | run out | 57 |
| R. Benaud | c May b Tyson | 34 |
| R.G. Archer | c Bedser b Statham | 0 |
| R.R. Lindwall | *not out* | 64 |
| G.R.A. Langley + | b Bailey | 16 |
| I.W. Johnson * | *not out* | 24 |
| W.A. Johnston | | |
| *Extras* | *b 11, lb 7, nb 1* | 19 |
| | (8 wkts, dec) | **601** |

1-51, 2-123, 3-325, 4-456, 5-463, 6-464, 7-545, 8-572

| | | | | |
|---|---|---|---|---|
| Bedser | 37 | 4 | 131 | 1 |
| Statham | 34 | 2 | 123 | 2 |
| Tyson | 29 | 1 | 160 | 1 |
| Bailey | 26 | 1 | 140 | 3 |
| Edrich | 3 | 0 | 28 | 0 |

## ENGLAND

| | | | | |
|---|---|---|---|---|
| L. Hutton * | c Langley b Lindwall | 4 | lbw b Miller | 13 |
| R.T. Simpson | b Miller | 2 | run out | 9 |
| W.J. Edrich | c Langley b Archer | 15 | b Johnston | 88 |
| P.B.H. May | b Lindwall | 1 | lbw b Lindwall | 44 |
| M.C. Cowdrey | c Hole b Johnston | 40 | b Benaud | 10 |
| T.E. Bailey | b Johnston | 88 | c Langley b Lindwall | 23 |
| F.H. Tyson | b Johnson | 7 | *not out* | 37 |
| A.V. Bedser | b Johnson | 5 | c Archer b Johnson | 5 |
| K.V. Andrew + | b Lindwall | 6 | b Johnson | 5 |
| J.B. Statham | b Johnson | 11 | (11) c Harvey b Benaud | 14 |
| D.C.S. Compton | *not out* | 2 | (10) c Langley b Benaud | 0 |
| *Extras* | *b 3, lb 6* | 9 | *b 7, lb 2* | 9 |
| | | **190** | | **257** |

1-4, 2-10, 3-11, 4-25, 5-107, 6-132, 7-141, 8-156, 9-181, 10-190
1-22, 2-23, 3-147, 4-163, 5-181, 6-220, 7-231, 8-242, 9-243, 10-257

| | | | | | | | | |
|---|---|---|---|---|---|---|---|---|
| Lindwall | 14 | 4 | 27 | 3 | 17 | 3 | 50 | 2 |
| Miller | 11 | 5 | 19 | 1 | 12 | 2 | 30 | 1 |
| Archer | 4 | 1 | 14 | 1 | 15 | 4 | 28 | 0 |
| Johnson | 19 | 5 | 46 | 3 | 17 | 5 | 38 | 2 |
| Benaud | 12 | 5 | 28 | 0 | 8.1 | 1 | 43 | 3 |
| Johnston | 16.1 | 5 | 47 | 2 | 21 | 8 | 59 | 1 |

Umpires: C. Hoy and M.J. McInnes

# CHAPTER TWO

# AMONG THE GO-AHEADS

## EARLY LIFE

## 1909 – 30

Let us go back to Monday the eleventh of August, 1919. To The Oval cricket ground in London.

Surrey, champions in 1914 when county cricket was last played, were playing Yorkshire, who were on their way to winning this first championship after the Great War.

Somewhere among the crowd that flocked through the main gates that morning were two young boys, travelling down from their home in Hampstead Garden Suburb. A ten-year-old Geoffrey Howard and his eight-year-old brother Donald. Anticipating their first sight of county cricket. Walking eagerly from the Oval underground station with their father and grandfather, towards the entrance where the Hobbs Gates now stand.

"We passed Bobby Abel's little stall," Geoffrey remembers. "At the end of the day, on our way out, my father stopped and bought me a bat. From Bobby Abel himself."

Bobby Abel – 'The Guv'nor' – was 61 years old by then, only three men above him in *Wisden*'s list of cricket's greatest run-scorers. In Sydney in 1892 he had opened the England innings with W.G. Grace and had carried his bat for a patient 132. But the young boy knew nothing of this. "He was just a small man with glasses, that's all I can remember."

Over a quarter of a century later, after another war, Geoffrey Howard returned to The Oval as assistant secretary, and in the Long Room there hung a photograph of Bobby Abel. "I remember Bert Lock the groundsman drawing my attention to the inscription under it. *'Surrey cricketer Robert Abel,'* it said. *'He was the father of four children and fielded at mid-on.'* That's all."

August 1919. Cecil Howard, his father, was the official shorthand writer for the Bankruptcy Court, following in the footsteps of his own father Ebenezer who for many years produced transcripts of parliamentary proceedings for Hansard. The day they went to The Oval, the stenographers at the Commons were recording the debate on a bill to check profiteering. "A consequence of war. Shortages create huge profits for the people who have got the things which are in short supply."

Elsewhere in the Commons, in a committee room, the Royal Air Force were demonstrating wireless telegraphy. A temporary aerial was erected on the roof of the House, and music played by a gramophone was transmitted from twenty miles away. *'The first piece,' The Times* reported, *'was taken from Tchaikovsky's 1812 Overture, and candour requires the admission that, though there was plenty of noise, there was little of music.'* There followed the song *'Take A Pair of Sparkling Eyes'* and *'some alleged poetry'*.

"I started myself some time after that. I made a wireless set with crystals, coils, bits of cardboard. I was picking up signals on a tiny coil of wire, the cat's whisker. I can remember sitting at home and shhh-ing the family so that I could get this faint sound of a human voice. 'Two L.O. calling.' From the BBC at Savoy Hill. It was so exciting."

So much change in one man's lifetime. "Think where we've got to in aviation. In the year I was born, Louis Blériot flew across the Channel for the first time and crash-landed on arrival. He only just made it."

Grandfather Ebenezer had often watched W.G. Grace in his prime. "Parliament didn't assemble till after lunch so he had mornings free to go to The Oval." He liked to tell his grandchildren of the day when he had seen the great magician Dan Leno playing in an exhibition match. "His bat had a trap-door in it and, when he played forward, he opened the trap. He was running up and down the wicket while the fielders were looking all over for the ball."

But Ebenezer Howard was more than a parliamentary stenographer with a passion for cricket. The social deprivation of Victorian London had been all around him in his childhood – "the city where wealth accumulates and men decay," one Home Secretary called it – and he spent his adult life developing ideas for a healthier and more humane urban environment. He set out his vision of slumless, smokeless cities in his 1898 book *'Garden Cities of Tomorrow'*, a work which rapidly established him as the founding father of the town-and-country planning movement.

Within five years of the book's publication, he had become managing director of the Garden City Association, developing the town of Letchworth in Hertfordshire. "It was a virgin site in 1903. By the end of 1919 they had a cricket club, theatre, museum, fire station, council offices, and on the perimeter all sorts of industry, even a factory that made the first tabulating machines. All those things had been developed in less than twenty years."

"He was not a masterful type," one colleague wrote, "but he projected an aura of benevolence, common sense and sincerity."

In 1919 Ebenezer Howard went with inadequate funds to an auction of land in Welwyn, and he persuaded the auctioneer to lend him the money necessary to bid successfully. He returned, trembling and in a cold sweat, but within a few years the second Garden City was inhabited. He raised donations from the rich and famous, including George Bernard Shaw who called him 'one of those heroic simpletons who do big things whilst our prominent worldlings are explaining that they are Utopian and impossible.'

"I remember holding Bernard Shaw's hand. I was uncertain who he was. I thought he looked like Father Christmas. And my grandfather knew Marie Lloyd. She lived near us in Golders Green. He pointed out her house to me. The music hall stars were such important people at that time."

*Oh, mister porter, what shall I do?*
*I wanted to go to Birmingham, and they've carried me on to Crewe.*

As well as the visit to The Oval, he recalls his first outing to the theatre. "It would have been during the war. We saw 'Peter Pan' one Christmas. 'If you believe in fairies, clap your hands.' How we clapped - and how we cried when Tinkerbell's light faded! Captain Hook was played by Gerald du Maurier, Peter Pan by a girl called Unity Moore. I'm sure I fell in love with her. But the odd thing was, I never heard anything of her acting again."

As they entered The Oval that day, they were part of a great crowd. "It was just the same in 1946. People had been deprived of cricket, deprived of entertainment. I think we sat at the Vauxhall end. I've got a memory of our stopping to watch the leading Surrey players in the nets. The seating was pretty rough in those days, uncomfortable and scruffy."

It was the hottest day of 1919, with the temperature in London reaching 91 degrees Fahrenheit. *'Experience on war service abroad,' The Times* reported, *'has taught large numbers of men the value of tinted glasses to protect their eyes from the glare.'*

Surrey won the toss and asked Yorkshire to field. *'Both Hobbs and Mr Knight batted brilliantly and made the attack, strong as it was, look perfectly simple.'* "I watched for what seemed like a long time. I saw Jack Hobbs out, but Donald Knight went on to a hundred. Wilfred Rhodes and Rockley Wilson bowled with enormous accuracy – so they proceeded at a very leisurely pace."

*Hobbs, caught Hirst, bowled Wilson, 41.*
*Knight, bowled Waddington, 114.*

"At lunch we walked around the perimeter behind the seats, as most people did. Because they've been sitting uncomfortably. We went behind the pavilion, and it just so happened, as we passed the players' entrance, Jack Hobbs was standing outside. He was wearing his M.C.C. touring cap and his blazer, as he always did. I got as near to him as I could, and I touched him. I just touched his blazer. He was obviously going to be a great hero of mine."

Cricket had cast its spell over the ten-year-old boy, though it was to be many years before the full consequences of that spell were realised.

"The next time I saw Jack Hobbs and Donald Knight together was in 1947, when I attended my first committee meeting as assistant secretary of Surrey County Cricket Club."

Jack Hobbs was already 36 years old in 1919, but he added 132 centuries to the 65 he scored before the war, the last at Old Trafford in 1934. "It was

George Duckworth's benefit match, and he persuaded Jack Hobbs to play as a favour, to attract a bigger crowd. 'I'll come and make a hundred, George,' he said, and he did. There are not many people in any class of cricket who could nominate a hundred at the age of 51."

May 1934. Hobbs, lbw Sibbles, 116. *'His innings began and ended amongst scenes of great emotion and support from the Lancashire crowd.'*

"Years later he told me that no one saw him at his best who had not seen him before the First World War."

Surrey versus Yorkshire, August 1919. 135 overs were bowled on that Monday, and the young Geoffrey rode home to Golders Green underground station with a new bat and a passion for this game of cricket.

Elsewhere in the crowd that day was another first-time spectator: a twelve-year-old boy who was also falling under the spell of the game. Ernest William Swanton.

*

Geoffrey was a happy boy at University College School, Hampstead, till the Christmas of 1919 when the great influenza epidemic brought the death of his mother, Bessie. "My father was so distressed, we never saw our house again. He closed everything up, and we moved to Letchworth Garden City. For a while we stayed with my aunt, then we took over my grandfather's house.

"My father made friends with the rector, whose wife had also died. He used to go across to the rectory for breakfast. He was the Reverend Gerard Kerr Olivier; he prepared me for confirmation. His son was Lawrence, but I never met him. He was away at St Edward's School in Oxford. Sybil, Lawrence's sister, acted in our school play. I played a Frog. I remember thinking she was a very beautiful girl."

By this time grandfather Ebenezer had switched his political allegiance from the Liberals to the Independent Labour Party, and the new garden city was full of radical thinkers and social visionaries. Theosophists, Quakers, Fabians; they all migrated there.

Geoffrey's school was St Christopher's, a child-centred experiment on the same lines as Bedales, and among his fellow pupils were Ralph Rowntree the chocolate maker's son, Ormonde the grandson of Lord Maugham, and Prince George Pushkin the son of a Russian émigré. The curriculum was largely a matter of choice, and subjects like mathematics took second place to handicrafts. "I learnt how to weave, how to repair boots and shoes, and I spent hours in the carpentry shop."

The close-knit family life of Hampstead Garden Suburb had been destroyed: his mother dead, his home moved, his father lodging in London during the week, leaving his brother and him to adjust to boarding school life, sleeping apart for the first time.

"We knew about the Lost Boys in Peter Pan. Now we were the Lost Boys."

What memories of school survive after eighty years? "On the first day we were picked up from Letchworth Station by the headmaster's wife in a pony and trap … The headmaster's name was Leighton. I can still feel his grip on the back of my neck … I had to be equipped with a lacrosse stick, but I never used it …I played cricket every available minute of the summer. I even used to sit in the elm trees and watch Letchworth's matches … We had a girl called Barbara Fenn. Bumpy Fenn, she was called, because she'd started to develop breasts. She got involved with a boy at the school and was expelled … How we used to look forward to Thursdays when it was fruit and nut and not burnt cauliflower au gratin … The forms were not numerically identified. I think I was in one called The Go-Aheads."

It was not a conventional upbringing and, through his long years of cricket administration, his quietly held political views were rarely those of his colleagues. "I never talked politics with cricketers. They are not really a tribe of thinkers about social conditions."

More than fifty years after his days in the carpentry shop, he retired to the Cotswolds and surveyed the disused cow shed next to his house. "I could make a cottage of that," he thought and, after five years of hard labour, he and his wife moved in.

When I arrived in the week of the general election of June 2001, I found a Labour Party poster in the little window beside the front door.

*

In 1920 there were two family outings to cricket in London. At The Oval they settled in the elevated seats in the East Mound Stand and watched the Surrey players take the field, followed by the Middlesex batsmen. "The first ball Jack Hearne got an edge and was caught at slip. He walked off, and the whole ground stood up and applauded him all the way back. He was 178 not out overnight, but I thought it was a very odd game."

Then on Tuesday the 31st of August they travelled by train to Lord's to see Middlesex play Surrey again. The championship programme was reaching its climax, with Middlesex needing victory to take the title from Lancashire. It was Pelham Warner's last match for Middlesex, and how the county's supporters longed that he would crown this ninth summer of his captaincy with his first championship title.

At four o'clock Surrey set off in pursuit of a target of 244, and at twenty past six their final wicket fell. The players carried Warner off, and the crowd began its celebrations. "I can see it as if it was yesterday. Plum Warner was up on the dressing room balcony, with his Harlequin cap on, waving to the crowd, and we were all over the grass."

In 1923 several of the Middlesex players were in Jack Durston's XI when they played Letchworth in a benefit match. "My father, my brother and I spent the whole week, with the groundsman, preparing the field. We had a side wheel mower with a box that tipped the grass out. I was only fourteen, but I played in the Letchworth team. I can remember going in late in the order. Fred Burton was bowling. A great Minor County cricketer. I scored this three, and somebody said, 'That's enough', and he bowled me out."

*Letchworth versus Jack Durston's XI, 1923*

*(Letchworth unless stated) Left to right, back row: Arthur Cuthbertson, George Redhouse, H. Goddard (Beds), Alfred Stark, S.J. Cook, A. Chadwick-Healey, Tom Diss, Leslie Garling, Alfred Webb. Next row: Parfitt (umpire), Unknown, Joe North (Middx), Unknown, Jack O'Connor (Essex), Unknown, Doc Gibbons (Worcs), P. Clarkson (Herts), A.C. Howard, P. Doult, Unknown umpire. Seated: J. Buckley (Beds), Unknown, Fred Burton (Herts), John Freeman (Essex), Jack Durston (Middx), Jimmy Cutmore (Essex), J.B. Wheatley (Middx), S. Fenley (Surrey), E.E. Denniss. On grass: Ernie Page (Beds), Geoffrey Howard.*

*"I think I've done jolly well to remember so many of them."*

By this time, his father had re-married, and he was at Alleyne's Grammar School in Stevenage, where his earlier years at St Christopher's left him at an academic disadvantage. "I struggled in mathematics but, when it came to carpentry, I was way ahead of them. I was having repeatedly to make cross-lap halving joints, which I'd done years before." He went on to captain the first eleven at cricket, where his headmaster reported, "He was capable, gentlemanly and able to hold his own."

Then a baby stepsister was born, and the change brought further upheaval.

"My stepmother was less than enthusiastic about Garden City life, our house was not big enough, and Father was tired of the daily rail journey into London. Also we were renting, and he was looking to buy and to settle."

In 1925 they moved to Edgware, a semi-detached house on an open field site developed by a local speculative builder. "Edgware in 1925 was little more than a village, almost rural, but it was ripe for development because the underground railway had just been extended from Golders Green."

For his father the journey into Holborn was an easy one, but life was harder for the two boys. "Donald joined Christ's College in Finchley, an impossible journey, and I had to accept a shift from schoolboy to unemployed school leaver."

The son of a court stenographer, the grandson of the great Ebenezer Howard. Even in those days of unemployment, there must have been openings for an intelligent sixteen-year-old with such connections. "My grandfather had plenty of influential and wealthy contacts, but he didn't believe in nepotism. And my father's influence was all in fields which he did not recommend. So I turned to the Situations Vacant and started writing letters."

Days at home with his stepmother and baby sister were relieved by the challenge of developing a garden and building a garage for "my longed-for motorcycle", when "suddenly out of the blue I found myself on the staff of H.K. Lewis and Company, medical publishers and booksellers." For six months he cut up and made ready the advertisements in the British Journal of Dermatology and Syphilis, with a monthly salary of £4 - 3s 4d. "Just a pound a week, but then in those days you could go to Lyons for lunch, get a cup of tea and a poached egg for sixpence."

In the offices at the Euston Square end of Gower Street, he shared a room with a director, R.J. Boothby, next door to the chairman's office. "I shall never forget the phone ringing one day when they were both out. It was the first time I had ever answered a telephone, and I was trembling with fear."

His father arranged him an interview for a job in banking, and in May 1926 he moved to Martins Bank in Lombard Street. He was never to look back to his time at H.K. Lewis till the day in the late 1960s when his secretary at The Oval brought in a message. "There's a Mr Boothby outside, wonders if you'd come and see him."

"All those years he must have kept his eye on me."

*

May 1926. "My first day in Lombard Street was the first Monday of the General Strike. My father arranged for me to get a lift in a private car to Marble Arch, then I walked. The Special Constabulary had a unit at Martins. I can see the chap now, reading the roll-call for the various jobs like driving the buses. 'Bromley-Martin,' he called out. Well, I knew Bromley-Martin was one of the directors. 'Where the bloody hell's Bromley-Martin?' 'I'm here, sir,' he said, rather quietly from the back."

Granville Edward Bromley-Martin, Eton and Oxford. He played cricket for Worcestershire at the turn of the century.

"People had no sympathy for the strikers, but I've always had a sneaking feeling for the underdog. We'd seen the Zeppelin that went down in flames in Cuffley in 1916. Ten or twenty crew and no parachutes. People all cheered, because they were Germans and they'd been killed, but my father and grandfather weren't like that. 'They're human beings as well,' they said. 'They have the same feelings.'"

At the outbreak of war his grandfather had even devised a plan to fly solo over Germany and drop a million leaflets calling on the German people to overthrow their despotic rulers. "A gorgeous notion," Bernard Shaw told him, "but entirely impracticable for a thousand reasons."

The miners stayed out till November, but the General Strike was over in a week and the 17-year-old settled down to his career in banking. "I wasn't good at maths at school, but it didn't ever seem to be a handicap." Others, who worked on the ledgers, looked after the figures. "There was a man at Westminster Bank. He would look down a ledger page with a big carry forward figure at the top and write the total at the bottom. As fast as your eyes could read the figures. And he wasn't alone in that. His brain was a computer." And outside work? "He drank fifteen or twenty pints of Guinness every night and died at the age of 40."

Martins was a private bank in the days when the City of London played host to many such institutions. "The entrants, the young people, all spent a year in what was called the Walks Department. We walked the City of London with cheques drawn on other private banks to collect on behalf of our customers. It taught me my way around. I was West Central One. I had the Moscow Narodny Bank on my walk, Credit Lyonnais, Banque Belge."

£90 a year, rising to £150 on his 21st birthday. "But I was very aware of the millions unemployed. When you got a job, with your employer making provision for your pension, it had a certain anchoring effect."

Martins Bank was owned by the Bromley-Martin and Holland-Martin families, but even their own sons began with a year in the Walks.

"The customer was all important. They could hand over their documents, their jewellery, anything, and the bank would look after it in the store room and make no charge. It was all part of the service. Now the customer is somebody to be milked. They even charge for writing letters and stopping cheques. But I suppose businesses have to change. They have to comply with the prevailing social conditions."

His local bank today is the HSBC in Nailsworth. "I was in there the other day, and the cashier was a girl, who had only just started. I said to her, 'I'd been in the bank four years before I was allowed to go to the counter.' In 1926 we had at least 200 people in the office, and only two were women."

In such a world of young men, it was inevitable that opportunities would arise to watch and play cricket. "I worked with a ledger keeper who used to manage to get down to The Oval for the start of play and stay there till lunchtime. He'd come out with a pass, which he gave to me so that I could go down in the afternoon. It was just five stations on the tube, and you were there.

"Martins Bank ran a side. We played matches over two evenings against other banks. And once a year we played our Liverpool branch. I remember playing on the Aigburth Ground at Liverpool, and I went out as runner for Granville Edward Bromley-Martin. 'You senseless arse,' he shouted. 'You'll run me out.'

"Then I was introduced to the Private Banks Cricket Club. The management didn't look favourably on you if you played for somebody else – not if they thought you were of any ability. Private Banks played at Catford, on wonderful wickets prepared by the old Surrey cricketer Fred Holland. He had three wickets to prepare for every Saturday, with his horse-drawn roller. He was a splendid chap. A real old professional. I remember being told off by the captain because I referred to him as Fred Holland. 'I suppose you mean Holland F.C., do you?'"

With five elevens in the field each Saturday, he started in the thirds and was playing for the first team by August. With a five-and-a-half day week ending at 12.30 on Saturday and the match set to start at two o'clock, "it was a struggle to get there in time, especially for some of the away matches, and you were lucky if you had any lunch. Some people cycled there with their cricket bag balanced on the handlebars or their bat strapped to the crossbar. But I ran for the train, and the first eleven had a van to deliver the kit." The cost of travel was not prohibitive, either. "Robert Holland-Martin was also chairman of the Southern Railway, and we could buy return tickets for eleven pence from an agent in the office."

Among his opponents that summer, when Private Banks played the Old Cranleighans, was the 19-year-old Jim Swanton. "At that time he was writing about schools cricket for the *Evening Standard* under the pseudonym Juventus."

August 1926. At The Oval Jack Hobbs and Herbert Sutcliffe scored centuries on a difficult wicket, and England won the Ashes for the first time since the war. That day Geoffrey Howard was playing at Blackheath during its cricket week. "Our captain was Horace Sercombe. He must have got me the day off. I wouldn't have dared ask myself. I can remember the news of England's victory filtering through while we were in the field, and Horace Sercombe signalled us to come into the middle. When we were all assembled, he gave three cheers for English cricket. I was so embarrassed. I think it was in that game that one of the Day brothers of Kent bowled under-arm at me.

"My life was almost totally devoted to cricket. I played evening matches in the week, half-days on Saturdays, whole days on Sundays, so I was always travelling home late to Edgware, often without a regular meal."

By the end of 1927 the family was moving again, this time to Bickley in Kent, where his father bought a site and had his own house built. "Father had always wanted to indulge his own rather eccentric ideas of the ideal home – so we had yet another virgin site to be turned into a garden. And this time we had to excavate the earth to create a sunken lawn."

*

Private Banks. Today they run just one Saturday side, most of their sports grounds sold to developers, but in 1926 there were five teams, with the first eleven containing several good enough to appear as amateurs in county cricket.

"It was the five-day week that killed the business house cricket. It started changing in the '50s. People went home on Friday evening, and they played for their local clubs."

The opening batsmen in 1926 were Tom Pearce and Arthur Childs-Clarke, both working for Brown, Shipley and Co. Tom Pearce was on his way to a long career at Essex, captaining them for eleven summers and scoring 22 centuries, while Arthur Childs-Clarke had already played for Middlesex and would return to first-class cricket in 1947 as captain of Northamptonshire. There was Ronnie Bryan, whose occasional appearances for Kent led to his taking a three-month sabbatical in 1937 to lead the county, and Dick Robertson from Coutts. "Years later, Tom Pearce said to me that, if Dick had had the same opportunities as Ted Dexter, he'd have played for England."

All the counties in the south had regular vacancies for good amateur cricketers. "When we went to watch Middlesex at Lord's in 1920, they only had five professionals." Essex had more vacancies than most. Tom Pearce, Tiny Waterman, the Midland Bank's Tom Smith, there was even one game for the Old Citizens' Cyril Hawker, later to become chairman of the Standard Bank and the husband of Tom Pearce's sister. "At one time, people used to say, 'Have you played for Essex this year?'"

Thirty years later Geoffrey Howard sat on an M.C.C. committee to clarify the definition of an amateur. "I was on my way to Lord's, and I bumped into 'Bill' Fender. 'I don't know why you have to have a committee for that,' he said. 'An amateur is a chap who says, 'I am available on that day and I will be playing.' Not 'if you pick me.'"

None of the bank cricketers played professionally. "There was a certain snobbery about that. The status of professional cricket was not that high."

In 1926 he made his first team debut. Then in 1928 Arthur Childs-Clarke left banking for the lead role in a touring production of R.C. Sherriff's *'Journey's End'*, and Geoffrey took his place as an opening batsman. "I can remember the first hundred I made. Nobody told me the protocol. I made about 120. When I came back, nobody clapped. I had to go and find out why. 'You get out when you've made 100,' they said. 'Let somebody else go in.'"

He was a young man, learning his way in life, and his colleagues at the bank introduced him to the entertainments of the capital. "When the bank closed, we would all go to the pub. Then somebody would say, 'What shall we do this evening?' At one time, I had seen every production in the West End – including first nights. And, if there was nothing to see at the theatre, we would go to the music hall: the Holborn Empire or the Alhambra in Leicester Square. I saw Max Miller a few times. The Cheeky Chappie."

*I'm known as the Cheeky Chappie.*
*The things I say are snappy.*
*That's why the pretty girls all fall for me.*

A colleague with a wealthy father introduced Geoffrey to his tailor. "I had a three-piece suit made that I had to pay for on credit. It was seven guineas, a whole month's salary. Imagine somebody today spending that much on a suit."

Cricket came first, though, in summer. "Whenever I got a chance, I nipped down to The Oval, to see really good players. Nothing to do with winning and losing. I saw Jack Hobbs, Wally Hammond, Don Bradman, and all around me were the people I played with in club cricket. We'd all gone down for the same reason. To see the best players. Just as I went to the theatre to see the best actors."

The BBC's first televised pictures would not be broadcast till 1935 so this was their only opportunity to study the masters. "I can remember watching Alf Gover bowling and being hooked regularly. In the same season he came down to play against the Private Banks, and he dropped one short at me. 'Here I go,' I thought. I didn't realise how much faster he was than the average club bowler. But I got some runs."

Then one Saturday the regular wicket-keeper was rushed to hospital with appendicitis, and he found himself taking over the gloves. "I did quite a lot of keeping in the years after that, and I loved it. I always stood up – but then we didn't have any Frank Tysons at the bank, though we did have some who were at least as fast as Alec Bedser."

*Private Banks Cricket Club, circa 1928*

*Left to right, back row: Geoffrey Howard, Clifford Black, Norman MacMillan, Dick Robertson, Bob Bryan, Malcolm Dawkins. Front row: Jack Murch, Tom Pearce, Eric Skinner, Gerald Foster, Gerry Horne.*

By 1930 his own chance of greater glory came.

"I played occasionally on Sundays for a wandering club, the Ferrets. They are long defunct now. They were run by a very enthusiastic chap; he had no idea how to play but he loved the game. We were playing Honor Oak Cricket Club, and because it was Sunday I was batting down the order. All the leading players – Tom Pearce and Hopper Levett among them – failed, and I went in and made a quick hundred. The captain of Honor Oak was W.T. Cook, the Surrey second eleven captain, and he asked me afterwards, 'Have you got any Surrey qualifications? If you have, you can come and play for me.' Well, I hadn't. I'd been born in Middlesex and lived in Kent. But I told my father and, because of his friendship with Patsy Hendren and Jack Durston, I got invited to go up to Lord's for a trial."

In the Lord's nets he faced Joe Hulme, the professional all-rounder who played soccer for England. "A lovely wicket to bat on. I found it so easy." Ronnie Aird, the M.C.C. assistant secretary, was behind the net and summoned him to his office. He was offered summer-time employment, for less than he was earning as a junior at the bank, and he declined it. "I didn't even discuss it with my father. I was so much enjoying the club cricket. I'd made so many friends. Friends for life, though I didn't realise it at the time. I enjoyed playing for the sake of the game. I didn't want to be a professional. I didn't realise then the extent to which professional cricketers enjoyed playing."

In June 1930 at Lord's, against Gloucestershire, he made his Middlesex debut as an amateur. Another Private Banks cricketer taking his fortnight's annual leave to play some county cricket. "Nigel Haig the captain took down the team sheet and gave it to the dressing room attendant for the printer. 'That's the team,' he said. 'Tell Joe Hulme he's twelfth man.' I felt awful. Here was I, pushing Joe Hulme out of the side. It did give me an insight into the life of a professional cricketer, that the captain could bring in an unknown amateur and leave out a seasoned professional with a cap."

It was many years before he met Joe Hulme again. "He couldn't remember it at all." It was what the professionals expected.

"I remember Ronnie Bryan telling us how, when he was captain of Kent, he called up Doug Wright from third man to bowl."

Doug Wright is the greatest back-of-the-hand bowler Geoffrey has ever seen. "I doubt if Shane Warne is as good. He bowls outside the leg stump, knowing they're not going to hit him. They play him with their pads. But Doug Wright, I can see him now. He bowled Tom Barling at The Oval with a googly, through the gate. Tom had made 100 and was looking to go on, he had a bat as wide as this table. He did the same to Lindsay Hassett. Unforgettable."

There they were in 1937. Ronnie Bryan, an amateur from the Lloyds Bank side, summoning Doug Wright, perhaps the greatest leg-break bowler in the history of the game. "Doug took off his cap, and he said 'thank you.'"

In the early years of the century these social distinctions were part of the way of life. "When I went to Old Trafford, George Duckworth told me stories about some of the old pros – like Dean and Cook, two great bowlers. They were unsophisticated, untravelled lads. They had to be sent back from the breakfast room in the hotel for coming down in braces, that sort of thing. They had to learn many of the ways of things from the amateurs."

By the middle of the century life had moved on. "The big difference between the professional and the amateur," Tom Pearce said, "is that the professional is better dressed."

By 1930, when Geoffrey Howard and his fellow amateurs went out from one Lord's dressing room and the professionals joined them from another, "you could feel the dichotomy was going to change."

Wednesday June the 18th. Middlesex, bottom of the table, versus Gloucestershire, the championship leaders. With the first day lost to rain, he was on the fourth day of his fortnight's annual leave when they started on Thursday morning.

Wally Hammond opened the batting for Gloucestershire. "I was a bit dismayed when Nigel Haig put me at extra cover. I'd seen Hammond hit nearly 200 at The Oval earlier that summer, and it was like he was firing cannonballs through the covers. I thought, 'What am I going to do?' But Wally batted for three-quarters of an hour and didn't hit the ball off the square. I don't think I even touched it. He was like that. A player of mood."

Later in the day, when the young Private Banks amateur came out to bat, there was a further surprise in store. "Beverley Lyon was the Gloucestershire captain. 'Take over for half an hour, Wally,' he said. 'I'm going for a hair cut.'"

This card does not necessarily include the fall of the last wicket.

2d. Lord's Ground

MIDDLESEX v. GLOUCESTERSHIRE.

(WED. no play), & THURSDAY, JUNE 18, 19, 1930. (Three-day Match.)

| GLOUCESTERSHIRE | First Innings | | Second Innings |
|---|---|---|---|
| 1 Hammond | b Durston | 6 | |
| 2 Sinfield | | 3 | |
| †3 B. H. Lyon | c Durston | 60 | |
| 4 Dipper | c Guise | 3 | |
| 5 Dacre | c Hendren | 95 | |
| 6 Neale | not out | 24 | |
| 7 Barnett | | | |
| 8 Stephens | Extras | 12 | |
| 9 Parker | | | |
| *10 E. T. Benson | | | |
| 11 Goddard | | | |
| Innings declared. | B , l-b , w , n-b | | B , l-b , w , n-b |
| | Total | 204 | Total |

FALL OF THE WICKETS.

1- 2- 3- 4- 5- 6- 7- 8- 9- 10

ANALYSIS OF BOWLING. 1st Innings. 2nd Innings.

Name. O. M. R. W. Wd. N-b. O. M. R. W. Wd. N-b.

| MIDDLESEX | First Innings | | Second Innings |
|---|---|---|---|
| †1 N. Haig | c Goddard | 17 | |
| 2 Lee, H. W. | b Goddard | 46 | |
| 3 Hearne, J. W. | c Benson | 10 | |
| 4 Hendren, E. | c Hammond | 7 | |
| 5 J. L. Guise | b Parker | 37 | |
| 6 G. C. Newman | lbw Parker | 9 | |
| 7 D. Russell | c Neale | 12 | |
| 8 Canning | not out | 21 | |
| 9 C. G. Howard | c Neale B Sinfield | 12 | |
| 10 Durston | c Neale | 15 | |
| *11 Price | c Sinfield | 0 | |
| | extras B , l-b , w , n-b | 6 | B , l-b , w , n-b |
| | Total | 185 | Total |

FALL OF THE WICKETS.

1- 2- 3- 4- 5- 6- 7- 8- 9- 10-

ANALYSIS OF BOWLING. 1st Innings. 2nd Innings.

Name. O. M. R. W. Wd. N-b. O. M. R. W. Wd. N-b.

Umpires—Huddleston and Denton. Scorers—Murrell and Bloodworth.

The figures on the Scoring Board show the Batsmen in.

Play commences at 11.30 each day.

Luncheon at 1.30 †Captain. *Wicket-keeper.

Stumps drawn 1st and 2nd days at 6.30, 3rd day at 6.

TEA INTERVAL—There will probably be a Tea Interval at 4.30-4.45 but it will depend on the state of the game.

GLOUCESTERSHIRE WON THE TOSS.

Standing so close to the bat at slip, Wally Hammond was the only professional to say much to him during that match. "Charlie Parker was bowling. I was an off-side player, and the ball was leaving my bat, which suited me. And Wally kept saying, 'You're doing all right.' Then I received a long hop from Reg Sinfield. I hit it up rather than down, and I was caught at deep square leg."

He still retains the scorecard where his Aunt Edith recorded in ink the detail of his dismissal.

*C.G. Howard, caught Neale, bowled Sinfield, 12.*

"I got a little round of applause from the members when I came in. I wasn't unhappy."

The next match was at Northampton where, after a long period of inactivity, Patsy Hendren came over to him. "Let's change places," he said. "You must be bored where you are." Immediately Jack Hearne sent down a full toss that the striker hit towards Geoffrey at deep square leg. "Suddenly I saw it in front of me, and I flung myself at it and caught it." *Wisden* called it *'an exceptional catch'*. "Patsy Hendren said he wouldn't have caught it."

The third and last match of his summer holiday was at Cheltenham. "I remember the coach stopping at Evesham on the way from Northampton and our eating some wonderful strawberries. Then we stayed at the Queens in Cheltenham. Just the amateurs. The professionals would all make their own arrangements. I dined with Nigel Haig the captain, and he invited Patsy Hendren and Jack Hearne to come over to the hotel and have dinner with us."

Dinner with the captain. "It was then that I discovered what had happened to Unity Moore, who played Peter Pan. She had married Nigel Haig."

Three matches, six innings, this was his full first-class career. The little round of applause at Lord's never grew louder, and he returned to the bank, to many happy years of club cricket, with never a thought in his head that twenty-five years later he would be at the heart of one of English cricket's greatest triumphs.

# CHAPTER THREE

# THE SECOND TEST

# SYDNEY

# DECEMBER 1954

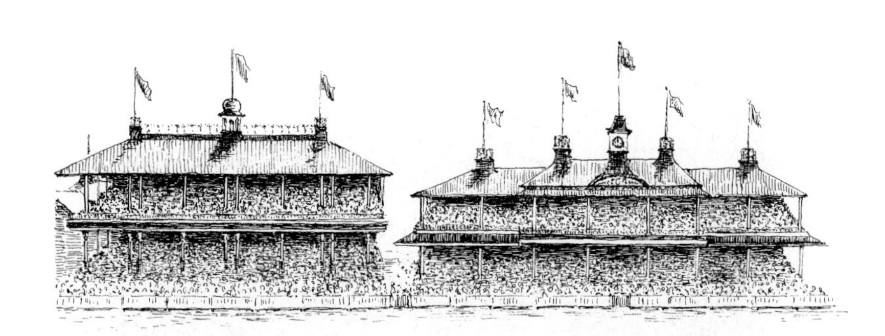

The second Test was due to start on Friday the 17th of December, and on Wednesday evening the M.C.C. tour party arrived at Melbourne railway station for the overnight train that would carry them the 500 miles to Sydney.

Since the end of the first Test in Brisbane, they had flown 340 miles north to Rockhampton for an undemanding two-day match against a country eleven, then 1,000 miles south to Canberra for what *Wisden* described as 'a gay charity match'. From there they flew south-west to Melbourne for their only serious contest before the Test, a match against Victoria. Now they were on the train, heading north-east to Sydney.

They had spent a night in the Oceanic Hotel in Sydney on the way from Rockhampton to Canberra, one of four hotels in four nights. Now they were beginning their final day of preparation before the Test by disembarking from an overnight sleeper and returning to the hotel.

Arthur Gilligan had captained M.C.C. in Australia thirty years earlier, when all the journeys were by rail, but he was not impressed by the arrangements made for Len Hutton's men. "In fourteen days between the first and second Tests," he wrote, "2,100 miles were travelled. It seems to me that there was far too much time spent travelling and not enough in practice."

At every stop there was baggage to be unloaded and re-loaded, hotel bills to be settled, local dignitaries to be greeted. It was a demanding schedule for the manager, and his fortnight was not made easier when in Canberra he developed a urinary infection that kept him overnight in hospital. "I had a tremendous urge to pee, but I couldn't do it. So they fitted a catheter and gave me a sleeping tablet." In the middle of the night he dreamt of his wanting to relieve himself and woke to find that he had let fly, cleared the catheter and created a puddle on the floor beyond the bed. The problem never recurred.

*The Prime Minister's XI match at Canberra*
*Robert Menzies seated centre, an uncomfortable manager in the back row.*

Four years earlier M.C.C. had sent two county secretaries, Michael Green and John Nash, to manage the tour, but such was their faith in the Lancashire secretary that for this tour he was a sole appointment, with a back-up team of two: Harold Dalton the masseur and George Duckworth who was doubling up as baggage master and scorer.

The masseur was an innovation, instigated by Trevor Bailey who insisted on Harold Dalton, his man at Essex. "They called him Woozer," Geoffrey recalls. "He was a pseudo-medic. He used to walk about with a stethoscope round his neck. I don't think anybody other than Trevor took him seriously. He used to love using his hypodermic needle. I can hear Tom Graveney walking by the dressing room door, shouting out, 'Give him the f---ing needle, Woozer.'"

George Duckworth, by contrast, was a man of great experience in the world of cricket. He had been part of Percy Chapman's victorious side in Australia in 1928/29 and, at Len Hutton's suggestion, he sat in on selection meetings. "He was an enormous help to the players. As soon as they were off the field, he'd come out of the scoring box and start telling them what they did wrong. And he was very good at cracking the whip. I remember Peter Loader using not very gentlemanly language about a Queensland reporter, and George stopped him. 'You're not to talk like that in front of the manager,' he said."

Early in the tour, Duckworth was put in his place himself – for suggesting that Fred Trueman should have been selected for the tour. 'DUCKWORTH GETS A WIGGING,' read the News Chronicle headline: 'Duckworth has been firmly told that he, like the players, is not permitted to give Press interviews. Only Hutton or Manager Geoffrey Howard can do that.'

But his confidence in the tour management was not shaken. "We had a yards-for-years sprint," Geoffrey recalls. "A one-hundred-yard race, where you got handicapped according to your age. So I started nine yards in front of Len, twenty-four in front of Colin. And I remember George. 'I'm backing the manager,' he said."

His faith was not misplaced.

George Duckworth's life since cricket involved all manner of activities, from radio broadcasting to organising Commonwealth tours of India, from pigeon breeding to running a small hotel, but his income came largely from his wife's shrewd management of their smallholding in Warrington. "Bessie ran the business, really. George just picked his way through life. She ran him. He'd have been done for without her." On the boat, George confided to the manager the details of his departure. "Typical of George. He didn't tell his wife he was going. He just left a note on the table, saying 'I'm going to Australia, I'll be back in April.' I doubt if she could have stopped him, but I think he wouldn't have enjoyed the turmoil that would have resulted."

It was the first of only two Australian tours that George Duckworth made as baggage master, and the veteran *Times* correspondent John Woodcock is clear about his worth. "There was no one on all the tours I went on who ever compared with George. He had wisdom, experience, humour, and the

Australians all knew him so well. Fergie, his predecessor, was just a scorer and baggage master. George was a great cricketer and a great character."

*Duckworth, Evans, Howard*
*"Three great keepers"*
*taken by John Woodcock*

But what did John Woodcock think of him as a baggage master? "If he was in charge of your cabin trunk, you knew that all would be well."

And as a scorer? "I remember a game in Bulawayo a couple of years later. It wasn't an important match. Peter Richardson was run out, going for his hundredth run. His score on the board was 99, his score in the book was 99. But George turned to his fellow scorer. 'We'd better just count that again,' he said. 'Oh that's funny, I make it 100.'" In *Wisden* Richardson sits on 44 centuries alongside Bert Sutcliffe and Vijay Merchant.

*

The selection committee for the second Test met on the overnight train. The manager, the captain, the vice-captain Peter May, Bill Edrich and George Duckworth.

Evans instead of Andrew behind the stumps. Graveney for the injured Compton. Bailey to open the innings instead of Simpson. That left room for a fifth bowler. But should they pick the four fast men who played at Brisbane and add one spinner? Or should they play a second spinner? At the heart of the decision lay their assessment of Alec Bedser's fitness.

The big man was the leading wicket-taker in all Test history, taking 30 in the series four years earlier and 39 in the Coronation Year triumph of 1953. But the shingles he had suffered at the start of the tour had left him below strength in the Brisbane Test, and he had not played in the only serious match since then.

'Broadly, what is being decided,' Jim Swanton wrote, 'is whether to take a chance on a recovery of form at Sydney, where he has not often had very great success, or whether to keep him in reserve this time, with an eye to launching him again at the New Year in Melbourne on the ground which has given him some of his greatest triumphs.'

Ian Peebles of the *Sunday Times* took the latter view: 'My personal inclination would be to reserve him for Melbourne, a favourite ground of his, and let him restart at full blast. This argument is supported by the fact that local opinion is that the ball will turn quite early in this match.'

"I don't think any of us realised how debilitating an illness shingles is," Geoffrey reflects. "It's an inflammation of the nerve ends, and Alec had it in his bowling arm. It was awful to look at, and he didn't report it for ages." Forty years later, the manager would experience the infection at closer quarters and learn just how strength-sapping it can be. "Poor Nora had it in her last months, and she had a terrible time."

They decided to name Bedser in the twelve but probably not to play him.

So which of the spinners should they pick? There was no Jim Laker – "His omission left me very unhappy," Len Hutton later revealed – so the choice was between the two Yorkshiremen, Bob Appleyard and Johnny Wardle, and the Glamorgan off-spinner Jim McConnon, who had spent the first Test in hospital after a blow in the groin.

All three were loners in their different ways. Wardle was a man intent on saving every penny for his family back in Yorkshire, Appleyard had spent six months lying on his side, single-mindedly fighting his way back from tuberculosis, and, unknown to the tour management, he had cracked a rib in one of the warm-up matches. McConnon was a quiet Catholic, ill at ease with the boisterous antics of fellow tourists like Bill Edrich and Godfrey Evans. "He and I used to go to Mass together every Sunday morning," the manager remembers. "He was homesick by the time we got to Aden on the way out."

They agreed that Johnny Wardle would play, and they debated the final place in the twelve. McConnon had played in the Victoria match while Appleyard had only appeared in the two-day game at Rockhampton. "Len was for playing Jim McConnon, but George and I opposed him. 'Put it this way,' I said. 'If Jim learns he's playing, he'll pull a muscle. And if Bob learns he isn't, he'll come and cut your throat.'"

It was decided. A week later at the Sydney Cricket Ground it was Jim McConnon who was sitting in his civvies in the front of the dressing room, alongside his manager, watching anxiously as the England fielders pressed for that last elusive Australian wicket. "He wasn't able to face it. He went off into the lavatories."

*

The train was completing its 500-mile journey from Melbourne, and the manager stirred in his compartment, woken by the voices of two Australians recovering from a late night drinking session.

"Hi, Jack, are ya in good nick?"

"Jees, how crook can yer be before yer die!"

The manager's ear was ever open for the local phrases, as his letters home illustrate:

*A great Aussie expression is "I beg yours?" All the emphasis being on the* <u>*yours*</u> *which comes down the nose. I'll do it for you soon. ... Another picturesque Aussie expression. "I am dragging my fur." Not feeling too good: not quite "feeling crook" but not "good thanks". ... They have an expression I like: "On the blink". It means just about to pack up: "my old car is on the blink." Very expressive – I dare say deriving from the use of oil lamps. You know how they blink and flicker when they are running out of oil.*

They were arriving in Sydney, the capital of New South Wales, a very different city from the sedate Melbourne. "Victorians prided themselves on their superiority over New South Wales, because they had never been a penal colony. Also Sydney had had a great influx of American servicemen in the war so it had become a much more modern sort of place."

But Sydney was not yet a great international city. Where the Opera House now stands was a tramway depot, the only high-rise building belonged to the Australian Mutual Provident, and the beaches did not yet attract planeloads of overseas visitors.

"I took out the first hospitality group in 1962/63. Twenty-one men, mostly over sixty. I remember during the match, it was eighty or ninety degrees, and this chap turned to me. 'Do you think there would be any objection if I took off my jacket?'"

Minor financial requests from the players were in the jurisdiction of the manager and, with a personal overdraft, perhaps Geoffrey Howard was not as generous as some would have liked. "Jim Swanton said I was too concerned to get a surplus for distribution to the counties."

Nevertheless, at Sydney, which was renowned for its oysters, he established a more liberal regime than his predecessor. "John Nash in 1950/51 had decided 'no oysters on the bill'. So, when Len asked the question, I had to say 'yes, oysters'. Brian Statham went for them like anything, I remember. 'Good for the moonk,' he said."

*

Friday morning was overcast and humid. The pitch had a green top and had sweated under the tarpaulins. For some observers they were ideal conditions for Bedser's bowling but, before the toss, Len Hutton told his Australian counterpart, acting captain Arthur Morris, that his eleven included Bob Appleyard.

It was a decision that did not impress Jim Swanton. 'Bedser was omitted in favour of a bowler who has been given only one brief spell of exercise in more than a month – a canter on a sandy showground in Northern Queensland. If it was proposed to play Appleyard here, he must in all sanity have been picked in the match preceding this at Melbourne.'

The England manager does not agree. "Bob Appleyard would have been a magnificent bowler without any practice at all. He was a natural bowler, with a hatred of batsmen."

As at Adelaide, when Denis Compton came off the plane and scored a century, the *Daily Telegraph* correspondent was certain that he was right –

though this time he left himself a means of escape. 'All in all, the leaving out of Bedser is a manoeuvre that can only be forgiven in the light of success.'

"Today's paper, tomorrow's fish-and-chip wrapper," the M.C.C. manager reflects. "It's very easy to go through life without making decisions. I remember saying to him one day, 'Your business is to criticise decisions. I have to make them.'"

"Will you miss Alec?" a reporter asked the England captain.

"Of course," Len Hutton replied. "I will always miss Alec."

This time it was Australia's turn to ask England to bat first, and the first day was as great a disaster as it had been at Brisbane. Trevor Bailey was bowled by Lindwall for a 35-minute duck, Peter May made five, and by lunch the score had reached only 34 for two, with Hutton in a cocoon of grim defence.

Worse was to follow. Hutton and Graveney took the score on to 58 with growing assurance, then the England captain played a fine leg glance, only to watch Alan Davidson – 'The Claw' – dive full length to his left and hold the ball an inch above the turf. According to Arthur Gilligan, 'it was one of the best catches ever seen on the ground'. "I thought it was four runs," Hutton complained as he returned to the dressing room. "You can't glance now without somebody catching you out."

'That was the key moment of the day,' wrote John Woodcock, 'for it buckled the main pillar of the English innings.' Soon after tea the scoreboard read 111 for nine, and the Sydney crowd was a-buzz with raucous excitement.

*Sydney, 18 December. Darling, I write very sadly. We had an awful day yesterday, and there really is no excuse. It was only very bad batting although they – Aussie – bowled and fielded jolly well. I feel very sorry for Len. In a way it is his fault because he is such a good player! If he appears to be in difficulty, they all think that it must be a good deal more than ordinarily hard and play an unnatural game with dire results. All our lads failed to hit the ball till John Wardle went in. He had lots of luck, but then he deserved to for using courageous and bold methods. At once the Australian bowling and fielding looked less capable or destructive.*

Wardle and Statham 'struck heartily at almost every ball', adding 43 in twenty minutes for the last wicket, most of them 'slashed, heaved, swirled and swept' by Wardle. With Australia so in charge, the Sydney crowd 'loved the frolic', with one over from Johnston despatched for 19 runs. Maybe, if they had known how tight the match would be by Wednesday, they would not have cheered so heartily.

At the front of the England dressing room, the manager sat glumly with the M.C.C. secretary, who had made his way via New Zealand to watch this Test: *Poor Ronnie Aird – fancy coming all this way for such an inept display.*

A heavy shower caused a delay, leaving Australia only 17 minutes to bat before the close. With Len Hutton's usual tardiness, that would have allowed time for just three eight-ball overs, but the England fielders sprinted to their places and, by a matter of seconds, they managed to fit in a fourth. Off that fourth over's sixth delivery Trevor Bailey got the ball to lift and fly off Arthur Morris's glove. At leg slip Len Hutton took the catch, it was 18 for one, and Jim Swanton clutched at a crumb of hope: 'It was a piece of ill-luck that may possibly have big consequences.'

*

The last Sunday before Christmas saw the temperature in the nineties and great crowds gathering on the Sydney beaches. The Father Christmas figures all sweated beneath their thick costumes, and the M.C.C. manager anticipated the big day with dread. *I can see an orgy of beer drinking and vast eating looming up, and I can't bear the thought.*

*

In the first Test at Brisbane, the young Frank Tyson had taken one wicket for 160 runs. But in the heat of that disastrous second day he had bowled off a shorter run, and the suggestion was made that he might stick with it. Some say that the idea came from Len Hutton, others that Alf Gover – covering the tour for the *Sunday Pictorial* – had spotted a dragging right foot in his approach to the crease. The bowler himself insists that he was only reverting to the run he had employed in his days in league cricket.

Whatever the cause, he bowled in the match against Victoria off a run of just six shuffling steps, followed by ten raking strides, and his return of six wickets for 68 was the best in his career to that point. Neil Harvey was among his victims in that match, and here at Sydney Tyson bowled the left-hander 'a horrible ball that he could only fend into gully's hands'. Benaud was uncomfortable, Hole was bowled by a yorker, and six wickets were down before Australia took the lead. Tyson even had the temerity to bowl a bumper at Australia's great fast bowler, Ray Lindwall.

Tyson, Statham, Bailey. Len Hutton rotated his three fast bowlers, with a few overs of relief from Bob Appleyard, but, after all the fuss over his choice of just four bowlers at Brisbane, he never required his fifth. 'Yet,' Jim Swanton noted, 'as he ran about at long leg, Wardle could reflect comfortingly that he had been England's top scorer.'

There were vital runs from Archer and Lindwall, but by close of play Australia had been dismissed for 228, a lead of just 74. Tyson, four for 45. Bailey, four for 59.

*Sydney, 19 December. We had a much better day yesterday and, having bowled well, ought to stand a chance of winning – if only the batsmen get some runs.*

Alas, on the Monday, Bailey, Hutton and Graveney were all gone before the deficit was cleared. Bailey failed again as an opener, Hutton fell to an uncharacteristically leaden-footed drive, and Graveney, in the words of John Woodcock, drove at his third ball 'as though he were well set in a September festival at Weston-super-Mare'. It was a shot that confirmed all his captain's prejudices, as Geoffrey Howard knew well: "I think Len would always have been looking for aspects of Tom's character to uphold his view that he wasn't reliable. 'He's got a red face,' he told me one day. 'I don't like red faces.'"

But Len did like his two young amateurs, Peter May and Colin Cowdrey, and his spirits revived as they batted steadily through the afternoon. 'They batted with unforced authority,' Alan Ross wrote, 'the one upright, flowing and lithe, the other powerful with the gentleness of strength. There was little to choose between them in the correctness of their technique, the natural assertion of their breeding.' 'In their differing ways,' Ian Peebles thought, 'they represent the best of the young English school and should be an influence in our cricket for years to come.'

Then in the final half hour, with the lead 97, the young Cowdrey, becalmed on 54 and suffering the restlessness of the Sydney crowd, spotted Benaud's googly and attempted to hoist it over the bowler's head. He was not there for the stroke, but he played it anyway and he watched the catch taken at mid-off. Then, according to Tom Graveney, "He sat on the pavilion steps and cried his eyes out. He thought he'd thrown away the Test match. And he was only 21."

The manager was the father of four girls back in Cheshire, and he read their letters from home with affectionate concern. How easy it was for him to make the same paternal relationship with the young men under his wing in Australia, especially with Colin Cowdrey who had so recently lost his own father.

*Sydney, 21 December. I did so feel for poor old Joy losing you in the London Road. Yesterday dear little old Colin Cowdrey was just the same. He had batted so beautifully and then get out to a bad shot – he just lost a bit of patience. The poor lad came back and wept. I felt so for him.*

George Duckworth's response to the shot was more robust. "The next time he saw Colin coming back from church," John Woodcock recalls, "George greeted him. 'Been to confessions?' he said."

At close of play Peter May was on 98, and England's lead was 130.

*

For Frank Tyson, this Sydney Test was the best game of cricket he ever played – though, for a while on Tuesday morning, he knew nothing about it.

He came to the crease after Lindwall had bowled May for 104. On Saturday, in his excitement, he had bowled a bumper at the Australian fast bowler, and now he found the hostility returned in kind. The ball reared up, he turned his head as he ducked, and there was a crack as the missile hit the back of his skull.

"I can remember seeing that," Geoffrey says. "I can remember hearing it, too."

Tyson lay on the ground as medical help arrived. "I was only dimly aware of the ambulance men and of being helped off the field."

"I went to the hospital with him. I was extremely concerned. He might have been badly injured. And we were pursued right into the hospital itself by photographers. I got very cross with them, I know."

*Sydney, 22 December. Life is full of managerial worries. Yesterday Frank Tyson took an awful crack on the head from Lindwall, and I had to get him off at short notice for x-ray – fortunately no damage. Now Reg Simpson has a temperature of 104°! The Doc says it is influenza: I got a bit scared thinking it might be polio. You know how easy it is to worry about such things.*

Within the hour Tyson – 'with his colour restored' – returned, to be bowled by Lindwall, and England were just 176 runs ahead with their last pair, Appleyard and Statham, together. But, as Wardle and Statham had done in the first innings, they added vital runs – 'Appleyard was upright and academic in defence, but Statham could not have played farther from his legs and body. With abandon he heaved, swept, edged and sliced. Like Wardle's innings on Friday he put Australia's bowling and England's attempts at organised batsmanship into somewhat uncomplimentary perspective.'

Appleyard, not out 19. Statham, caught Langley, bowled Johnston, 25. They had added 46, three more than Wardle and Statham had added in the first innings, and Australia's victory target was 223.

By close of play they had reached 72 for two, and opinion divided between those who thought the match well-balanced – 'It would take a brave man to predict with confidence which side will win,' John Woodcock wrote – and those who expected the home side to win – 'Australia need only 151 for victory with eight wickets in hand,' Denys Rowbotham wrote in the *Guardian*, 'a task it is difficult to conceive her not accomplishing.'

The manager's letter home made clear which of the two views he took: *We shall, I am afraid, lose, but that cannot be helped. We don't have a lot of luck off the field and even less on it. To say that the Aussie batsmen have been lucky against Tyson and Statham is to put it very mildly! Harvey is really apprehensive facing Tyson and none too happy with Brian – our Brian.*

*

It had been fourteen weeks since they had boarded the boat at Tilbury, and there were fifteen more before their plane would land at Prestwick. Christmas was only three days away.

To spend Christmas in the shadow of a second defeat, with so much touring time still to follow, was a dismal prospect, but at least for the manager there were moments when he knew that the tour was about more than winning cricket matches – as he said in a letter home the previous week.

*Melbourne, 15 December. Yesterday I went with Brian Statham, Vic Wilson and Harold Dalton our masseur to cheer up the patients at a police hospital. Darling, it was me that needed cheering in the end. They were all wonderful – not one word of complaint: I had to struggle very hard against a tendency to weep. Those in the iron lungs, darling, were simply wonderful – such courage and fortitude I have never witnessed. How can one worry about the result of a cricket match when such things exist to be borne?*

*

A week later, on Wednesday the 22nd of December, he was watching with alternating alarm and excitement as the second Test worked slowly towards its climax. There were four of them sitting at the front of the England dressing room – though they went down to three when Jim McConnon decided to take refuge in the lavatories. There was Geoffrey himself, watching the Sydney crowd growing by the hour and knowing how the success of the tour depended on England levelling the series. There was Ronnie Aird, hoping for triumph in the first Australian tour of his M.C.C. secretaryship. And there was Henry Sayen, an elderly American who had become something of a lucky mascot since he had turned up at Lord's in 1953 and offered the players prize money for their runs and wickets. "£3 for 30 runs, £5 for 50, £6 for 100," he declared. "£1 for a wicket, £1 for catches or stumps, £5 for most spectacular play. All bonuses to be doubled on the last day."

That was the game in which Watson and Bailey saved England with four hours of determined batting, and the American parted with his money with delight: "It was like going to the races and trying to lose," he wrote later. The following winter he turned up in Kingston, Jamaica, and this time it was Len Hutton, with a magnificent double century, who profited most from his enthusiasm.

A letter from Ronnie Aird thanked him for his kindness, adding, 'You certainly seem to give the boys extra strength when they need it. I wonder if you will be able to go to support them in Australia. I think they will need all the support they can get there next time.'

Henry Sayen needed no more encouragement. Defying doctor's orders to rest after major surgery and enduring a flight made long and arduous by a faulty plane engine, he arrived in Sydney full of the romance of his new-found love affair with English cricket – quite unlike his fellow American, Groucho Marx, whom Ronnie Aird had entertained at Lord's one April morning. M.C.C. were playing an uneventful match with Cambridge University and, after about an hour, the American became satisfied that he understood the basic rules: "Okay," he said, "so when do they begin?" Then after lunch, the M.C.C. secretary hailed a taxi for his guest. As it drove off, Marx wound down the window. "And don't forget to cable me the result of that contest."

On that Wednesday morning at Sydney, Henry Sayen had barely arrived in what he called "the locker room" when Frank Tyson sent the stumps cartwheeling behind first Burke, then Hole. Rattled by the blow to his skull, the fast bowler was bristling with menace: "My hesitant shuffle was more like a bull pawing the ground, so eager was I come to grips with the enemy."

"It was the quickest bowling I've ever seen," Tom Graveney says. "I've no doubt about that."

It was 77 for four, and the game was no longer tilted Australia's way.

For an hour Harvey and Benaud steadied the innings, 'Harvey hemmed in, Benaud struggling'. Then Len Hutton turned to the slower bowling of Bob Appleyard, and Benaud, celebrating the relief from pace, mistimed a sweep shot, sending the ball high towards square leg. 'The ball seemed to be up in the air a long time,' Jim Swanton wrote. 'No doubt it swung about in the wind.'

'Frank' went up the cry of the fielders, and the fast bowler, resting from his first spell, misjudged the ball in the wind. "There was that heart-stopping moment when I realised that I had gauged it wrongly, and I completed my effort on one knee, the ball clutched in my hands three feet from my body and inches from the turf. In the dressing room, Geoffrey Howard was doing a dervish of delight."

Perhaps this was spectacular play qualifying for a £5 bonus.

118 for five at lunch. Another 105 to win, and Neil Harvey batting with increasing mastery. "I don't think any of our digestions felt that good," Henry Sayen reckoned.

After lunch, in fifty minutes of the finest pace bowling – Tyson downwind, Statham up – Australia lost four wickets for 27 runs, and the contest was all but over. *Darling, every time a wicket fell, we rushed round the dressing room hugging each other and making the most awful din!*

But it was not over. Patiently Neil Harvey worked almost all the strike, with the number eleven, Bill Johnston, facing just seven deliveries in eight eight-ball overs. 'Harvey played like a genius,' John Woodcock reported, as the crowd became more and more tense. 'Women grew hysterical, and the spectator in front of your correspondent mistook his dark glasses for his pipe.'

Frank Tyson had been bowling for ninety minutes and, according to John Woodcock, 'he was almost on his knees.' "My run became to seem longer with each ball I bowled, and I did not seem to be able to pull the extra fast one out of the bag."

Then Harvey hit the last ball of a Bailey over for four – 43 to win – and, with Johnston at last on strike at the start of an over, Len Hutton turned for one more effort from Tyson. The number eleven survived the first two deliveries, then swished one-handed at the third, sending the ball to the fine leg boundary to reduce the runs required to 39. Fewer than the 43 Wardle and Statham had scored for the last wicket in the England first innings. Fewer than the 46 Appleyard and Statham had added in the second.

As they retrieved the ball, Brian Statham approached the bowler. "Try one a little closer to the body, Frank, and a little shorter." The advice was followed, the ball made the faintest of contact with the bat's edge, and there was Godfrey Evans claiming the catch that levelled the series. Tyson, six for 85, and Henry Sayen on hand to throw a grand party at Prince's.

*Darling, Did you enjoy that wonderful Christmas present we sent you? My word! We beat them and was it exciting!! I have never known such a time. I just cannot tell you how pleased and happy we all are. It has made the tour: just what we needed to pull the binder tight and hold us all together. But what we all think about is you at home. You must have dreaded switching on to find the result. And then what joy – just to think of it now brings tears to my eyes.*

In Sydney that afternoon was his predecessor as Lancashire secretary, Major Rupert Howard, who had managed the tours on either side of the war. *Can you believe that Rupert, coming all this way, missed the finish by going to a lunch – a lunch of all things! Oh dear, how stupid can you be.*

The team had come together, not just the extroverts like Edrich and Evans but even the loners like Wardle, as Frank Tyson acknowledged. "In the whole match he only bowled four overs but, as each Australian batsman was dismissed, he ran eagerly to the wicket and insisted on polishing the ball for the fast bowlers."

For Jim Swanton, though, the decision to omit Bedser was still unproven. 'Argument may long wax as to whether England would have won more easily had Bedser been there, or perhaps in some opinions whether they would have won at all. At the least it must now be admitted that his omission was feasible.' Perceptively he devoted his column on the following day to ways that Len Hutton could be relieved of some of the burdens of captaincy.

But these were not thoughts that troubled the tour party as they gathered for their Christmas lunch. "A hilarious party," the manager remembers. "Best to draw a curtain over it. Just say it was hilarious. By the time the dinner was ready to be served, the waiters had gone home."

After lunch, some of the party went swimming on the beach, and John Woodcock recalls George Duckworth running into rugby league friends among the lifeguards. "Norman Preston, the editor of *Wisden*, was swimming perfectly innocently, and George said to them, 'Let's have an incident. Go and pick up Norman as though he were in trouble.' So they all went out and brought old Norman in, and he was shouting away. 'No, no, no, there's nothing wrong with me.'"

John Woodcock has lived all his life in Longparish in Hampshire, and I drove Geoffrey across to meet him once more.

"I've spent seventeen Christmases in Australia, Geoffrey. I've been out there with every England side in the last fifty years, and your tour was the happiest of them all. It was so well managed, you were so level-headed, and you only had George Duckworth to help you – though, of course, he was incomparable."

Geoffrey Howard managed the happiest England tour of modern times. Yet only eight years earlier, when the news from the first post-war tour of Australia was all of disappointment and defeat, he had been sitting at a desk in a London bank, restlessly wondering if he should take up farming or teaching.

# AUSTRALIA v ENGLAND – SECOND TEST

Sydney. 17, 18, 20, 21 & 22 December 1954

ENGLAND WON BY 38 RUNS

## ENGLAND

| | | | | |
|---|---|---|---|---|
| L. Hutton * | c Davidson b Johnston | 30 | c Benaud b Johnston | 28 |
| T.E. Bailey | b Lindwall | 0 | c Langley b Archer | 6 |
| P.B.H. May | c Johnston b Archer | 5 | b Lindwall | 104 |
| T.W. Graveney | c Favell b Johnston | 21 | c Langley b Johnston | 0 |
| M.C. Cowdrey | c Langley b Davidson | 23 | c Archer b Benaud | 54 |
| W.J. Edrich | c Benaud b Archer | 10 | b Archer | 29 |
| F.H. Tyson | b Lindwall | 0 | b Lindwall | 9 |
| T.G. Evans + | c Langley b Archer | 3 | c Lindwall b Archer | 4 |
| J.H. Wardle | c Burke b Johnston | 35 | lbw b Lindwall | 8 |
| R. Appleyard | c Hole b Davidson | 8 | *not out* | 19 |
| J.B. Statham | *not out* | 14 | c Langley b Johnston | 25 |
| *Extras* | *lb 5* | 5 | *lb 6, nb 4* | 10 |
| | | **154** | | **296** |

1-14, 2-19, 3-58, 4-63, 5-84, 6-85, 7-88, 8-99, 9-111, 10-154
1-18, 2-55, 3-55, 4-171, 5-222, 6-232, 7-239, 8-249, 9-250, 10-296

| | | | | | | | | |
|---|---|---|---|---|---|---|---|---|
| Lindwall | 17 | 3 | 47 | 2 | 31 | 10 | 69 | 3 |
| Archer | 12 | 7 | 12 | 3 | 22 | 9 | 53 | 3 |
| Davidson | 12 | 3 | 34 | 2 | 13 | 2 | 52 | 0 |
| Johnston | 13.3 | 1 | 56 | 3 | 19.3 | 2 | 70 | 3 |
| Benaud | | | | | 19 | 3 | 42 | 1 |

## AUSTRALIA

| | | | | |
|---|---|---|---|---|
| L.E. Favell | c Graveney b Bailey | 26 | c Edrich b Tyson | 16 |
| A.R. Morris * | c Hutton b Bailey | 12 | lbw b Statham | 10 |
| J.W. Burke | c Graveney b Bailey | 44 | b Tyson | 14 |
| R.N. Harvey | c Cowdrey b Tyson | 12 | *not out* | 92 |
| G.B. Hole | b Tyson | 12 | b Tyson | 0 |
| R. Benaud | lbw b Statham | 20 | c Tyson b Appleyard | 12 |
| R.G. Archer | c Hutton b Tyson | 49 | b Tyson | 6 |
| A.K. Davidson | b Statham | 20 | c Evans b Statham | 5 |
| R.R. Lindwall | c Evans b Tyson | 19 | b Tyson | 8 |
| G.R.A. Langley + | b Bailey | 5 | b Statham | 0 |
| W.A. Johnston | *not out* | 0 | c Evans b Tyson | 11 |
| *Extras* | *b 5, lb 2, nb 2* | 9 | *lb 7, nb 3* | 10 |
| | | **228** | | **184** |

1-18, 2-65, 3-100, 4-104, 5-122, 6-141, 7-193, 8-213, 9-224, 10-228
1-27, 2-34, 3-77, 4-77, 5-102, 6-122, 7-127, 8-136, 9-145, 10-184

| | | | | | | | | |
|---|---|---|---|---|---|---|---|---|
| Statham | 18 | 1 | 83 | 2 | 19 | 6 | 45 | 3 |
| Bailey | 17.4 | 3 | 59 | 4 | 6 | 0 | 21 | 0 |
| Tyson | 13 | 2 | 45 | 4 | 18.4 | 1 | 85 | 6 |
| Appleyard | 7 | 1 | 32 | 0 | 6 | 1 | 12 | 1 |
| Wardle | | | | | 4 | 2 | 11 | 0 |

Umpires: M.J. McInnes and R. Wright

# CHAPTER FOUR

# THE MAN WHO GOT AWAY

## WAR AND PEACE

## 1930 – 46

Geoffrey Howard was not restless in August 1939.

He was a married man, with a six-month-old daughter, living in his first family home and earning a secure living at the little branch of Martins Bank in Maidstone. "I was the second senior," he says, "but there were only three of us there. The manager, myself and a girl."

He had played plenty of sport in his nine years in Kent, representing Club Cricket Conference against the West Indians in 1933 and appearing several times for the county at rugby union. "I was a left wing three-quarter. One of the things I was said to be good at was cross-kicking but, looking at the way they play these days, I don't think I'd ever get the chance to make a kick."

*Club Cricket Conference XI v West Indies, May 1933*

*Left to right, standing: umpire, Cecil Pogue (Private Banks secretary), Lionel Recordon, Nobby Hunt, Arthur Grimsdell (Tottenham Hotspur footballer), E.A.C. Thompson (founder of Club Cricket Conference), umpire.*

*Seated: I. Chapman, Geoffrey Howard, Ronnie Bryan, C.B. Fordham, Sid Newnham, H.T.O. Smith. In front: Geoff Cornu, Malcolm Dawkins (twelfth man).*

*Missing is R.V. Thornhill: "Dizzy Thornhill – typical of him, he's not there!"*

He had met Nora Le Plastrier, the younger sister of the Chief Clerk's wife at the Chislehurst branch. For three years they had been engaged, while he saved one hundred pounds, and during that time he paid many visits to the public telephone box near where he lived. "On a quiet evening you could get quite a few minutes for two old pence – before the operator's voice broke in. 'I shall have to cut you off soon.' Then it would be, 'I am afraid I have to cut you off now, caller.'"

By August 1939 they were a settled couple, living in a semi-detached, redbrick Victorian house, for a rent of fifteen shillings a week. Number One, Tower Villas, Bearstead, three miles east of Maidstone. Three rooms on each of the two floors, and a small garden at the back. "A nice little place to start your married life."

But, on the morning of Thursday the 24th of August, their family life in the heart of the Kent apple orchards was to be broken into – and by a much harsher voice than an apologetic telephone operator.

There was no newspaper delivered – "The bank had a copy of *The Times*, and I read that. In fact, because it was never that busy there, I read far more of it then than I've ever read since." – and there was no radio set tuned to the morning news. The first sound in the house might even have been the postman as the mail dropped through their letter box. "I can still see the doormat and this envelope lying on it – and my opening it, never anticipating what it contained."

The previous year he had volunteered as an auxiliary airman. "The feeling was that, by joining, we might prevent the war. We might daunt the Germans with the strength of our opposition. And we had a certain amount of confidence in the Prime Minister and his relations with Herr Hitler. Nobody realised the extent to which he was having his arm twisted."

During evenings and occasional weekends Geoffrey learned the skills of aircraft maintenance. "I knew a little about internal combustion engines but nothing about practical engineering. You would be given a rectangle of mild steel, and you had to reduce it to a given dimension with a file and micrometer. If you were half of a thousandth of an inch out, you got it thrown back at you."

Then at the start of August 1939 he was sent on a fortnight's camp in Dorset. "I did my fourteen days and came home, thinking I'd be on a weekend basis thenceforth. We were still hoping that the war wouldn't happen."

Thursday the 24th of August, 1939. The cricket page of *The Times* reported a century for Len Hutton at Dover, following his 165 in The Oval Test the previous day. Such achievements seemed suddenly insignificant. With German troops massing on the Polish borders, the headline on page ten sent shock waves across the nation. 'RUSSIA AND GERMANY SIGN NON-AGGRESSION PACT IN MOSCOW.' The King was on the train back from Balmoral, Parliament was preparing to grant emergency powers to the Government, and Lord Halifax, the Foreign Secretary, would address the nation on the wireless that evening.

The previous Sunday Geoffrey had turned out for Aylesford Paper Mills cricket team, as he did when he could throughout that summer. The Paper Mills were the Maidstone bank's leading customers, and his last match before the war was at Meopham, near Dartford, on the village pitch where W.G. Grace once played.

In the churchyard of the next village, Thurnham, lay the grave of Alfred Mynn, the greatest cricketer before Grace, and now in his own village of Bearstead lived the old Kent leg-spinner, Tich Freeman, the only man ever to take 300 wickets in a season. The second greatest wicket-taker in the history of the game, he had moved there after his retirement in 1936, to a house he called 'Dunbowlin'.

Thursday the 24th of August, 1939. Geoffrey Howard picked up the envelope on the mat and read its contents. Nothing in his life would ever be the same again. "I found my papers there. Report immediately, that day." A farewell to his wife Nora and their baby daughter Frances. Then a quick visit to the bank where he returned his keys to the manager George Jeffery and kissed his young colleague Marjorie Kay goodbye. "You've waited a long time to do that," she said.

At Dover that day Yorkshire's Hedley Verity took nine wickets, and Kent's only resistance came with a century from their captain Gerry Chalk. Within four years they would both be dead, Verity of gunshot wounds in Sicily, Chalk when his plane was brought down over northern France, his body remaining undiscovered till 1989.

"I would earnestly hope," Lord Halifax told the nation on the wireless, "that in face of all the consequences of a resort to force, and before any step is taken which cannot be retraced, reason may yet prevail."

That night the young auxiliary airman slept on the concrete floor of an aircraft hangar at RAF Detling. Early on Friday morning of the following week German tanks crossed the Polish border. By then Nora and Frances had moved to a rectory in Uppingham. Away from Kent and the south-east where the bombs were expected to fall.

"I got a compassionate 24-hour pass on September the third, and I drove up to see them. In an old Austin 12. I was in the rectory, listening to Chamberlain on the wireless. 'The country is now at war with Germany. We are ready.' I went to the church, told the rector and heard him announce it to the gathering. Then I turned on my heels, left the car with Nora and took the train back. It was really traumatic. I thought possibly I'd never see her again."

On the journey back to camp, he travelled across London in a bus, and in Trafalgar Square the sirens sounded. "I really thought that it was starting, that we were going to be bombed right then."

Some of his colleagues never did see their wives again. "One of the first things I had to do was to go down to the coast, somewhere near Hastings. It was a sunny day, and we'd lost an aircraft. The crew were all friends, and I had to pick up little bits of them and put them into bags. They were volunteers like me, but you had to face the next day and carry on."

There followed the months of the Phoney War. Nora moved to Letchworth with her sister, also with a young baby. Then in January 1940 she returned to Bearstead, and he got permission to sleep out of camp. For three months he worked long days, sometimes nights, Nora adapted to the constraints of rationing, and they maintained a domestic life. Then he was posted to Liverpool to help organise balloon barrage. The furniture went into storage – "We didn't see a stick of it again till 1945" – and they embarked on a life of movement and uncertainty.

Tower Villas, Bearstead. Twenty-five years later he and Nora would travel on from his father's funeral to view once more their first family home, but it was gone, bulldozered to make way for a larger property. "But the barmaid at The White Horse was still there. 'Good afternoon, Mr Howard,' she said."

All across Liverpool hundreds of hydrogen-filled balloons, attached to power-operated winches, floated into the sky, to ensure that German planes could not engage in dive bombing. "If they had, they would have been so accurate that they'd have put the port out of action." Pilot Officer C.G. Howard was responsible for the co-ordination of sites, crews and transport while Nora lived in a village in Cheshire. "I didn't see her much," he remembers. "But I certainly did visit her there because she became pregnant."

In June came news of the evacuation of Dunkirk, followed by the fall of France. "I saw General De Gaulle walking into the Adelphi Hotel in Liverpool, with what remained of the Free French Army. He was immaculately turned out. A very impressive figure."

Then the bombing of Liverpool began. Nora moved down to her sister's in Guildford, and the full horror of war came home to Geoffrey. "The people in Liverpool had it very rough. They had no possibility of retaliation. They were there to be bombed." Next door to where he was quartered, a father and mother were killed, their two young children surviving, and everywhere at night, as Pilot-Officer Howard rode in the sidecar of a motorcycle, he passed major fires. "The most dramatic was the Custom House. You could see the fires encircling the big dome, then suddenly it caved in. Plop. Bombs were dropping all around. People were so very brave."

There was no cricket, but there were occasional trips to the theatre. Tommy Trinder provided music hall entertainment, and one night Geoffrey joined the audience at the Liverpool Playhouse to watch Shaw's *'The Millionairess'*. "There was an air raid going on, and it was pretty intense. Edith Evans was the female lead, and she came forward. 'If any of you feel that you must go,' she said, 'by all means, go. The show goes on.' Nobody left."

Gradually the worst of the bombing passed and, with Nora expecting their second child in the New Year, he was sent on compassionate posting to Chessington in Surrey. "I was in a trench with an air raid going on, and a message came through to say that Joy had been born." There followed a posting to Weybridge where barrage balloons protected the Vickers aircraft factory.

But the theatres of war moved and, when the bombing stopped, the anti-aircraft gunners and barrage balloon operators had little to do. "Can you imagine the life of an anti-aircraft gunman when there's nothing to shoot at, or any likelihood? Gunners used to say, 'What are the three most useless things in the world? Men's tits, the Pope's balls and anti-aircraft guns."

At least it allowed time for some cricket. He had played through the '30s, as a batsman and wicket-keeper, mostly for Private Banks – though the move to Kent led him to try other clubs. "I played one season at Town Malling, but it was ten miles from Maidstone and I couldn't always get there on time. Then I played at The Mote, but their best side played all day on Saturday, which I couldn't do. So I went back to Private Banks, probably '37 and '38. Then in '39, when Nora was pregnant, I played for Aylesford Paper Mills. It was a very different cup of tea from London club cricket. The grounds were more sophisticated, better looked after in London, because the banks put in so much money. And there were more outstanding players. But Kent is a cradle of cricket, and the Paper Mills had a wonderful ground. We played villages, but it was a good standard."

It was not the standard that Tom Pearce, his opening partner at Private Banks, had gone on to play. From 1933 to 1938 Tom shared the captaincy of Essex, scoring 1,000 runs in 1936 and making 85 for the Gentlemen against the Players at Lord's, against Gover and Verity. He had left banking for the wine and spirit trade. "He was employed by a fellow called Tray Grinter. He became a director eventually. Their main product was Stone's Ginger Wine."

Their paths had separated, but from time to time they crossed. There was the Sunday when they opened the batting once more, for the Chislehurst President's XI. "I can see him now wearing his Essex blazer." And the Tuesday afternoon when he found time to slip away to the cricket at Leyton and saw Tom win the match against Worcester with the ball. "And he wasn't much of a bowler." A first-class career of 250 matches yielded him just 15 wickets at a cost of 61.8 each but, with Geoffrey Howard watching in disbelief, he took four for twelve that day.

The bombing of Liverpool, the dead friends on the coast at Hastings, the constant moving of his family. It was strange to hold a cricket bat again. But one day, when he found himself in Southend, he improvised an indoor cricket net on the pier, and he found that batting still came easily to him. "It was a wooden floor, and the ball came off the bat, woof! It was the most wonderful experience."

His PT officer at that time was Bob Gregory, the Surrey opener, and, with a lull in the bombing, they were soon playing together for the squadron.

Wednesday the 18th of June, 1941. For the first time since his Middlesex debut in 1930, Geoffrey Howard stepped out to bat at Lord's. Against an R.A.F. Biggin Hill side, led by the old England captain A.E.R. Gilligan. "It was one of those days when everything went right." *Wisden* records the score: *No 2 Balloon Centre 249 (C.G. Howard 105)* "Arthur Gilligan came on himself at the end, and I hit one straight back at him, which he caught. He then asked me to play for his R.A.F. XI at Aldershot."

Thursday the 26th of July, 1941. With German troops approaching Moscow and the Japanese preparing for an assault on Singapore, Aldershot staged a two-day cricket match, thirteen of the participants first-class cricketers, among them Denis Compton. "I remember being somewhat surprised. He got a few runs, but he didn't dominate. Not as I had seen him dominate at The Mote five years earlier."

*Wartime cricket at Lord's. C.G. Howard the non-striker: "Look - no gloves."*

Kent versus Middlesex, July 1936. *D.C.S. Compton, caught Chapman, bowled Ashdown, 87. Caught Levett, bowled Freeman, 96.* "I couldn't believe it. He was just 18 years old, and he murdered Tich Freeman. When he was out, he came in, twirling his bat, as if to say, 'What do you expect? I'm the great Compton.' He was a lovely, modest chap, but he was very aware of his ability."

At Aldershot, Geoffrey's innings of 40 was the second highest in the match, behind the Surrey keeper George Mobey's 44. This was a pleasant way of passing a war, but it was not quite what he wanted. "I'm ashamed to confess what I did. I was a married man, with two small children, and I volunteered for flying. I thought I wasn't being sufficiently aggressive; I wanted to be in contact with the enemy. It was a dreadful thing to do."

By Christmas he was on official flying training at Torquay, his family nearby, but the R.A.F. discovered a regulation that debarred him as too old. So he went up to the Mull of Galloway to train as a navigator. "Then my conscience began to prick me. I thought, it's one thing flying these machines, it's quite another being flown around by a 19-year-old. So I went to see the CO. 'I really feel I ought to drop out,' I said, and he entirely agreed with me. 'In your circumstances,' he said, 'I'd do the same thing.'"

The decision was reinforced when he stumbled by accident on the instructor's report on his pupils. "Against my name it said that I was very slow on the uptake, compared with the younger ones." What aspects of navigation did the 32-year-old banker find so difficult? "I could manage the operational side. What I struggled with was the arithmetic."

A holding unit in Uxbridge. Then he was posted to Sheerness, this time to organise the air-sea rescue launches. Now he was a Flying Officer, with the vital task of protecting the convoys going down the Channel. But again he grew frustrated, and this time he volunteered to go into the launches himself.

"A lot of the time you longed to be more active. Every one involved in that war has his own story, his own problems. And in my case I made a lot of them for myself. When you enter the services, people say to you, 'Don't volunteer for anything, just go where you're sent.' And I volunteered not once but twice."

Christmas 1942 was spent in Stranraer, learning boat handling and sea navigation. And his family? "They were in Bromley or Aylesbury or Guildford. I don't remember. Nora moved 21 times in all during the war. And moving by rail in wartime, with heavy trunks, wasn't easy. There were no porters. Many a time she was helped by soldiers."

By 1943 Geoffrey Howard was receiving instruction for entry into the Catholic church. "Nora had had Joy in a Benedictine nursing home, and she'd been so impressed by the nuns that she had become a convert. And I felt, 'Well, there's no point in my not converting.' So I used to meet with Father Burke of Leatherhead whenever and wherever I could. We met one time at the café in Victoria Station. But I was insufficiently prepared. I don't think I ever fully believed in things like transubstantiation and, although I could see the virtues of confession, I never really accepted the priest's right to grant absolution.

"I was standing outside the church in Leatherhead one day, and Father Burke waved to this man across the street. I asked him who it was, and he said, 'Oh, that's the local heretic.' He was an Anglican vicar. What a ghastly thing to say! I should have taken that as a sign that Catholicism was not for me."

For many years he struggled to maintain the faith, looking for Sunday mass wherever he travelled, even in India, but eventually his Catholicism faded away. "I said to Jim Swanton the last time I saw him that I'd been confirmed into both the Anglican and Catholic churches, but that I was no longer a member of either. 'Oh yes, you are,' he said. 'You're there for life. You can't get out of it.'"

The war continued. He served for a while in Grimsby, then at Gorleston near Great Yarmouth where they supported the United States Air Force in their daylight bombing raids. At the beginning of June 1944 the signal came to go down to Calshot on Southampton Water. "Everywhere we went there were landing craft full of soldiers. Sick as dogs they were, the weather was terribly rough. At Calshot the armada had to be seen to be believed."

Tuesday the 6th of June was D-Day. "It was all so quick. We were briefed overnight and went at dawn. An incredibly bad briefing, too. I hope the others were better. When we eventually came within sight of the shore, we dropped anchor. There was nothing else to do. 'Await further instructions.' When we got up in the morning, we were aground. Nobody had told us about the tides."

There at Arromanches the tugs towed in great concrete blocks, and a complete artificial harbour was built. "It was a wonderful sight. It was up in two days. Then they had this thing called PLUTO, Pipe Line Under The Ocean, huge pipes laid across the Channel."

Back and forth he went in his air-sea rescue launch. One time they lost their propellers and were towed back. The next time they hit a submerged tank and had to keep their course without any rudders.

"I remember, when we were sent to look for a dinghy, we were fired on by the shore batteries. Then one night German one-man submarines set off all these depth charges. A terrific noise all night long. The following morning I went aboard the supply ship, and they'd got a handful of submariners on board. They looked little more than schoolboys, and they were terrified. But in the end the opposition died away. I'll never forget the noise of the barrage when we were bombarding Caen. Shore-based batteries, sea-based batteries, battleships, all firing. Then all air-sea rescue vessels were recalled. Because there was no opposition from the air."

In a little shop in Port-en-Bessin he discovered that the French had not seen coffee for years. "A lot of people were operating a black market so, when I found myself back in Calshot, I bought some coffee and took it over to them. I thought I was going to make some money. The woman took the coffee, smelled it and rushed upstairs. There was such a family celebration that I walked out of the shop. I was just pleased to share their happiness."

His next posting was at Newhaven, operating in the Channel. Then from December 1944 to September 1945 he was in Alexandria, preparing for onward transmission to the Far East. A Flight-Lieutenant by this time. One day the daughter of Greek friends brought him a French newspaper, and he read the news of the bombing of Hiroshima. 'LA GRANDE CHALEUR,' read the headline. After that they were not required in the East.

He played three cricket matches in those nine months, on matting wickets, and in one of them he faced the New Zealand fast bowler Tom Pritchard. "I played and missed, again and again. He made the ball do so much off the matting, and at a considerable speed, too." His equipment was not much help, either. "I had a NAAFI bat. I kept it after the war and, when I next played, at The Oval in 1947, Bob Gregory looked at it. 'That's not a bat at all,' he said. 'That's a plank.'"

In the final weeks, when he was Acting Squadron-Leader, they filled in forms requesting training for peace-time work. "I put myself down for teacher training. And I can remember one of my men filling his in, saying he wanted to be considered as an applicant for public hangman and would like to go on a course as soon as possible."

For two weeks he went on a preliminary teaching course in Cairo, and he soon realised how much work it entailed. "I had to address my fellow students, and I didn't realise the extent to which you have to prepare. I went up gaily to talk about garden cities, and I completely dried up. I was looking at all these people, who were waiting for me to say something, and I couldn't think of a word to say."

In six years, he had gone from being number two of three in a quiet provincial bank to having charge of a thousand men, "not all of them capable of looking after themselves." With the war over, not all his fellow officers looked forward to a return to the civilian roles they had left behind. "I remember being visited by an Establishment committee, who were going round the Middle Eastern units deciding how to shrink them. 'Well, I'm amazed,' this chap from the Treasury said when we'd finished. 'You're the only one so far who doesn't want more men.'"

Back in England in September, with ninety days' leave, the family were reunited in a new home in Upminster in Essex. "I don't suppose I did very much. I just enjoyed being at home."

In 1939 he had had a settled life. A nice home and a first child, a steady job with a pension, an afternoon of cricket each weekend in summer. Family life brought him great joy, but the prospect of a return to banking brought no such pleasure. "I went for an interview at Lombard Street, and this chap made it quite clear that he thought it a pity I was coming back. They'd got it nicely organised without us. They didn't want people coming back who were senior to them in service. In Alexandria I'd been used to people saluting me wherever I went. I spent a day taking King Farouk of Egypt to sea on one of our boats. And here I was, back in the bank, and this chap took a cigarette out of his pocket and threw it at me."

*King Farouk of Egypt at a display of life saving by Air-Sea Rescue Services, Acting Squadron Leader C.G. Howard behind his right shoulder.*

Sir Ebenezer Howard had inspired the garden city movement. Geoffrey had been a Go-Ahead at St Christopher's School in Letchworth. In six years he had risen from Aircraftsman to Acting Squadron Leader. Now he was back in the world of banking, where promotion was rare and slow.

His first posting was as Head Cashier at the Hanover Square branch of Martins Bank in the West End. "It was a very much bigger bank than Maidstone, but I'm bound to say that I slightly resented those who hadn't served in the war and who had mopped up the chances of promotion." He had not been that at ease with his banking career before the war, now he struggled to focus on it at all. "I can remember answering the telephone one day, and I said, 'Marine Craft Unit, Alexandria.'"

Balloon barrage, air-sea rescue launches, pilot training, a squadron in Alexandria. War had brought so many assignments. Now it was time to find the one that would bring him fulfilment in peacetime. Like his grandfather, restlessly looking beyond stenography, Geoffrey Howard sought an alternative to this world of ledgers.

First there was the option of teacher training. "I was called for an interview by the Essex county education board, and it really went well. I was accepted, but I heard nothing, absolutely nothing at all. So I got irritated and started to look for other outlets."

Then there was the idea of farming. "I went to see the chairman of the National Farmers' Union. How I got to an interview at that level, I've no idea. And he talked me out of it. 'You haven't got enough capital,' he said. 'You go back to your job and look after your family.'"

There was a trip to Cornwall to meet three ex-officers planning to restore the Lost Gardens of Heligan. "I spent a weekend there, and I was prepared to put my release money into it. They were going to buy an Admiralty fishing boat and do sea-fishing as well. But I didn't altogether like them, so I talked myself out of it."

He even applied for re-instatement in the RAF. "I passed the medical and got accepted. But I'd have gone out and served with UNRRA, the United Nations Relief and Recovery Association, in Germany, and that put me off. I would probably have had to leave Nora and the children at home."

"I remember one afternoon at the bank, I was talking on the telephone to my brother, about my restlessness, my difficulty reconciling myself to civilian life. Suddenly I realised there was no noise about me. Everybody had gone home. And I hadn't noticed. I was so absorbed in the conversation."

The one thing that did not feature in this post-war life was playing cricket. Private Banks were re-forming, and they asked him to re-join. "I'm sorry," he said. "I'm not playing any more. I've had six years away from my wife and children. I can't go off every Saturday afternoon and play cricket. I want to go home." And their response? "They thought it was odd, but I maintained it."

How strange sometimes are the twists of fate!

"And, by maintaining it, I found myself going into first-class cricket."

The Essex captain in 1946 was his old friend Tom Pearce. The first fixture was at Taunton, where Somerset set Essex 383 to win and Tom, arriving at the wicket at 75 for four, *'gained a powerful mastery of the bowling'* with a winning 166 not out. Then on the Saturday Geoffrey called at Ilford on his way home from the bank. And Tom Pearce – "I can see him coming out of the pavilion now, just as I knew him, no batting gloves." – *'drove and pulled vigorously'* on his way to another century. "He wasn't a great player of spin bowling, but between mid-off's left-hand and mid-on's right hand, he could be pretty devastating."

Geoffrey Howard had watched Surrey at The Oval as a boy. He had played for Middlesex, and he had lived and played club cricket in Kent. Now he was in Essex. "I remember writing to Tom, saying 'Can I become a member?' I was thinking that I might have to do all sorts of things to qualify, and all you needed was a guinea. So I joined Essex as a member. Bought a tie."

Essex, with a mixture of old and new – Sonny Avery and Dickie Dodds, the cousins Smith and Trevor Bailey – finished in eighth place, and Tom Pearce scored five centuries. *'Enthusiasm among members ran high,' Wisden* records, *'and increased attendances were reflected in a satisfactory balance sheet.'*

In the autumn Tom Pearce was laid up in Romford Hospital after a road accident, and Geoffrey called on him. "A friendly visit, nothing in mind. But not long afterwards he came on to the phone. 'How would you like to be secretary of Essex? Because, if you would like to, I think I can arrange it.'"

Brian Castor, who had so keenly developed Essex's policy of playing all round the county, was taking over at The Oval and, with farming forgotten and no news from the Essex Education Board, Geoffrey expressed enthusiasm. "Tom suggested that he could say 'I've got the man you want' and they would have to accept it. But in the end they decided, as committees do, that they would advertise it."

At the Great Eastern Hotel in Liverpool Street, he sat before them. "Sir Hubert Ashton was in the chair. It was one of those absurd interviewing bodies; there must have been twenty there. I answered all the questions. Then one said, 'What experience do you have in preparing wickets?' A very odd question. I said, 'The only answer I can give to that is that I haven't any.' And with that the meeting concluded."

There were three candidates short-listed: Geoffrey Howard from Martins Bank, the old Northants amateur T.B.G. Welch and Robert Paterson, who had played that summer for Essex. "I was fairly light-hearted because I'd still got this teacher training in mind."

Then came the telephone call from Brian Castor at The Oval. "I'm sorry, but they've appointed Robert Paterson. But how would you like to come here as my assistant?"

Back in Upminster, he reported to Nora. Their third child Ursula was born by now, and he weighed the attraction of a life in cricket against his loss of pension and the junior nature of the post.

"I don't think I'll do it," he resolved. "Being the secretary's one thing, but being the assistant secretary's something quite different."

"Oh well," Nora replied. "It's your decision. But, if you do decide to go back to the bank, stop grumbling about it."

Through six long years Nora had moved all over England, keeping the family together, and "she was wonderful, she never complained."

"Stop grumbling about it." Her words jolted him into a new life.

By February 1947, he was once more walking through the gates of The Oval. "I was coming up to 38 years old. Not a very good time to start a new career. I'd never have done it but for the war. I would have accepted the banking, gone on till I was 60 and taken the pension."

He would have retired in January 1969, from a Martins Bank that was about to be taken over by Barclays. "I was one of the only ones who left. The others all soldiered on, sometimes bitterly regretting it to the end of their days. But I had become a restless soul. Like my father and grandfather."

A new life lay ahead of him. Two years at The Oval, then on to Old Trafford where he would spend sixteen years as secretary. "Lancashire had their account at the District Bank in Manchester. Whenever I went in there, the Chief Cashier always said to me, 'Ah, here's the man who got away.'"

# CHAPTER FIVE

# A CLUB RUN BY AMATEURS

# THE OVAL

# 1947 – 49

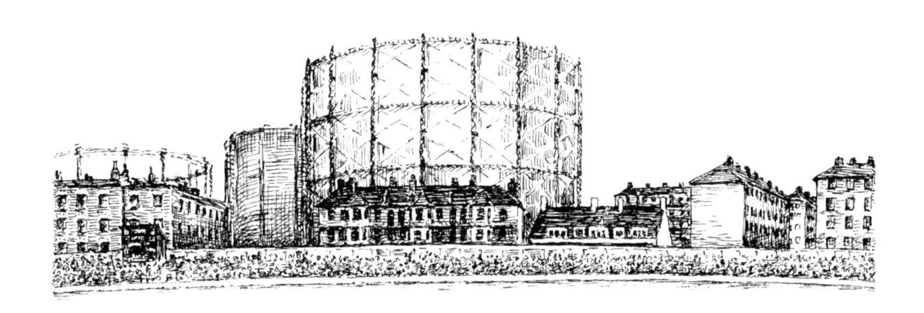

The Private Banks cricketers of 1927 had spread into the county cricket of 1947. Tom Pearce was captain at Essex, Arthur Childs-Clarke at Northampton. Now Geoffrey Howard was assistant secretary at The Oval. Fred Holland, the Banks' groundsman, was a Surrey man, and he was quite clear about the relative merits of the three assignments. "Of all the cricketers who've passed through here," he told Geoffrey, "you've got the best job."

The best job perhaps but certainly not the easiest. The Oval had suffered extensive damage, requisitioned by the War Ministry and accommodating in sequence a prisoner-of-war cage, a barrage balloon and an assault course. Alan Davey, the secretary, spent six years working from his home in Wimbledon and, when he returned in the winter of 1945/46, he oversaw the laying of fresh turves across the whole playing area. Bert Lock the head groundsman employed shilling-an-hour volunteers from the locality, and there was great relief when the summer began and the square played truly. So truly that, in only the second first-class match, Sarwate and Banerjee of India, batting at numbers ten and eleven, both scored centuries. The only recorded instance of this in the whole history of cricket.

On Monday the third of February Geoffrey Howard began his new life, but it was a full two months before the green grass from Gravesend Marshes became visible beneath the thick snow that paralysed Britain that winter. The ground staff prepared composts in a few dry areas under the Vauxhall Stand, but mostly they spent their days in the Long Room, with Bert Lock instructing them how to sew up the decaying nets.

"The Oval was in such a run-down state, and there wasn't much one could do. Because of the weather and because of the post-war privations. You could see things that were shrieking out for repair, but you couldn't get the materials, let alone the labour. The Oval is a very proud place, you can't help feeling it, but in those days it was much scruffier than Lord's."

The pavilion was heated by coal fires, and coal was scarce. So it was never warm. "You had to be content with the ambient temperature." The water heating system had mostly broken down, and all round the ground the lavatories were in a state of disrepair. The seating, the scoreboards, the bars, they all cried out for remedial work, and it fell to the new assistant secretary to organise repairs as materials became available. An assistant secretary who was entering a world "about which I knew hardly anything or anybody at all. I had never even been to a committee meeting before."

At Martins Bank he had been frustrated by the mundanity of his work. Now he was in another world. "It was a revelation, the people I suddenly found myself mixing with on equal terms. At a very early committee meeting, the door opened and everybody got up and made a great fuss of the man who came in. 'Harry, how wonderful to see you.' It was the Earl of Rosebery, and they all called him Harry. He was captain of Surrey before the First War, when he was Lord Dalmeny. 'The only sensible thing I did for Surrey,' he said, 'was to give Jack Hobbs his cap.'"

Committee meetings were once a month, at four o'clock on a Thursday afternoon, always with Mr H.D.G. Leveson Gower in the chair. "Pronounced

Loosen Gore. Henry Dudley Gresham Leveson Gower. He was a stockbroker, but I don't think he was an awfully good one. He ran the Scarborough Festival each year, and they used to say that he got more money from that than from his business."

By 1947 Leveson Gower was 74 years old. A short man, he was known as Shrimp. But what he lacked in height, he made up for in importance. A former England captain, the younger brother of Earl Granville, he had served for twenty-five years as chairman of Surrey's cricket committee. "He was the éminence grise. He ran the club. Oh Lord, yes, he was God's brother Alf."

*Sir Henry Leveson Gower*

At the first committee meeting attended by the new assistant secretary, the subject of the captaincy was on the agenda. In 1946 the county had appointed Major Nigel Bennett, an undistinguished club cricketer but the only amateur they could find. There is a story that they had being looking for Major Leo Bennett and had become confused when his namesake arrived to renew his membership, though Geoffrey thinks that might be apocryphal. Whatever the truth, Surrey slipped to twelfth place, as low as they had ever finished, and they looked for another captain for 1947.

There were several past captains involved in the running of the county club. Not just Lord Rosebery (1905-7) and Leveson Gower (1908-10) but Errol Holmes (1934-38) and Monty Garland-Wells (1939). Sometimes even Percy Fender (1921-31), though "he had been deliberately sidelined because of his total antipathy to Shrimp, who never called him anything but 'Thender'."

In 1946 Percy Fender, already aged 53, was proposed as second eleven captain, but Leveson Gower commanded a majority for his alternative proposal of the Honourable Bobby Blades, the young son of fellow committee member Lord Ebbisham.

"Lord Ebbisham. He usually only came to the second eleven matches. 'Where have I left my umbrella? I can't find my umbrella.' I spent quite a lot of time in 1947, going round the pavilion, trying to find his umbrella."

Amateurs with time to play cricket were hard to find in post-war England, and by 1947 there were no obvious candidates beyond the committee table.

"The discussion went on and on. All the people who might be approached. Then Errol Holmes, who was a member of the committee, said, 'Well, I am prepared to take on the captaincy again, as long as I am paid.' There was a gasp, then a silence that had to be heard to be believed. The thought of Surrey being captained by a professional! 'What do you mean by that, Errol?' 'I haven't got the resources to do it in any other way.'"

The minutes of the next committee meeting in March record the outcome: *'Pleasure was expressed that Mr E.R.T. Holmes had found it possible to accept the captaincy.'*

"He looked for somebody to pay him, somebody who wasn't anything to do with Surrey or cricket, and an Indian, who was involved in the insurance market, gave him a job. Tommy Chopra. After that, I think, he was paid by the *Daily Express*."

The finance sub-committee minutes add a further detail: *'It was agreed to recommend that Mr E.R.T. Holmes be allowed a first-class return fare to Oxted for all home matches.'*

"Errol Reginald Thorold Holmes. He married Leveson Gower's niece. He should have been born a hundred years earlier. He was a sort of aristocrat in manners and thinking. He looked one, too, with his M.C.C. Overseas cap, with the George and Dragon, and his Free Foresters blazer."

Meanwhile, at his first ground sub-committee meeting, Geoffrey Howard listened to discussion of the deteriorating tarpaulins, the dangerous footway between the pavilion and the Tavern, the inability of the Post Office to attend to the wiring to the scoreboard telephone, and the difficulty in finding a motor roller. The heavy roller in use weighed 3½ tons and took eight men to move, but *'a quotation for 12 months delivery of a suitable roller from Aveling Barford Ltd at £800 was considered too expensive.'*

With the pavilion never warm and snow all over the playing surface, this was another world from Martins Bank in Hanover Square. "I had twenty years' seniority there, and the pension was non-contributory. I left with just one month's salary and the ninety pounds the R.A.F. had paid me on completing my service. One of my brothers-in-law said, 'You must be mad.' He was dead right. But looking back, I've got no regrets."

Officially the new recruit's position at The Oval was as assistant to the secretary, not assistant secretary. It may sound a minor difference, but it was an important one to the committee. The previous secretary, Alan Davey, had announced his resignation at the end of a committee meeting in July 1946, as a result of still being on the same salary – £850 – as he had received before the war, and Bill Haseldene, the assistant secretary, had resigned, disgusted that he had not been promoted. So there was to be no idea in the mind of the new assistant that he might succeed Brian Castor.

"If ever a man looked the part, it was Brian. He was large, beautifully dressed with black hand-made brogue shoes, with his monocle dangling. It's hard to imagine a more impressive figure. But it wasn't long before I realised that he did need an assistant."

Charles Bray, who became cricket correspondent for the *Daily Express*, played for Essex in the 1930s, when Brian Castor was secretary there. "He loved to do all the spectacular things," Charles used to tell. "Like ringing the five-minute bell at lunchtime. So one day at Leyton a couple of us shortened the rope. When he went to ring it, he couldn't reach."

Brian Castor was Surrey secretary from 1947 to 1957, but a little part of his heart stayed in Essex. "Whenever the ticker tape machine went," his assistant remembers, "the first score he would look at would be Essex."

He was born in 1889 and served in the First War in the King's Royal Rifles in German East Africa. Then he managed a theatrical touring company led by the comedian Leslie Henson before becoming secretary at Essex. In the 1930s Geoffrey knew him as a keen and able Sunday cricketer with a wandering side, the Musketeers. A large man in every sense. But at the outbreak of war he rejoined the Army, being posted to Singapore where he served in the Military Police. He was 52 years old when it fell to the Japanese, and he spent 3½ years as a prisoner-of-war, his weight down to ten stone by the end."

Like most prisoners of the Japanese, he did not talk much about the experience, "only how they kept the game of cricket going. Wilf Wooller, Freddie Brown. They manufactured a ball from rope and string, and they had one copy of *Wisden*." The long years of captivity left him longing to return to the England he knew before the war, not this England in which he found himself in 1947.

"He wasn't looking forward at all. He was just upholding the traditions he'd grown up with. And he suffered, as a lot of people did in those days, from the indignity of being governed by the Labour Party. He used to write letters to *The Times*, signed 'A Tory'. What did he call Edith Summerskill? 'That acidulated bitch.' He called me a Communist. Anybody who wasn't a Tory was a Communist. We worked in the same office, and one day he got irritated with me to the extent that he swept his glasses off and threw them at me. It was near the end of the day, and before long we were both on our hands and knees in the half-light, searching for the glasses and laughing at ourselves."

For all their incompatibility, the new assistant had come to The Oval at Brian Castor's instigation, and a thread of affection always ran through their relationship. "He was so generous to me, such a good friend, and he was very good at laughing at himself."

At Surrey County Cricket Club it was the assistant secretary whose political sympathies were not the norm, as he discovered when the annual dinner was addressed by the Home Secretary, James Chuter Ede. A little man with a Chaplin-like moustache and a homburg hat, he sometimes sat in the public seats filling in a schoolboy's scorebook. "When he arrived before the dinner, nobody wanted to speak to him. 'Chuter Ede? Corporal in the First War, wasn't he?' Then he gave a most wonderful speech about cricket and, of course, everybody wanted to talk to him afterwards."

In April the snow melted, and the cricketers returned. The Surrey side was in transition, the pre-war team of Gover, Barling, Fishlock, Gregory, Squires, Parker and Watts starting to make way for a younger generation: the Bedsers, Laker, McIntyre, Fletcher, Surridge and Lock. Under Errol Holmes' captaincy, the changes were at times painful, but he was not a man to worry unduly about the sensibilities of the professionals.

"It was his instinct to be a leader, not his training. So he was not without prejudice."

In the bound minute book of the cricket sub-committee are his confidential end-of-season comments on the players under his charge:

*Barling is well past his best and getting slow in the field. Is rather "gutless" but has great ability. .... Gover is "finished" and will only do harm to himself and his county by carrying on. .... Fishlock is not so young as he was. Also very deaf and sometimes I feel a little "light-headed". ... Parker's temperament is hopeless for a bowler, he cannot bear to be hit about and upsets the whole side. A difficult chap and needs handling. ... Lock is very young and very pleased with himself, but he has possibilities.... At the beginning of the year I found Bedser A.V. rather swollen-headed, but with firm handling this will not recur. But firm handling is essential.*

Only Jim Laker emerged uncriticised:

*A real "find". He is a finished cricketer and will never let you down. Full of "guts" and a thorough Yorkshireman, who is very popular with the rest of the Surrey side.*

"Errol was a black-and-white chap. He was all for you or all against you. He had great faith in Jim Laker, but he didn't like Tom Barling."

Not all his opinions were at one with those of the Surrey coach, Andrew Sandham. "I was sitting in my office, a good long way from the nets, and I saw the young players, the prospective professionals, practising. And I thought,

'That little chap looks as though he can bat.' I looked more closely, and it was Andrew Sandham. At the age of 57. A perfect example of how to play."

In the 1947 *Wisden*, Sandham's 107 centuries put him in eighth place in its list of hundred-makers, but he was powerless to stop Errol Holmes trying to turn the Australian John McMahon from an orthodox slow left-armer to *'this funny stuff bowling'* or to save Tom Barling: *'Can the club afford to let him go until the 2nd XI has been built up?'*

"Tom Barling was a bit of a loner, but he was a beautiful batsman, with an enormously broad bat. He was probably as good a player at the end of his career as he'd ever been." In the Surrey side from 1927 to 1939, he returned in 1946 to be one of only seven men in the country to top 2000 runs. He added 1600 in 1947, and a useful start to 1948 can have left him with no inkling of what was to happen at the end of June when he arrived in the dressing room for the match against the Australians. "In those days everybody wanted to play against the tourists. Not like the rag, tag and bobtail the counties put out now. Errol didn't even take him to one side. It was just, 'Barling, you're twelfth man.' He was absolutely shattered."

It fell to the secretary's assistant to complete the business. "I had to be the one to tell him he was finished, and I made the not-very-intelligent observation, 'Don't worry, Tom. This door has shut, but sooner or later another will open and you will forget all this.'"

The following summer, when Geoffrey was the new secretary of Lancashire, Tom appeared in his office at Old Trafford. "He was thoroughly pleased with himself because he'd got two jobs. He was coach at Harrow, and he was working for Lillywhite Frowde, who made cricket bats and tennis racquets."

Though he did not know it, there were influential figures beginning to notice qualities in the new assistant secretary. "I can remember finding Plum Warner wandering around in the Long Room, and I looked after him for the day. He, Shrimp and the Lancashire chairman Tommy Higson had all been Test selectors in the 1930s."

While Brian Castor provided the public face of the club's administration, his assistant worked hard behind the scenes on the many and varied tasks that came to the secretary's office, first and foremost the repair work: "We were constantly having to get the plumber in for burst pipes."

Then there were the second eleven and Club and Ground sides to be organised: "I sent the card inviting Peter May to play his first second eleven match. At Norwich in 1948. There'd been a lot of talk about the two young amateur cricketers, Peter May and Colin Cowdrey. They both had Surrey qualifications, Peter from school, Colin because he was living with his uncle and aunt in Sutton. The committee decided to concentrate first on Peter because he was three years older. Geoff Whittaker played in that match at Norwich. I remember asking him afterwards what he thought of Peter. 'Not bad for an amateur,' he said."

On match days there were sometimes decisions to be taken about the closing of the gates: 30,000 in the ground one August Saturday to see Middlesex make 537 for two, Compton and Edrich adding 287 in just 2¾ hours: "What wonderful batsmen they were. They didn't just wait for bad balls to hit." In June, the gates closed at Lord's on the Saturday of the Test, and thousands crossed London to fill The Oval for the Surrey-Glamorgan game. "A good proportion of them would be standing or sitting on the grass. It could be very uncomfortable. I'd say to Brian, 'I think we ought to close the gates', and he'd say, 'It's up to you.'"

An attempt was made to stamp out the practice of members passing their tickets out to friends. "I remember seeing little Shrimp standing by the Hobbs Gates, raising his bowler to a friend in the street and popping through his ticket. I told Brian. 'It's got to stop,' he said. He was very anti-Shrimp. But I don't think he ever took it further."

There were distinguished guests to entertain. Field-Marshal Montgomery attended the first day of the Surrey-Australians match in May 1948. "I was deputed to receive him. I can see it now. He got out of his enormous armoured Rolls Royce. A corporal driver came round, opened the door for him, and he stepped out and drew himself up to salute. But there was nobody there at all. I took him into the pavilion and spent the whole day with him. He never stopped talking. 'You've got to attack,' he kept saying. 'They're not attacking.'"

The twelve-year-old Duke of Kent came later in the summer with his tutor Lord St Leven. "I sat with them all day. After lunch I had to take him over to meet Don Bradman and, because I was used to my own young children, I took him by the hand and walked him across the room. He said, 'You know, I'm quite a big boy, sir.'"

Then there was the visit of Wally Hammond in May 1947. Surrey were entertaining the South Africans, and the England captain, just back from touring Australia and crippled by lumbago, presented himself at the secretary's office where Geoffrey sat alone. "I must have given him some tickets or something. As he was going out, I said, 'What are you doing for lunch?' He said, 'I've got no arrangements.' So I gave him a ticket for lunch and tea. I left the office and, when I came back, there was Brian, looking really irritated. 'Did you give Hammond these tickets? ... Well, you shouldn't have done. I've taken them away.'"

Like Tom Barling's dismissal, the sequel took place in Geoffrey Howard's office at Old Trafford in 1949. "Wally Hammond came in during the Test match, and I gave him lunch and tea tickets. He said, 'You're not going to take them back, are you?'"

Life at Brian Castor's side was full of such moments. "I used to ask if I could play odd games for Club and Ground, and always he would say, 'Yes, of course.' Then the day before, I would say, 'Brian, you haven't forgotten that tomorrow I won't be here.' 'Oh dear, oh dear,' he'd reply. 'What am I going to do without you? I wish you weren't going.' Then he'd let me go, and I'd feel thoroughly disloyal. But the day after, he'd turn round and lend me fifty pounds. He was such a nice, kind chap, you couldn't help liking him. But he was difficult.

"He gave me a ticket to the Lord's Test. He lived in St John's Wood. A substantial, two-bedroom flat, right opposite the ground. Number One, Grove End Road. He paid a pound a week rent, including electricity. 'At lunchtime,' he said, 'go round to my flat and Phyllis will give you a meal.' I'd never met her, and we sat down to this lovely lunch she'd prepared, in the course of which she said to me, 'How do you get on with my husband?' and, before I could reply, 'Awkward bugger, isn't he?'"

Brian Castor's sister had married the actor Donald Wolfit – "He had no time for him, used to call him Wolfit" – while he himself had married into the Medawar family. Phyllis's brother was Sir Peter, winner of the Nobel Prize for Medicine, and Peter's son was a Cambridge mathematician, just the chap Brian thought he needed to relieve him of his most burdensome task. "The fixture list for the whole country fell to Brian to do, and it drove him barmy. He'd sit there with his pencil and rubber, then suddenly he'd throw the whole thing down. So he sent it to his nephew, but it soon came back with a note saying, 'This is not a mathematical problem.'"

Through the summer of 1947 Brian Castor courted the touring South Africans in the hope that he would be appointed manager of the M.C.C. tour there in the winter of 1948/49. Such an appointment was the pinnacle of every secretary's ambition, and he had South African connections from his service in the First World War. "The South Africans had told him they wanted him, but it didn't happen. Michael Green of Worcestershire was appointed. He was a much quieter, calmer man."

Surrey rose from twelfth to sixth under Errol Holmes' captaincy in 1947. Then in 1948, with Errol Holmes sharing the captaincy with the young amateur Michael Barton, they came within four points of winning the championship for the first time since 1914. If only they had not dropped those two catches when Middlesex won by one wicket at The Oval, with Jim Sims hitting 36 not out: *'Fortune favoured him, for he was twice dropped when ten runs were needed with the last pair together.'*

Some of the players criticised Errol Holmes' captaincy that day, but Brian Castor in the secretary's office was quicker to find fault when Michael Barton was in charge. "Brian used to sit there in his swivel chair, muttering imprecations about his ineptitude. 'Why the hell doesn't he ... ?' He wrote the criticisms down on bits of paper."

The great Surrey side of the 1950s was starting to take shape. Jim Laker, Alec and Eric Bedser, Arthur McIntyre, Stuart Surridge and David Fletcher were capped players while Tom Clark and Bernie Constable were starting to come through. Tony Lock was away on National Service, the slow left-arm bowling in the hands of John McMahon, Peter May was making his second team debut at Norwich, and a 17-year-old Ken Barrington had joined the ground staff. "They thought he showed promise as a leg-spinner, but he was really taken on to learn the art of groundsmanship." *'His bowling was rather disappointing,'* read Andrew Sandham's perceptive end-of-season report, *'but he is a good bat for his age.'*

Laker and Lock. "If they wanted somebody to bowl to in the nets," the secretary's assistant remembers. "I'd go and have a bat. Jim was the older, more experienced cricketer. I had no trouble with Tony Lock, who didn't spin it much in those days, but Jim Laker was a different cup of tea. He bowled consistently at your off and middle stumps, and you'd get in a routine. Then suddenly one would go the other way, and you hadn't spotted it. He had that wonderful gift of the ball that leaves the right-hand batsman. And he had flight. But he was a fairly lazy chap, really. You couldn't see him rolling up his sleeves and digging a hole in the ground. He'd get somebody else to do it and light up a cigarette. The two things at which he shone were spin bowling off a very short run and sitting in a commentary box, giving his views."

Eric and Alec Bedser. "Eric always lived in the shadow of Alec. But he might have been an equally famous cricketer. If Jim Laker had not been such a good off-spinner, he would have done the double several times. 'If I'd been captain,' Bob Gregory told me. 'Eric Bedser would have been top of the bowling averages.'"

Jim and Tony, Alec and Eric. "I was on such good terms with all the players. I remember Brian Castor telling Alec off for calling me by my Christian name. Even Jack Hobbs called me Mister Howard."

Surrey was run by amateurs, and the professional cricketers learned to know their place. "'You're servants of the club,' Brian Castor used to say. The professionals weren't allowed in the members' bar. 'The eyes of the world are on you,' Errol Holmes told them. 'You can't afford to be seen drinking with the members.' They had to go out to the Surrey Tavern."

Membership of Surrey was not just a matter of paying a subscription. It was limited to 5,000 men, 400 boys and 450 ladies and girls, and it required two proposers, with each applicant's name presented to the full committee. Like holding a bank account or being granted a mortgage, it distinguished you from those of lower rank.

"You need a proposer and a seconder," one bewildered fourteen-year-old boy was told when he arrived in the general office in the summer of 1947. "My dad had given me ten shillings and sixpence to buy a schoolboy membership," he remembers, "and I didn't even know what a proposer and seconder were. But just at that moment Geoffrey came into the general office, and he caught hold of Errol Holmes and Bob Gregory. 'These two will propose and second you,' he said."

"What's your name?"

"Stewart. Michael Stewart."

Over half a century later the assistant secretary and the schoolboy sit together in the Committee Room, two former presidents of the club, and they reflect on this lost world of gentlemen.

"I signed for Surrey in Brian Castor's office," Micky recalls. "Peter May came in, and I knew him from Army cricket. 'Hallo, Peter,' I said. 'Hallo,

Micky, I'm glad you're joining us.' Then, after I'd signed the contract, he said, 'I've got to go now. All the best, Micky.' 'Thank you, Peter.' And Brian jumped in. 'You mean Mister May.' I was a professional now."

"Members could ring The Oval on non-match days," Geoffrey says, "and request a net, and I would have to provide bowlers from the playing staff. I wonder what would happen today if a Surrey member rang up and said, 'I'd like to have a net.'"

Alf Gover was a Test cricketer, the only fast bowler to take 200 wickets in two consecutive seasons. He had been an officer in the war, but his status at The Oval was among the unranked, as the minutes of the finance sub-committee meeting of December 1948 make clear. The subject was the investment of his benefit money.

*'Gover's Investments. A letter was referred to which had been received from Gover, drawing attention to the serious drop in the market value of his holding in 2½% consols and to the capital appreciation of his holding in British Electric. Gover asked that the latter be sold, but it was decided to inform him that the committee did not think the present moment a proper time to sell.'*

By this time Percy Surridge, Stuart's father, had joined the committee. "Percy's father was the Golden Dustman. He got the contract for clearing the dustbins in Wandsworth with his horse and cart. Then more horses and carts. Then he happened on the contract for removing the spoil when they excavated for the Underground. So he got lots and lots of carts and lots and lots of barges, and he took the spoil to Essex where he started planting willow trees. And from the willow trees grew the bat industry. He put all his money into buying property around south London. If I drove around that part of London with Stuart, he was always pointing out properties they owned."

When Michael Barton retired at the end of 1951, the committee could once more find a captain from their own. Stuart Surridge led them for five years, and in each one of them he won the championship. By then Geoffrey Howard was well-established at Old Trafford. "I liked Brian Castor very much, but by the end of my first year at The Oval I had my eyes on the secretaryship of any county."

At Lord's the secretary, Colonel Rait Kerr, wanted a second assistant to take on the backlog of maintenance, and Geoffrey Howard was persuaded to apply. "RK was a disciplinarian. We all had to sit in the Long Room and write an essay." At the end of the day he took a bus with another candidate. "Goodbye," they said. "I don't suppose we shall meet again." But his fellow passenger – surveyor and estate agent Jim Dunbar – was M.C.C.'s choice.

A member of the Surrey committee, Charles Killick, pointed out to him that Lancashire was advertising for a secretary. "He was a theatre chap and a Lancastrian himself, and he told me I should apply. But I didn't want to apply for another job I wasn't going to get. 'I think I know the north well enough,' I said, 'to be certain it will be a Lancastrian who gets that post.' 'Yes,' he said, 'I'm sure you're right, but you should apply.'"

The District Bank, High Street, Manchester. In the large reception room of the manager's office, Surrey's assistant secretary sat before the full Lancashire committee, with Tommy Higson in the chair. "I was totally relaxed because I was certain I wasn't going to get it. It can be quite an advantage."

Was it his relaxed manner that day? His reputation for quiet efficiency? A word from Charles Killick? A behind-the-scenes endorsement from Plum Warner and 'Shrimp' Leveson Gower, who had once been Test selectors like Tommy Higson?

In two years Geoffrey Howard went from being number three at a branch of Martins Bank, earning £550 a year, to being the secretary of Lancashire County Cricket Club, with its Test match ground. His salary started at £850, with the promise of £1,000 within three years.

"I want to tell you," Tommy Higson wrote the following Spring, "you got the job on your personality alone. I feel you are the right man for Lancashire people who will like your ways." Tommy Higson was in his 49th year as a committee member, and the letter was written with a shaky hand on his 18th day in bed. "I hope you will reign long – after I have gone."

The letters of congratulation are still in Geoffrey's possession, among them the expressions of regret from the men he was leaving behind at The Oval. "Everyone will miss you," Leveson Gower wrote. "No one more than I. You have been a great stand-by and a great help to me personally for which I shall always be grateful. One final request to you: please remember I am "Shrimp" to you, not Mr L.G."

"We shall miss you very much at The Oval," Bobby Blades wrote. "In fact I don't know what Brian will do without you."

It is easy to feel the claustrophobia he must have felt as assistant secretary, sharing that office with Brian Castor. But their friendship endured. "He stayed quite a few times with us in Manchester. There was a shortage of sweets, and he always brought the children bags full of coconut ice that Phyllis had made."

Brian Castor died in October 1979, in his ninetieth year. "The cremation was at Kensal Rise, and Peter May stood up. 'Do you mind if I say a few words?' And when he was talking, I thought, 'I'd like to say something, too.' But the chance didn't arise. He was awkward to work with, but my memories are all of a man I was fond of."

"He wasn't somebody the players felt they could talk to," Micky Stewart says, "but I do remember, after I was married, when the children had measles, he rang up twice a day to see how they were. Morning and evening."

"He would sit at the window of the office," Geoffrey recalls, "looking out at the cricket. If the telephone rang, he would turn in his swivel chair and answer it. Then he would throw down his pen. 'Aaah,' he would say, 'I wish I didn't love this game so much.'"

# CHAPTER SIX

# THE THIRD TEST

# MELBOURNE

# DECEMBER 1954 – JANUARY 1955

"I can see Len now. He was sitting up in his bed with a woollen vest on, staring at the wall."

"I don't think I can play today," Hutton said. "I'm not feeling too well."

It was Friday the 31st of December, the third Test was scheduled to start in less than two hours, and the England captain had lost his will for the battle.

'He was feeling unwell,' his official biographer Gerald Howat records, 'with fibrositis and a cold, white as a sheet and shivering.'

But that is not how anybody else in the room remembers it.

"He seemed to be in a very disturbed state," Denis Compton wrote, "as if suddenly things had got too much for him, and he couldn't or wouldn't go on."

"Come on, mate," Godfrey Evans cajoled.

"Come down to the ground at any rate," Bill Edrich suggested.

"Let's put it this way," Geoffrey Howard says. "If somebody had said, 'The hotel's on fire', he'd have been out of bed and down the stairs as quick as any of us."

*

The day after Christmas, with the team still recovering from their 'hilarious' party, they had caught the train to Newcastle for a three-day country match. But their captain had not gone with them. "He went ahead to Melbourne on his own. He wanted to think things out for himself."

Peter May scored a century for the fourth successive match, Wardle and Appleyard took wickets, and *Wisden* records that 'M.C.C. gave a joyous display.'

Yet all the while their captain sat in his room in the Windsor Hotel in Melbourne, trying to focus his mind on the challenge of the forthcoming Test. It was Thursday afternoon before his team arrived to join him.

"Basically," the manager believes, "it all amounted to one thing. 'How am I going to tell Alec that he's not playing?' That was the thing that was preying on his mind."

The idea before the second Test had been, in the words of Ian Peebles, 'to reserve Bedser for Melbourne, a favourite ground of his, and let him restart at full blast.' But, after the superb bowling of Tyson and Statham at Sydney, Bedser could only regain his place at the expense of Wardle – and that meant disturbing the shape of a winning team.

*

Len Hutton grew up in Fulneck, west of Leeds, in a family steeped in Moravian Presbyterianism. He was not an active worshipper – "I don't remember Leonard showing any signs of ever wanting to go to church" – but he had internalised their belief in discipline, hard work and self-sufficiency and he practised the 'stillness' that for centuries had been a hallmark of the sect.

'What Moravians have said about stillness,' an early Yorkshire believer wrote, in the days when their settlements were attacked by angry mobs, 'has either been strangely misunderstood or strangely misrepresented. They mean by stillness that we should endeavour to keep our minds calm, composed and collected, free from hurry and dissipation."

*

On the eve of the Melbourne Test, the England captain sat drinking coffee with Bob Appleyard, and he watched as Compton, Edrich and Evans came down the steps, dressed up for a night on the town. "Look at those three," he said to his fellow Yorkshireman. "They'll say they need to relax. But this is the time to be thinking about the match."

From Sunday, when they went their separate ways at Sydney, to that Friday morning when he would not get out of bed, he had done little else but think. But what was he thinking?

"I can remember on the voyage out," Geoffrey says, "there were times when I would retire to my cabin with a tin of toffees and a book. But I can't imagine Len doing that. He'd just have sat in his room with the radio on, staring at the wall."

*

A stillness of mind and deep powers of concentration were at the heart of Len Hutton's batting. In 1938 he had stayed at the crease for 13¼ hours to set a new world Test record score of 364. Then after the war he had carried the fragile England batting for years, adjusting his technique to compensate for a left arm made two inches shorter by a gymnasium accident.

Denis Compton scored sparkling runs with a carefree abandon but Hutton carried the responsibility, never more than in the Caribbean the previous winter. The first professional cricketer to lead M.C.C. overseas, he endured a stream of attacks for his diplomatic faux pas and his inability to keep his more wayward team members under control. Yet, after losing the first two matches, he hit 169 at Georgetown, 205 at Kingston, and the series was levelled.

At the start of the summer of 1954 Len Hutton had scored 6,665 Test runs at an average of 61.71. "His powers of concentration at the wicket were enormous," Geoffrey says, "and the statistics are wonderful. But not as wonderful as seeing him bat. He was such a beautiful stroke-maker."

But the Caribbean tour had taken its toll, and in the summer of 1954 he was bowled for nought in the first Test and took a month out of cricket. His replacement as England captain, David Sheppard, was an amateur, and there were many in cricket's ruling circles – not least the selector Walter Robins and the Surrey trio of Errol Holmes, 'Shrimp' Leveson Gower and secretary Brian Castor – who advocated that Sheppard should take charge in Australia rather than the professional Hutton.

Apart from any other consideration, Hutton, whose official title on the tour was captain of the M.C.C. side, was not even a member of Marylebone Cricket Club, an anomaly about which he was very sensitive. "We were going out to a function one night," the manager recalls, "and I was wearing my M.C.C. tie. 'I'd rather you didn't wear that,' Len said to me."

*Captain and Manager*

In the press, Jim Swanton was quick to express his reservations about professional captains, as he had done in 1952 before Hutton's first appointment:

> When professionals have been called upon to lead representative sides, they have not usually taken particularly easily to the job. There is no strong reason why they should since, whereas they have risen to the heights by concentrating all their energy and effort on succeeding in their own particular departments, the secret of captaincy lies in seeing the game as a whole, in appreciating the feelings of the other ten players, and in always taking the unselfish part.

For the England manager, however, the issue was more complex. On the one hand, he regarded much of the attitudes of Swanton and his old Surrey bosses, Brian Castor and Leveson Gower, as outmoded snobbery. "I think Jim would have been upset if anybody had said he wasn't a snob. He was proud of it." By the mid-1950s the certainties of social class were fading. "I remember Jim telling me how he'd been travelling by rail one day in Kent, and some chaps had got in, drinking and making a great noise. 'I suppose you realise this is a first-class carriage,' he said. 'Yes, we do, mate,' they replied. 'Do you want to see our tickets, or would you like to show us yours first?'"

But, on the other hand, the England manager knew that Len Hutton had had no background of training or experience for the responsibilities he carried. "The captaincy of the English cricket team was the most important office in all sport. It meant a lot to Len, but he'd never been captain of Yorkshire. He was very confident of his own ability as a player but, till the later stages of his career, I don't think he ever saw himself as a leader. They say that in 1953, when Freddie Brown played at Lord's under his captaincy, he called Freddie 'Skipper'. He'd been captain for over a year, but he still hadn't got used to it. Deep down, I think he had an inferiority complex.

"He relied a great deal on Dorothy and, by Melbourne, he was missing her terribly. There were times on the tour when I had to pack his bags for him because he wasn't ready. I remember asking him at one point if he'd had any letters of congratulation. 'I've been unindated,' he said. He wasn't a great user of words. 'Unindated.' And he opened up his case and there were hundreds of them. 'Give them to me,' I said. 'I'll write a stereotyped letter of thanks, and you can just top and tail them all.'"

Len Hutton could speak entertainingly at the various functions, and he was always immaculately dressed. But he needed time away from the limelight, time when he did not have to be Len Hutton, M.C.C. captain.

"I was sitting in the Windsor Hotel with him and Johnny Wardle, having a drink, and this Australian sat down at our table. He was full of grog, and he asked Len who he was. 'My name's Joe Soap,' Len said, and this chap spent the rest of the evening calling him Mister Soap."

By the morning of the first day it had all got too much for him.

*

The manager summoned a doctor.

"He was recommended back in London. 'This is the chap you should see if you need medical help in Melbourne.' And I got him to examine Len."

"There's nothing really wrong with you, Mr Hutton," he said. "You'd better get up, have a shower and some breakfast and get down to the ground to play."

Today there would be a sports psychologist on hand to help him through the crisis. "He was depressed, but in those days people didn't talk about depression like they do now. You were expected to get on with your life."

The small gathering in the room waited for the captain's reaction.

"Len didn't look overjoyed at the doctor's opinion. I think he'd made up his mind that he wasn't going to play, but he did as he was told."

With Compton, Evans and Edrich returning to their rooms, the manager quietly offered the captain his assistance.

"If you like, I will tell Alec Bedser he's not playing."

"No," Len insisted. "It's my job."

Nearly half a century later Geoffrey Howard wonders if perhaps he should have insisted. 'The secret of captaincy lies in appreciating the feelings of the other players,' Jim Swanton had written, but it was not lack of appreciation of Alec's feelings that was the difficulty here. "Len knew he was going to hurt Alec, and Len didn't like hurting people."

The world was moving forward. Only eight years earlier, M.C.C. had toured Australia under the management of Major Rupert Howard and the captaincy of Wally Hammond. "They travelled around together by car while the team struggled with the trains. They drove from Brisbane to Sydney with Len and Cyril Washbrook in the back, and the only word they spoke all journey to them was when Wally passed back his cigarette. 'Light that for me, will you?'"

Then in 1950/51 they were under the captaincy of Freddie Brown, with six amateurs in the party. "If Freddie had still been England captain, he'd have taken Alec to one side on the eve of the match. 'I'm afraid I'm going to have to leave you out,' he'd have said, and Alec would have accepted it. 'Right, thank you for telling me.' Alec was used to the master-and-servant relationship. It was much harder to take from Len."

*

At the ground the England captain asked Denis Compton to take Alec Bedser out to the pitch and to see how he felt about bowling on it.

They pressed their thumbs into the ground, and the bowler gave the only reply he was ever going to give. "Yes, I reckon I can bowl well on that. I'd like to play." And he added, "If I do, I'll be trying."

As Compton later wrote, 'It was always a certainty that Alec would be trying.'

Hutton had no stomach for the decision, but his senior players were all of the same mind. Evans, Edrich, Compton: they all told him that he should leave out Alec. But they left it to the captain to find the best way of telling him.

"I can see it clearly to this day," Geoffrey Howard says. "It's a vivid picture in my mind. I'd been delayed at the hotel, and I'd only just arrived. The team list was pinned to the back of the dressing room door. Alec was standing in front of it on one side, Johnny Wardle on the other. They were both changed and ready, both with their blazers on, looking at the list to see who was playing."

'It seems extraordinary to write Bedser off in favour of a bowler who in Sydney was used for only four overs all told,' Jim Swanton fulminated. 'The occasion seemed to call for some sort of accompanying statement, not a mere dropping half an hour before the start.'

"As the Australians took the field," Denis Compton wrote, "you couldn't help feeling a kind of gloom about things, with Len apparently exhausted and without all his usual nerve, and Alec so tactlessly, even woundingly, omitted from the side."

Compton was returning after his injury in the Brisbane Test but, when he was struck a painful blow on the thumb by Miller, with the ball looping up for a catch, the score was 41 for four and the gloom had deepened.

*Melbourne, 1 January. We cannot seem to keep free of trouble. Denis took an awful crack on the thumb from Keith Miller, who bowled really wonderfully. Thank goodness Denis's thumb is only badly bruised and he can bat. We don't really mind if he can't field. We can put a better one in – Vic Wilson!!*

Edrich 4, May 0, Hutton 12, Compton 4.

"It would have been better in some ways," Geoffrey thinks, "if Len had batted down the order. When he failed, going in first, he felt a terrible sense of irresponsibility. That day at Melbourne he was so dejected. He sat there in the corner of the dressing room, still with his pads on, brooding. Out in the middle Colin started to set about the Australian bowling. We were all watching through the little window and, before very long, when he heard us clapping, Len came out to see what was happening."

'Cowdrey played a lovely innings, full of delightfully timed strokes,' an Australian correspondent wrote in *The Times*, 'but his execution was no more perfect than his grand temperament for the desperate situation.'

"Len took his pads off, sat beside us and started to cheer up."

Cowdrey's fifty, a fifty partnership with Bailey, the team's hundred, the clapping became more frequent – and at the heart of it all was the young man, just turned 22, whom the England captain had decided was a winner. 'I'll look after him,' he had told his father at Tilbury, and there had been tears in his eyes when he had said that brief 'I'm sorry' after the telegram had arrived at the Palace Hotel in Perth.

While I was writing this book, I drove Geoffrey to Lord's to watch M.C.C. play the Melbourne Cricket Club, and for a while we sat with Colin's eldest son Christopher. "I think my father really loved Len," he told us.

The mood on that first day at the Melbourne Cricket Ground was transformed. Hutton was no longer a broken man. The masterful batting of his young protégé had cleared the gloom and despondency that had enveloped him and his team since early morning.

"It was a wonderful innings," Geoffrey recalls. "I can see him now, hitting Lindwall past mid-off."

By the evening session Colin Cowdrey was driving Archer to the sightscreen to take his score to 97. Then the next ball he played to leg for three and, in the words of Alan Ross, 'all Melbourne seemed to shout the runs on. The crowd cheered long and movingly. Cowdrey smiled with pure pleasure, a smile of disbelief.'

Ten minutes later he was bowled for 102, and by the close England were all out for 191. 'It will need another supreme effort in the field,' John Woodcock wrote, 'if England's losses are to be retrieved.'

*Melbourne, 1 January. Had a very pleasant evening with Ronnie and Viola Aird last night. Organised by me to keep Len's mind off his worries. He is dead out of form and doesn't look half a batsman at the moment. Colin Cowdrey's hundred was in every way wonderful. And he is such a dear lad. Wonderful cable to him from Plum Warner. 'Cowdrey, Melbourne, Magnificent, Warner.'*

When the Test was over he returned to the subject of this cable, this time enjoying his ear for the Australian dialect.

*Hobart, 10 January. Did I ever quote to you Plum Warner's telegram? 'Cowdrey, Melbourne, Magnificent, Warner.' Great economy both of style, expression and cable charges. He should have replied, 'Warner, Lord's, Good on Yer, Cowdrey.'*

*

Part of the ground was out of bounds, with a stand in the middle of construction for the 1956 Olympic Games, but on the Saturday there were 65,000 spectators present on a day of stifling heat. In five hours of play they watched with increasing discontent as the English team managed just 54 eight-ball overs, where the previous day the Australians had bowled 68. Repeatedly in the middle of overs Hutton conferred with his bowlers and re-set the field, so that the fast bowlers could stay fresh for longer and, at one stage after tea, they had reduced Australia to 134 for seven.

'At this point,' Jim Swanton thought, 'the English effort slackened somewhat, partly because of the natural weariness of the bowlers, but also as it seemed because Hutton was disinclined to risk England batting before the close.' The fielding was at its worst: 'There was an amount of fumbling that no school coach would have allowed to pass unreprimanded, while the throwing was as haphazard as ever.' By close Australia had recovered to 188 for eight, just three runs behind.

The pitch – 'different altogether from the days of the old black marl' – was providing a less and less consistent bounce, and the cracks were starting to appear in the heat. With a rest day to follow, Swanton was unable to predict how it would behave when they returned on Monday. 'I wish I could give any worthwhile indication as to how the wicket is likely to play after the weekend, for upon that largely hangs the result of the match.'

Geoffrey Howard sits in his living room forty-six years later, and he recalls his inspection of the surface before they left the ground. "There was a piece of the pitch, bigger than that mat over there, and you could stand on one corner of it and work it round. It was loose. A great lump with cracks."

*Melbourne, 1 January. Dear Mother and Dad, We stand here at the end of the second day of the Test match with what must be at least an even chance of winning. We must get these last two wickets reasonably cheaply and then go all out for a substantial total. I would like to see them take their last innings on a thoroughly worn wicket with lots of runs to get.*

*

The heat on that Sunday was the greatest that Geoffrey had ever experienced – greater than in Alexandria in the war, greater than anything in six months in India. A northerly wind was blowing down from the heart of the continent, and there were bush fires spreading everywhere. "The atmosphere was as thick as the air inside a pottery kiln," Frank Tyson wrote.

On the beach the wind was blowing up the sand, which was so hot that it stung the face. The Windsor Hotel had no swimming pool so the manager spent the day in the Melbourne suburbs, well away from the cricket ground.

On Monday morning he described the conditions in his letter home.

*Melbourne, 3 January. I am finding it hard to get down to anything at the moment. The heat is simply terrific and conditions awful. There is a fiery wind blowing – just exactly like opening an oven door – and yesterday the day temperature was 105°. It only fell to 98° in the night but strangely enough I slept well, though many did not.*

On that Monday the clouds built up, the heatwave passed, and the temperature fell into the comfortable seventies. But the state of the pitch was not at all as the players expected.

"When they went into the field in the morning, Len looked down at his boots and found little bits of mud sticking to them. 'Look,' he said. 'The wicket's been watered.'"

The Laws of Cricket. 1947 Code – 2nd edition. Section C – The Care and Maintenance of the Pitch. Law 10, final sentence: Under no circumstances shall the pitch be watered during a match.

With relative ease, on that Monday morning, the Australian tail created a first innings lead of 40, and the out-of-touch Hutton summoned all his powers of concentration to take England to 88 for one at tea. 'Hutton has batted since Brisbane,' wrote Alan Ross, 'rather as one who, long word-perfect in several languages, now seems increasingly to hanker for the dictionary.' 'The crowd began to bait Hutton for his slowness,' Swanton reported, 'but they took his side when he made the gesture of offering them his bat.'

After tea he was lbw for 42, Cowdrey played on for seven, and it was left to Compton, with a swollen right thumb, to stay with Peter May while the young vice-captain, with a fine exhibition of driving, reached 83 not out. According to John Woodcock, it was 'an innings of rare beauty and class' while Jim Swanton admired its 'confidence and maturity'. At 159 for three, England's lead was 119, and it remained to be seen whether the future behaviour of the pitch would render that a lead of significance.

'The wicket was definitely not watered,' the groundsman said in a statement. 'It was a very humid night and the wicket sweated. When the covers were removed at seven this morning, the wicket was quite damp. The tarpaulin has a tendency to draw moisture and close cracks. It will be in favour of batsmen tomorrow, and I am quite confident it will last six days.'

The *Melbourne Age* newspaper, however, had received a telephone call that told a different story, and it went into print with the headline, 'Test pitch watered during game.' It was enough for the *Daily Telegraph* in London to run a front page news item, written by Jim Swanton and carrying the sub-headline, 'POSSIBILITY MATCH MAY BE VOIDED': 'If there is proof, the question arises whether the result of the Test match should be allowed to stand in view of the transgression of the laws and playing conditions.'

"The official curator," Geoffrey explains, "was a nice chap, but he'd brought in a curator from a local club to help him. And in club matches, at the end of play on a Saturday, he would have watered his wicket automatically. So, when he saw all the cracks, he must have decided to water it. I'm sure the official curator knew about it."

On the Tuesday England reached 279, with Peter May making 91, and Australia, requiring 240 for victory, finished on 75 for two. They were scores that would have been unimaginable if the pitch had been left to crack in the heat on Sunday.

Meanwhile the Victorian Cricket Association and the Melbourne Cricket Club spent Tuesday carrying out their own investigations, and at close of play they issued a statement: 'After a searching inquiry it is emphatically denied that the pitch or any part of the cricket ground has been watered since the commencement of the third Test match on Friday, December 31.'

"That was not true," Geoffrey says. "Neil Harvey told me that he'd seen it happening. There'd have been a terrible to-do if it had worked to the Australians' advantage, but in the end it didn't. We made 279 in the second innings, and we'd never have got that if it hadn't been watered."

*Melbourne, 4 January. This Test is simply terrific. I wish you could have seen Johnny Wardle. He got 30 off two overs and nearly drove us mad with delight. Of course it had to end, but he made a most valuable 38. In addition our share of the gate will be well over £20,000 so whatever happens we shall have achieved a good deal. After this match I think that all our takings – more or less – will be profit. Rather a pleasant thought.*

The flexible personal overdraft that he had negotiated three months earlier in Perth was finally to be cleared, and he had even persuaded Jim Swanton to lend him his assistant, Margaret Harper, to help type some of the many letters he was having to write.

"How much easier I would have found it to manage the tour if M.C.C. had provided me with the two things I didn't have – help and money."

At Sydney Australia had ended Tuesday's play on 72 for two, requiring 223 for victory. Now in Melbourne they were 75 for two, requiring 240. 'So far,' John Woodcock wrote, 'this game has run a course curiously parallel with that one, and it seems that tomorrow may be another day for the gnawing of parasols.'

'On the face of it,' Jim Swanton thought, ' England would seem to have as good a chance this time as last. Yet the wicket seems to have withdrawn all favours from the fast bowlers who, manfully as they tried this evening, could only occasionally get the ball to come off with any real ginger.'

For Swanton there was one England bowler ideally suited to such a pitch – 'Bedser would have been the chief danger if England had availed themselves of his services' – and, in his absence, the general view seemed to be that their best hope lay with Bob Appleyard, whose four overs before close had yielded the wicket of Favell with a quick off-break. But, prior to this Test, Appleyard had bowled just 13 first-class overs in six weeks, and once more the *Daily Telegraph* correspondent was shaking his head at the ineptitude of the tour management's planning.

"Part of the problem," Geoffrey reflects, "was that we had eighteen players. It was too many."

*

Wednesday the 5th of January 1955. The series was in the balance. The winners here would be 2-1 up with just two matches to play, and the Melbourne crowd filled the ground for a fifth time. 50,000 of them took the total match attendance over 300,000 and set a new record for any cricket match in Australia. Mr. C.G. Howard's overdraft was a thing of the past.

"The crowd had all arrived with their packed lunches and their eskies full of beer, to have a day out to watch England lose."

Despite the speculation that Appleyard would be the key bowler, Hutton turned first to his two young fast bowlers, Tyson and Statham. They had won him the match at Sydney, and his whole tour strategy had been to exploit the Australians' unease against real pace. He had had enough years of suffering at the hands of Lindwall and Miller. If he could beat them with pace, it would be the sweetest of revenges.

Tyson came from the Richmond end, a little uphill and into the breeze, and Neil Harvey clipped his first ball to square leg for two. It had been Harvey who had threatened to take the match away from them on the last day at Sydney, but off the seventh ball of the day's first over he glanced the ball towards fine leg with confidence, and Godfrey Evans – 'with a leap like a flying trapezist' – took what even the laconic Len Hutton called 'a wonder catch'. "It was magnificent," the England manager remembers. The score was 77 for three, and the mood of the morning was set.

In Tyson's third over Benaud hooked at a ball outside his off stump, a wild swing that saw him under-edge the ball down into his wicket – "That was a very bad shot" – then four balls later Miller got a touch to an out-swinger. 'Hutton, at second slip, jumped and parried it and Edrich, at first slip, tumbled to his right and caught the ball just off the ground.' The score was now 87 for five, and the England captain's mood was euphoric: "I felt like a jockey riding a runaway Derby winner," he wrote later.

'The crowd sat silent,' Alan Ross wrote. 'The sun spilled down, its heat ignored in this sudden freezing of pleasurable anticipation.'

Brian Statham was at his relentlessly accurate best. "I don't want to take anything away from Frank Tyson's performance," the manager says. "He was magnificent. But Brian always got a lot of wickets for the bowler at the other end. He gave nothing away, and the Australians like to get on with it. They don't like maiden overs."

Statham took two wickets himself that morning – Hole, caught flashing, and Archer, yorked – but it was Tyson who claimed all the headlines. Maddocks, bowled first ball. Lindwall, lbw to his second. Finally Johnston, caught by Evans 'leaping horizontally like a dolphin'. According to Alan Ross, 'It was a catch to raise the roof in other circumstances; now it merely shook down the curtain."

Australia had collapsed from 75 for two to 111 all out, with Frank Tyson leaving the field with figures of seven for 27. "I was bowling in a daze," he wrote later. "It was as if I were watching another bowler." With Len Hutton not even having to consider a change of bowling, there had been no role for Swanton's danger man, Bob Appleyard.

'Tyson put his arm round Statham,' Alan Ross wrote. 'Together they walked off the field through the avenue made for them by their ecstatic colleagues.'

The crowd of 50,000 had seen 99 balls bowled in 80 minutes of play. "They were stunned into silence," Geoffrey recalls. "The whole thing was over so quickly. They just sat there in their seats, eating their lunch and drinking their beer, while we celebrated in the dressing room. It was the most magic day of my life."

The champagne was set to flow – "but, for some reason, I couldn't find anywhere that sold it. But Keith Tolhurst, the old Victorian cricketer, said, 'Leave it to me.' And I never had to pay for any of it." Even Brian Statham forsook his glass of beer for the fizz. It was the middle of the night in England, but by 6.30 in the morning Mrs Violet Tyson was opening her front door to neighbours keen to congratulate her on her son's triumph. "The house hasn't been empty all day," she later told the *Daily Telegraph.*

What a change of mood there had been in the six days since Len Hutton had sat in his bed, resisting his colleagues' attempts to raise his spirits.

*

The days passed. Between this Melbourne Test and the fourth at Adelaide, the tour moved to Tasmania, and the manager's letters home savoured the excitement in Australian style.

*Launceston, 14 January. The children seem to have had a wonderful time, and I am so glad. Dear little things – they do deserve it - so do you for having to do so much for yourselves while Daddy does it for others – for ENGLAND!!! How about that now? Isn't it a beaut thought? My oath it is!*

He had eighteen cricketers to look after in Australia – and four daughters back in England. The youngest of them, Rosalind, was just six years old.

*Adelaide, 21 January. Your letter came yesterday. I did love dear little old Rosie's remark that I was their Daddy and not the cricketers'.*

They had arrived in Adelaide via Mount Gambier, where they had stayed three nights and played a South Australian Country XI. But it seems that, even after the triumph of Melbourne, the captain was still looking to find some inner stillness.

*Mount Gambier, 19 January. Len pushed off straight to Adelaide from Tasmania – he wanted to be alone! He is an enigma: so often when alone he switches on the radio and sits looking at the wall!! He will never change so long as he plays cricket. None of us knows him, and none of us ever can do so, I think. He just cannot let you in on himself. It is useless to expect that he will do so, although some of the selectors at home thought it possible. He is full of sterling worth and a very good fellow: such a pity he won't really let you get to know him.*

*Len Hutton and Peter May*

*"So typical of Len. People would ask him, 'What would you like to drink?' and he'd say, 'You haven't got such a thing as a cup of tea, have you?'"*

*

At John Woodcock's house, we sat around the table.

"I dare say you had your problems with Len, Geoffrey, because he did sometimes seem to speak in riddles. But you worked well together. You were sympathetic when he needed sympathy. He knew just where he was with you, that was the great thing."

"Every now and then," Geoffrey said, "Len would lose the thread of what he was saying. 'You know what I mean,' he'd say. Cyril Washbrook used to say, 'If he says, 'You know what I mean', that's when he doesn't know what he means himself.'"

*

Geoffrey Howard the manager and Leonard Hutton the captain. Six months they spent together, at the helm of one of English cricket's greatest successes. But their paths never crossed intimately again.

*None of us knows him, and none of us can ever do so.*

Over twenty years later, Geoffrey was embarking on a new life, retired from his position as secretary at The Oval and looking for new projects.

"I wanted to write a biography of Len. I spoke to him, to seek his permission, and I remember what he said to me. 'Nobody knows me better than you, Geoffrey.'"

The story of Hutton's cricket was effectively over at the end of this tour. He played a few county matches for Yorkshire in the summer of 1955, then retired to work for the *London Evening News* before going into public relations for J.H. Fenner and Company, a firm which supplied manufacturing equipment to industry.

"I don't think he ever intended to go on after that tour. He'd been in touch with the *Evening News*. They were making him an offer to write for them, with an amanuensis. For Len, that would have seemed like an easier living with more money. And a motor car. 'Is there a full tank of petrol?' he asked when they delivered it.

"There were only three things in Len's life. Cricket, family and money."

And perhaps the cricket had become the hardest to handle.

"Len was a Yorkshireman through and through. When he batted, his objective was never to give the bowler a chance. Not like Denis. Denis was an entertainer. At some of the smaller games, he'd look out at the crowd. 'There aren't many people here,' he'd say. 'I shan't be out there long.' You couldn't imagine Len saying that. He was a perfectionist, and it took such immense concentration."

*He will never change so long as he plays cricket.*

"After he retired, he was much more relaxed, much more communicative. I might even venture the possibility that he was happier."

*

How different Len Hutton's later life might have been if, on that New Year's Eve, his manager had not called the doctor to his bedside, if they had left him to stare at the wall in his hotel room.

"Peter May would have been captain, of course, and I don't suppose he'd have had any idea that Len was so troubled. So he'd have been in a state of shock. Peter would have played Alec, for certain, and he'd have had to find another batsman. Reg Simpson, probably.

"I wonder if Reg would have done as well as Len did in that second innings. That 42 that Len scored, with Peter May, was a real captain's innings. They dug in at a point when we could have lost the game very quickly. But it's all speculation, isn't it? The fact is that we managed to get Len out of bed."

So the M.C.C. cricketers arrived at Adelaide 2-1 up in the series, one victory away from the winning of the Ashes. Who would have thought it? Len Hutton the builder's son, who had worked his way to greatness through discipline, hard work and self-sufficiency; Len Hutton, who spoke in riddles and felt uneasy with his manager's M.C.C. tie; he was one match away from going into history as one of English cricket's most successful leaders.

On the eve of the fourth Test, as the manager wrote home, he knew that his man was in shape for the challenge.

*Adelaide, 27 January. Len really means business and is determined to make a lot of runs. We all pray that he will do so.*

# AUSTRALIA v ENGLAND – THIRD TEST

Melbourne. 31 December 1954, 1, 3, 4 & 5 January 1955

ENGLAND WON BY 128 RUNS

## ENGLAND

| | | | | |
|---|---|---|---|---|
| L. Hutton * | c Hole b Miller | 12 | lbw b Archer | 42 |
| W.J. Edrich | c Lindwall b Miller | 4 | b Johnston | 13 |
| P.B.H. May | c Benaud b Lindwall | 0 | b Johnston | 91 |
| M.C. Cowdrey | b Johnson | 102 | b Benaud | 7 |
| D.C.S. Compton | c Harvey b Miller | 4 | c Maddocks b Archer | 23 |
| T.E. Bailey | c Maddocks b Johnston | 30 | *not out* | 24 |
| T.G. Evans + | lbw b Archer | 20 | c Maddocks b Miller | 22 |
| J.H. Wardle | b Archer | 0 | b Johnson | 38 |
| F.H. Tyson | b Archer | 6 | c Harvey b Johnston | 6 |
| J.B. Statham | b Archer | 3 | c Favell b Johnston | 0 |
| R. Appleyard | *not out* | 1 | b Johnston | 6 |
| *Extras* | *b 9* | 9 | *b 2, lb 4, w 1* | 7 |
| | | **191** | | **279** |

1-14, 2-21, 3-29, 4-41, 5-115, 6-169, 7-181, 8-181, 9-190, 10-191
1-40, 2-96, 3-128, 4-173, 5-185, 6-211, 7-257, 8-273, 9-273, 10-279

| | | | | | | | | |
|---|---|---|---|---|---|---|---|---|
| Lindwall | 13 | 0 | 59 | 1 | 18 | 3 | 52 | 0 |
| Miller | 11 | 8 | 14 | 3 | 18 | 6 | 35 | 1 |
| Archer | 13.6 | 4 | 33 | 4 | 24 | 7 | 50 | 2 |
| Benaud | 7 | 0 | 30 | 0 | 8 | 2 | 25 | 1 |
| Johnston | 12 | 6 | 26 | 1 | 24.5 | 2 | 85 | 5 |
| Johnson | 11 | 3 | 20 | 1 | 8 | 2 | 25 | 1 |

## AUSTRALIA

| | | | | |
|---|---|---|---|---|
| L.E. Favell | lbw b Statham | 25 | b Appleyard | 30 |
| A.R. Morris | lbw b Tyson | 3 | c Cowdrey b Tyson | 4 |
| K.R. Miller | c Evans b Statham | 7 | (5) c Edrich b Tyson | 6 |
| R.N. Harvey | b Appleyard | 31 | c Evans b Tyson | 11 |
| G.B. Hole | b Tyson | 11 | (6) c Evans b Statham | 5 |
| R. Benaud | c sub (Wilson) b Appleyard | 15 | (3) b Tyson | 22 |
| R.G. Archer | b Wardle | 23 | b Statham | 15 |
| L.V. Maddocks + | c Evans b Statham | 47 | b Tyson | 0 |
| R.R. Lindwall | b Statham | 13 | lbw b Tyson | 0 |
| I.W. Johnson * | *not out* | 33 | *not out* | 4 |
| W.A. Johnston | b Statham | 11 | c Evans b Tyson | 0 |
| *Extras* | *b 7, lb 3, nb 2* | 12 | *b 1, lb 13* | 14 |
| | | **231** | | **111** |

1-15, 2-38, 3-43, 4-65, 5-92, 6-115, 7-134, 8-151, 9-205, 10-231
1-23, 2-57, 3-77, 4-86, 5-87, 6-97, 7-98, 8-98, 9-110, 10-111

| | | | | | | | | |
|---|---|---|---|---|---|---|---|---|
| Tyson | 21 | 2 | 68 | 2 | 12.3 | 1 | 27 | 7 |
| Statham | 16.3 | 0 | 60 | 5 | 11 | 1 | 38 | 2 |
| Bailey | 9 | 1 | 33 | 0 | 3 | 0 | 14 | 0 |
| Appleyard | 11 | 3 | 38 | 2 | 4 | 1 | 17 | 1 |
| Wardle | 6 | 0 | 20 | 1 | 1 | 0 | 1 | 0 |

Umpires: C. Hoy and M.J. McInnes

# CHAPTER SEVEN

# IN THE NORTH

# OLD TRAFFORD

# 1949 – 51

Old Trafford had much in common with The Oval in 1949. They were both Test match grounds – indeed, they were two of the three premier grounds of England. In the previous twenty years there had been seven summers when only three Tests had been held, and on each occasion they had been allocated to Lord's, Old Trafford and The Oval.

The pavilions were similar, both designed in the 1890s by Thomas Muirhead of Manchester: the 'piano nobile' Long Room on a raised ground floor, the balcony above it, the same brickwork and elevations. The Oval design was more generous, but it was not difficult for the new secretary to find his way about his new place of employment.

Both grounds were recovering from extensive war damage, and for his first two years he had to work out of the President's Room while his own office was rebuilt. In 1945 the chairman, Tommy Higson, had launched an ambitious reconstruction fund, hoping to build a new pavilion and increase the ground capacity to 40,000, but less than half the £100,000 target was raised so, as at The Oval, much of the secretary's time was taken up supervising renovation and repair work.

There were differences, though. The playing area at Old Trafford was smaller, but beyond it there was far more land, with two practice grounds and a huge car park, "all dirty and dusty, not tarmacked as it is now."

Surrey County Cricket Club were tenants of the Duchy of Cornwall, but Old Trafford was a freehold site belonging to the Lancashire County and Manchester Cricket Club. "There was even within the curtilage of the ground an area set aside for the Manchester Gun Club, for clay pigeon shooting. We used it as a car park in summer and as a lacrosse pitch in winter. In the end it was sold for a ten-pin bowling alley."

In April 1949 Geoffrey Howard took up his new post, taking lodgings for three months while he made arrangements for his family to join him. "I lived in a chummery, as they call it in India, with two sons of a local MP and quite an eminent surgeon. They taught me a lot about life in and around Manchester. One of the things I rejoice about in my life is that I got to know the north of England and the people who live there."

"I feel you are the right man for Lancashire people who will like your ways," the chairman had written on his appointment, but not everybody in the club shared his enthusiasm.

"I knew you were a Catholic," one member told him. "And I knew you were a southerner. Now I've found out that you're a Londoner. And booger Londoners."

His predecessor was Rupert Howard, who had been secretary since 1932 and who had been a Major in the war in the Royal Army Pay Corps. He had managed two M.C.C. tours of Australia, and at the age of sixty he was passing the reins to his southern successor so that he could concentrate on his textile business in Ashton-under-Lyne.

On 13 April 1949, at the Midland Hotel, the new secretary attended his first committee meeting. "Before I arrived, the minutes were all hand-written. I had to persuade the committee to have them typed and circulated. I can remember taking the book home to my digs in Sale and sitting in my bedroom, writing them up. Because there was never any time during the day."

Fifty years on, the leather-bound volume sits in a grey steel cabinet in the old umpires' room in the pavilion. In Geoffrey Howard's hand it records, *'It was unanimously agreed to co-opt Major R. Howard to all committees except the match committee.'*

"I expect you'll find it will help you," Tommy Higson said.

The gesture was well-meant, but it created a fault-line that produced tremors throughout the new secretary's sixteen years at the club. Rupert Howard had retired from day-to-day duties, but he wanted still to exercise influence. He lived in Sale, next door to Geoffrey's lodgings, with his wife and two sons. Nigel was 23 years old and was beginning his first summer as Lancashire captain. Barry, 22, was captain of the second eleven.

Major R. HOWARD

It was with a deep sense of regret that Major Rupert Howard resigned the Secretaryship of the Club last December for business reasons. The Club owes much to his capable administration over a period of sixteen years. He is succeeded by Mr. Cecil Geoffrey Howard, former Assistant Secretary to Surrey County Cricket Club.

Mr. Cecil Geoffrey Howard took up his duties as secretary of the club in succession to Major Rupert Howard on April 10th.

Educated at St. Christopher's School, Letchworth, and Alleynes School, Stevenage, Mr. Howard served in the R.A.F. as a Flight-Lieutenant. For the past two-and-a-half years he has been assistant secretary to the Surrey County Club.

Apart from his administrative connections with the game, Mr. Howard played in three County championship matches with Middlesex in 1930, and has frequently assisted Surrey 2nd Eleven in Minor Counties' Championship games. He is 40 years of age.

*from the Lancashire year book for 1949*

The management structure was not unlike that at The Oval, but some of the lines of command seemed to have become muddled. "The chairman of the ground committee, Dr Bowling Holmes, went around giving instructions, without even telling me he was on the ground. I would go out and I'd say to somebody, 'Why are you doing that?' and they'd say, 'Dr Holmes told me to.'"

Anxious to follow correct procedures, he rang the M.C.C. secretary, Colonel Rait Kerr, for guidance. "Unfortunately RK rang Rupert Howard to tell him that I'd made the enquiry – which was a pity."

The chairman, Tommy Higson, was an autocrat. It was a style of leadership that Geoffrey Howard recognised from his two years under Leveson Gower at The Oval. But, compared with the Lancashire chairman, 'Shrimp' was the mildest of democrats. The Manchester solicitor, whose intermittent cricket career had begun in the previous century, was in his 49th year on the Lancashire committee, his 18th as chairman, and he expected to get his own way. "I can see him chairing a cricket committee meeting while a match was going on. He would give them something to discuss and go off to watch the cricket. Then he'd come back and tell them what their decision should be."

One committee member was a local schoolmaster, Donny Davies, who had played amateur football for England and wrote occasional articles for the Manchester Guardian under the pseudonym 'Old International'. "There had been a leak to the press, and they were trying to establish who had been responsible. It became quite acrimonious. Tommy Higson practically accused Donny Davies. He was so rude to him that Donny got up and walked out. When the row was all over, I made a few inquiries and I found out that the leaker was none other than Tommy Higson himself."

The Lancashire chairman was a man of great stature in the community, and his religious beliefs had taken him to the verge of converting to Catholicism, as his new secretary had done. But beneath all this there was a mischievous sense of humour. "He won a bet to see the Cup Final at Wembley without a ticket. He got on his train at Carnforth, went down and, as he approached the first challenge, 'How good to see you!' he said. 'Wife and family well?' Straight through. And once he was through, he went to the secretary's Office. 'I'm chairman of Lancashire County Cricket Club. T.A. Higson. Where do I sit?' He sat with the directors. Had lunch with them. Came home and collected his winnings."

Within two months of his appointment, the new secretary found himself at Old Trafford on the Saturday morning of the Roses match. "It was an absolute eye-opener. There was such an intense rivalry. I was staggered by the attendance and the atmosphere. I took my normal morning train to Warwick Road, and I had to walk past these huge queues."

The Superintendent of Police appeared in his office. "You must open immediately. There's a lot of distress outside. People have been here all night, and there are no lavatories."

The telephone rang on the desk, and the chairman's voice came down the line. Acquainted with the police's advice, his instruction was clear: "You're not to open till I get there."

Time passed, and there was no sign of the chairman. "I've got to put pressure on you," the Superintendent said, returning to the office. "The situation is serious."

"Well, of course, in the circumstances," the new secretary responded, "we must open."

"Hardly had I done so than in came the chairman in high dudgeon. He told me what he thought of me, and he finished up saying, 'This would never have happened in your predecessor's time.' So I got on my high horse. 'Mr Higson, if I am to run the job in accordance with my predecessor's methods, you must put them on paper. Otherwise I'll make my own decisions.' And he never said another word."

The packed house saw Len Hutton score a faultless double century, on his way to 1294 runs in June, the highest monthly total in the history of the game, though Geoffrey has a clearer memory of his innings in the return match at Headingley. "Play had started when we arrived and, when we went through the gates, there was absolute silence. We wondered what on earth had happened and, after a while, we enquired. ''Utton's out. Run out for nought.' My word, it mattered."

It mattered, too, in Lancashire where the county had gone fifteen years since the last of their seven championship titles. At The Oval Surrey had not been champions since the First War, and there was not the expectation or emphasis on such success. Lancashire, however, had won three summers in a row in the 1920s and again in 1930 and 1934, and their ageing chairman longed for another taste of glory.

Harry Makepeace was the coach. A Yorkshireman by birth, he had played for Lancashire before the First War and in the great years in the mid-1920s. Regularly, in the new secretary's first summer, the telephone would ring in his office, and the chairman would come through, loud and clear. "Can I speak to Makepeace?"

"I had to go all over the ground to find him."

Tommy Higson was an old man. "He had two objectives: to be on the committee for fifty years and to secure the championship for Lancashire one more time before he died."

Neither was achieved. On Wednesday the third of August, the day after the Roses match at Headingley, with Lancashire languishing in an unprecedented fifteenth place in the table, the chairman died at his home in Grange-over-Sands. "I hope you will reign long – after I have gone," he had written to his newly-appointed secretary in the Spring, and within the fortnight Geoffrey Howard found himself reciprocating the old chairman's kindness. "His widow came to live with us. We had her for quite a few weeks." Nora and the four children were still settling into the home Geoffrey had bought for them all in Altrincham, adjusting to another fresh start, when Frances Higson joined them – and she was not an easy guest. "She was used to issuing orders – and having them carried out."

The chairman was dead. Lancashire had as disappointing a season as any in their history. Even the celebrations that accompanied their long-serving fast bowler Dick Pollard's thousandth wicket for the county were muted by the awareness that the last few had come very slowly.

The county year book struck a gloomy note:

> *Meteorologically the glorious summer with its hard-baked pitches glaringly exposed Lancashire's deficiency in pace bowling, a weakness that became tragic because of Pollard's inability to produce his best form. By the resignation of Kenneth Cranston, the team was not only shorn of an accomplished all-round cricketer but of a well-seasoned captain. Nigel Howard stepped into the breach heroically; but the burden carried on his young shoulders – made more arduous by criticism – so affected his performance in the field that he too shared in the general decline.*

*Dick Pollard, Nigel Howard, Cyril Washbrook*

Ken Cranston played only two summers of first-class cricket, but so successful was he that he played eight Tests, even captaining England in Barbados when Gubby Allen was injured. His retirement, to enter his family's dental practice, left Lancashire with the same quandary as Surrey had experienced two years earlier.

Nigel Howard was the only amateur playing regularly in the side, but at 23 he was still finding his feet, and Denys Rowbotham in the *Manchester Guardian* argued for the appointment of Cyril Washbrook, a professional. At committee Donny Davies advanced the same view – *'Mr H.D. Davies spoke at length on the comparative merits of professionals and amateurs, supporting the appointment of a professional.'* – but he found no seconder. "The world wasn't thinking that way," Geoffrey Howard reflects. *'A further resolution that the captaincy be offered to N.D. Howard, and that the committee back him up with all the help he may need, was passed, 21 votes being cast in favour with one against and four members refraining from voting.'*

Each night the new captain went home to talk over the day with his father, Major Rupert, and between them they began to launch the plan that would bring a revival of the county's fortunes in 1950.

They needed a fast bowler to replace Dick Pollard, and in late August 1949 a young National Serviceman called Frank Tyson appeared for the second eleven against Northumberland at Old Trafford. A rail strike led to his late arrival on the ground, he took nought for 19 in five overs, and he pulled a muscle in his back. By the time he had recovered from a sprained ankle and a broken leg, it was the summer of 1951, and it fell to the secretary to write the letter that closed the door on the young Lancastrian. "I didn't know him at all. At that time a lot of people were being recommended as fast bowlers."

> *Dear Tyson,*
>
> *Thank you for your letter. I am sorry to say that I am afraid I cannot be of any help to you this year. We have extended invitations for the remaining second eleven matches this season, and this, with our existing professional staff, means that there will be no opportunity for you this season.*
>
> *Yours sincerely,*
>
> *G. Howard*

Lancashire had missed the very match-winner they were searching for, a man who within four years would be good enough to bowl England to victory in Australia. What an irony it was that, at the fast bowler's hour of greatest triumph, his manager should be the author of this letter - and sharing the glory that day at Sydney should be his fellow Lancastrian Brian Statham.

Tyson and Statham. What an opening attack that would have been on the county circuit of the 1950s!

But in August 1949 the committee was preoccupied with the great gap that had been left by the death of its all-powerful chairman.

The committee consisted for the most part of two distinct groups. In class terms they were the Gentlemen and the Players, except that to a large extent it was the Gentlemen who had played the game.

There was Leonard Green, who had captained the county to their three championships in the mid-1920s. An all-round sportsman, he had also played rugby and hockey for Lancashire. He held a Military Cross from the Great War, was a Colonel in the Territorial Army, and owned a textiles company in Clitheroe. He introduced the new secretary to the Free Foresters Cricket Club, handing on to him the blazer which still hangs in Geoffrey's wardrobe.

There was Myles Kenyon, an Old Etonian who was the High Sherriff of Lancashire, county captain from 1919 to 1922, a director of Martins Bank. "He spent his life at the top. A natural leader both in terms of his own character and his status in society. He had a country house in Stow-on-the-Wold where he had a private ground and an invitation eleven, the Fosseway Club, with its own blazer and colours. I remember talking to his wife about Frances, my eldest daughter, and she asked me, 'Is she out yet?' He was 'the Squire of Milnthorpe'. They say he sat below the pulpit and, if the parson went on too long, he'd look at his watch, purse his lips and gently whistle."

There was Alan Boddington, an Old Rugbeian, who kept wicket for the county before George Duckworth. He was a stockbroker, his family the owners of Boddington's Brewery in Manchester, and he often played with Myles Kenyon at the Fosseway Club – along with Gubby Allen and Errol Holmes, whom in the Spring of 1950 he joined on the M.C.C. committee. "Leonard Green and Myles Kenyon wanted him to become the Lancashire chairman, but he said he didn't want to do it."

So the chairmanship fell to one of the Players, Doctor John Bowling Holmes, a general practitioner. "He was the one who wanted it most badly. He was already a director of Manchester City Football Club, and his wife was very ambitious for him. He was a very nice chap, but he had no real knowledge of cricket. Every six months he went down to Lord's to the Advisory County Cricket committee, and he hadn't a word to say.

"He went on a Mediterranean cruise with his wife. I asked him what ports he'd called at, and he couldn't remember. 'I didn't go ashore,' he said. 'I don't like foreigners.' And he was the chairman of a county cricket club.

"He certainly had no idea how to make use of a chief executive. He expected me to spend all day saying, 'If you hold on a minute, I'll confer with the chairman and come back to you.' One day he said, 'I want you to tell me everything, no matter how unimportant it may seem to you.' So I phoned him. 'I'm just going to have a pee,' I said."

Doctor Bowling Holmes was one of a coterie of Freemasons, small businessmen whose influence was extensive on the committee. The new secretary took charge of the ground improvements, and he found himself struggling with all kinds of irregular contractual arrangements. In the post-war world of rationing, there were great advantages to being part of the Masonic network. Materials in short supply could be obtained, restrictions by-passed. But the new secretary found himself in trouble when he insisted that the county took on the direct employment of two carpenters from Bolton. "They'd been working off a debt they owed to one of the committee, and I was accused of empire-building. But I was only restoring power to the club."

With his son as captain and the chairman weak, Major Rupert Howard grew in influence. He was not on the match committee but, for the summer of 1950, he persuaded them that the groundsman should not water or roll the wicket in the week before a match. The county had a trio of young spinners – Roy Tattersall, Malcolm Hilton and Bob Berry – and it was judged that dusty, cracking wickets would be to their advantage.

The following winter he turned his attention to the position of assistant coach, manoeuvring the appointment of Derbyshire's Stan Worthington in place of the old Lancashire keeper George Duckworth. "Stan had been on Gubby Allen's tour of Australia in 1936/37, which Rupert had managed. George was a great character and he had a tremendous knowledge of the game. But I think Rupert thought that Stan, as an all-rounder, would be a better coach."

Again the former secretary was using his influence beyond his formal position in the club. "Everything he did was for the good of Lancashire cricket. He wanted the county to be champions again. But he was such a puller of strings, such a schemer. He could never accept that other people had different ways of doing things."

In early June 1950, the West Indians arrived in Manchester. On the dusty Old Trafford wicket, with the temperature up in the eighties, they beat the county by an innings and 220 runs, with the young left-arm spinner Alf Valentine taking 13 wickets. It was for the West Indians a perfect build-up to the Test that would be played on the adjoining strip, but they grew alarmed at the absence of any preparatory ground work.

On the morning of the match there were cracks everywhere – it was like a broken road, one commentator suggested – and Eric Hollies bowled a leg-break that pitched on middle and leg and bounced and turned so much that umpire Frank Chester called it a wide.

Geoffrey recalls an early delivery from Ramadhin that leapt over Len Hutton's head, over Clyde Walcott keeping wicket and ran away for four byes. Rupert Howard was sitting next to him. "Perhaps we've overdone it," he said.

It was in the middle of this match, the busiest days of Old Trafford's summer, that the staircase for the reconstructed secretary's office arrived. "I told them to come back the next week, but the builder was a member of the committee so I had to withdraw my objection."

Controversy over the state of the square reached a head on Wednesday the 12th of July when Sussex arrived with their usual side – three seamers and two spinners – only to find themselves batting on a dusty track against a Lancashire side with four spinners and no pretence of seam. They lost by an innings inside a day, with all twenty wickets falling to Greenwood and Hilton, with Berry bowling just three overs and Tattersall, the country's leading wicket-taker, not even coming on.

*'Much comment was caused by the change in the Old Trafford pitch,' Wisden* recorded, *'but Lancashire had made known their intentions in advance.'* Fifty years on, their secretary reads the words with some disbelief. "Did they? I can't remember informing the other counties."

After a lifetime in cricket, he reflects on the argument. "I can't remember a time when pitches haven't been controversial. Too good or too bad. Too fast or too slow. Ernest Tyldesley always said, 'There's only one true pitch on which cricket should be played, and that is coir matting on a properly prepared surface.' Sydney Barnes said the same. Good batsmen can play on them, poor batsmen can't."

In fairness, nine of their 16 championship victories in 1950 came away from Lancashire, and in mid-summer they found a fast bowler to replace Dick Pollard: a young Mancunian called Brian Statham. A National Service colleague had got him a trial at Old Trafford, and the secretary watched alongside Harry Makepeace and George Duckworth. "I know I made a hit with the secretary," the bowler wrote. "He was standing next to Harry behind the nets. One delivery went through the back of the net and caught him in a very tender spot."

By June Statham was in the first eleven. In August he took five for 52 in the Roses match. At the end of the summer he was in seventh place in the national bowling averages, and in the middle of winter he flew to Australia to reinforce M.C.C.'s injury-hit party. "Nigel Howard fought to have Brian Statham in the Lancashire side. He wanted him from the outset."

The last match of their programme was at The Oval. They only required first innings points to secure the championship, but it was not to be. Both sides ground out the dullest of draws, and all Lancashire had to wait on the result of Surrey's last match against lowly Leicestershire. A win for the London county would give them a share of the title, but it looked for a while that the weather would frustrate them. "I remember Rupert Howard offering prayers for rain." Then the Surrey bowlers got to work on the damp wicket, and Lancashire had to share their glory.

It was their first title since 1934. There was a celebration dinner, and the players were given little silver cigarette boxes. Perhaps, if they had known that they would not win it again in the next half-century, they would have celebrated with greater enthusiasm, but somehow the events of that final week made it seem more like a championship half-lost than half-won.

With Statham, Tattersall, Hilton and Berry all England bowlers by the start of 1951, and with an experienced batting line-up of Washbrook, Place, Ikin, Wharton, Grieves and Geoff Edrich, the years ahead were full of promise. Lancashire was once more a force in the land, and in July M.C.C. acknowledged this by appointing Nigel Howard captain for the winter tour of India, Pakistan and Ceylon, with Geoffrey the manager. *'The two are not related,' The Times* added to the announcement.

It was effectively an England second team tour but, with Freddie Brown planning to step down from the captaincy and no obvious successor among the amateurs, there was an opportunity for the young Nigel to stake a claim to the captaincy beyond the winter tour. At Lord's he led the Gentlemen against the Players and, though he scored just one run in his two innings, the family was filled with anticipation.

For Geoffrey Howard, in only his third summer as a county secretary, this recognition by M.C.C. was a glowing tribute. In the meantime, his main concern was not with the playing strength of the county side but with the ongoing challenge of developing the ground and balancing the budget.

The surplus in 1949 was £3,437. In 1950, with gate receipts reflecting the excitement of the championship challenge, it was £3,993. But in 1951 it fell to just £1,936. The secretary was looking to improve the ground, create a first-class workforce and raise the income, but the instinct of his committee was always to reduce expenditure.

"I can remember discovering what a pittance my secretary Mavis was being paid, and she had carried the can for quite a long time after Rupert Howard had gone. So I went to the committee and asked for an increase for her. Their first question was, 'Has she asked for one?' The second was, 'What would she get if she was working at the Town Hall?' She was worth twice what they paid her, but they didn't agree to it."

Then there was Alf Wilkinson, who worked with pride and thoroughness around the ground. "He was the most valuable chap I ever took on. He repaired and pointed the boundary wall all round the ground, and he took down all this awful asbestos cladding they'd put up in the new members' dining room, replaced it with brickwork. He was the best servant the club ever had. I put in for an increase for him, which they reluctantly granted, and one of the committee, Albert Rhodes, went straight out to talk to him. 'Alf, I'm surprised at you,' he said. 'I should have thought the honour of working for Lancashire County Cricket Club would be sufficient.' Imagine saying a thing like that! He hadn't even asked for the increase. He was a lovely, blunt Lancastrian, and he said, 'You know, Mr Rhodes, the honour of working for Lancashire doesn't help me pay my bills.'"

Fifty years have passed. The £40,000 budget has become one of £6 million, and the staff is more than twice the size it was in the early 1950s. "But I don't suppose they've got anybody there like Alf. He was a wonderful chap."

I drive Geoffrey to Edgbaston where he is reunited with the woman who joined him as his secretary in 1956, Rose FitzGibbon, and with her colleague, Sheila Delve. Rose stayed at Old Trafford for forty years, rising to become the first female secretary of a county cricket club. She and Sheila knew the family atmosphere that he engendered among his staff, and she knew the opposition he had to overcome.

"They say that the day after you left for that tour of India, Rupert Howard came into the office and demanded to go through the Wages Book."

"Did he? Did he indeed?"

We sit eating our picnic lunch in the committee room of the well-appointed Edgbaston pavilion, and he reflects once more on that Lancashire committee. "They were wonderfully hospitable people, and I loved my years up there. But I think that they were sentimental about Old Trafford. They didn't really cherish it."

# CHAPTER EIGHT

# A TOUR OF INFINITE VARIETY

# INDIA, PAKISTAN AND CEYLON

# 1951 – 52

The tour party set off by train from St Pancras Railway Station on their way to Tilbury Docks. A group of sixteen cricketers was accompanied by two journalists, Edgar Turner and Leslie Smith, and one manager, Geoffrey Howard. There was no baggage man, no masseur, no scorer. "We didn't even have a scorebook with us."

For England's leading players, there had been two six-month tours in the previous three winters: to South Africa in 1948/49 and to Australia and New Zealand in 1950/51. With the West Indies now strong enough to beat the full England team, the tour of India was the obvious one to miss for those who wanted a break.

They were all missing: Hutton, Washbrook, Bedser, Compton, Evans. Not one of the party that had set out for Australia a year earlier was selected. In their places the 16 M.C.C. tourists at St Pancras possessed 34 Test caps between them, and their captain and vice-captain, Lancashire's Nigel Howard and Derbyshire's Donald Carr, were both set to make their England debuts – with a manager who was learning the ropes.

Colonel Rait Kerr, the M.C.C. secretary, was there to see them off. Geoffrey had never been to India, and he had no job description or set of instructions to prepare him for his experience. "I didn't have anything that could be called a briefing. I left my desk at Old Trafford in the afternoon, got together for dinner in the hotel at Paddington and was on the train and boat the following day."

"Well, good luck, old boy," Rait Kerr said, leaning his head into the first-class railway carriage. "Rather you than me. I can't stand educated Indians."

This was M.C.C.'s first trip to India since 1933/34, the first since India had become independent in 1947. The old British provinces, based on local princedoms, had given way to modern states while the Muslim regions to the East and West had become the separate nation of Pakistan. It was less than four years since half a million people had been slaughtered in the bloodshed that accompanied the partition, and the two countries co-existed now in an uneasy truce.

India had played twenty matches in its twenty years as a Test-playing country, and it had not come close to winning any of them. So, although there was disappointment in India that none of the great names of English cricket would be on view, there was no great anxiety at Lord's that the players selected would be inadequate to the task. Rather, there was a hope that some would gain experience and advance their claims to a regular England place.

There was Tom Graveney, the stylish, young batsman from Gloucestershire. There was Frank Lowson, Len Hutton's opening partner for Yorkshire: "He was a beautiful player. He modelled his batting on Len. If they played today, wearing helmets, you'd be hard put to identify which was which." And there was Don Kenyon, who was already scoring 2000 runs a season with regularity. There were the two Lancashire bowlers, Brian Statham and Roy Tattersall, who had flown out in the middle of the Australian tour the previous winter, and there was Don Brennan, the Yorkshire keeper who had displaced Godfrey Evans for the last two Tests against South Africa. Ahead of all of them, in the unfamiliar Indian sub-continent, lay the rare opportunity to establish themselves as Test cricketers.

Perhaps Nigel Howard wondered whether his charmed rise to the top might go further still. Freddie Brown had retired from the England captaincy at the end of the summer, and there was no obvious successor among the ranks of the county captains. A successful tour, and who knows? He could be captain of the full England side the next summer.

And his manager? Geoffrey had no clear idea what lay ahead in India, but the thought crossed his mind that a trouble-free tour might lead to his managing the next tour of Australia, as his predecessor at Old Trafford, Rupert Howard, had done.

Frances was twelve, Joy ten, Ursula five and Rosalind three. In January, when he worked out the benefits of his long absence from them, his enthusiasm for a second appointment seemed at a low ebb.

*Darling, I don't think I would go to Australia if it was offered – not unless it was very highly paid. This job is a much harder task than Australia can possibly be, and I get less out of it than anybody!! I lose £300 from Lancashire, get £650 from M.C.C., pay £300 income tax – net £50. The players get the same as I do and lose nothing of their home pay, and the amateurs get £250 tax free. Honour? Glory? Doubtful. Six months away from home – certain!*

*Left to right, standing: Jack Robertson, Don Kenyon, Donald Carr, Roy Tattersall, Cyril Poole, Tom Graveney, Nigel Howard, Brian Statham, Geoffrey Howard, Don Brennan, Derek Shackleton, Frank Lowson. Kneeling: Dick Spooner, Malcolm Hilton, Fred Ridgway, Allan Watkins, 'Dusty' Rhodes.*

After a cheerful boat journey of two weeks, they arrived at Bombay on the second of October. They were *'Howard's willow-wielding ambassadors'* in one newspaper headline, and each of them was garlanded. "They were all a bit bewildered, suddenly finding themselves the centre of national interest."

Narayan Karmarker, the Indian Board's liaison officer, arrived – 'an educated Indian' in Rait Kerr's terms – and he handed over a bundle of rupees that the manager carried around with him. "I had to pay for everything out of it, like all the chitties from the dhobi wallahs for our laundry."

With Karmarker at his side, he was soon learning the local customs. "The dhobi wallah would call in the morning for your shirts, and you'd have them back in the evening, beautifully finished. He'd give them to the women, who would take them down to the river, beat them on the rocks and get the dirt out of them. It was a wonderful service. One of the joys of India."

Then there was the dhersi wallah. "He would come and take your measurements in the morning, offer you his selection of cloths and by the next day you'd got a made-to-measure suit. We all had trousers made. Lightweight cotton ducks."

The financial records were scrupulously kept by the manager – though not scrupulously enough for the accountant at Lord's. "'Have you got all the receipts?' he asked. He had no idea. Many of the dhobi wallahs were quite unable to read or write. They provided a wonderful service but, if I'd kept all their chitties, I'd have had a trunk full."

With Karmarker to guide him, there were no problems. "And he was such a good companion. He'd played tennis for Baroda. I had a real struggle when I played him."

No sooner did they begin net practice in Bombay than Cyril Poole, the left-handed batsman, fractured a finger. He had been a late replacement for Jack Ikin – "I got him on the tour. He made a beautiful hundred at Old Trafford, against Brian Statham at his best." – and his injury gave the manager his first chance to discover the reality of life beyond the cricket grounds.

"I had to accept the recommendation to take him down into the bazaar where an Indian doctor was operating. The conditions were unbelievable; there were flies everywhere. It took a long time. They had to break the finger and do it again. They gave him quite a substantial anaesthetic. I took his watch while he was being operated on, and I held his hand the whole time. He was so drunk with anaesthesia, it took him hours to come round – and, when he did, quite suddenly, he looked at me and said, 'Here, you've got my bloody watch.'

"He came out with a newspaper folder with tablets. I asked the High Commissioner what they were. 'They're penicillin,' he said. 'It's the latest treatment. Everywhere you go in India, you'll be given penicillin.'"

The first weeks were undoubtedly a shock to many of the players. Leslie Smith in *Wisden* recorded that the first match in Bombay 'took place under extremely hot and humid conditions', so extreme that Tom Graveney abandoned his first net after only five minutes – "and I like the heat." The following day he batted three hours for a powerful century, but support was limited. According to Leslie Smith, 'a number of players tired after a short stay' at the wicket.

The three-day match ended in a draw, and the following morning the party flew north to Ahmedabad. "The hotel there was very crude," the manager remembers. "Jack Robertson and Roy Tattersall turned their backs on their breakfast for a moment, and a monkey ran in and took it. There was a vulture sitting on the windowsill, too."

The modern cricketing tourist might find it hard to imagine a six-month trip to India with a management team of just one, with the support of one Indian liaison officer. There were diplomatic functions to attend, and a multitude of things to be supervised: accommodation, travel, baggage, laundry, emergency health problems, all to be accompanied by detailed financial records and all in a foreign land without modern five-star hotels – "It was hit or miss as far as we were concerned. We took what we were given. Now they would reject it out of hand." – and without comfortable aircraft. "Sometimes we travelled by train or coach, but mostly we flew in a twin-engine Dakota."

I received a telephone call from Geoffrey one day just after we had started talking about this tour. "I've been reading my letters to Nora," he told me, "and there's something in them that I seem to have forgotten."

"Oh?" I asked with curiosity. "What was that?"

"Well, it seems that sometimes, when we flew, I took the controls of the aircraft."

*Ahmedabad, 9 October. We arrived by air yesterday, landing about mid-day. It is 275 miles north of Bombay. We did not see a lot as we flew at 10,000 feet right over the clouds, but it was very smooth and free from bumps. I had about half an hour at the controls.*

*Amritsar, 18 October. We arrived here yesterday about lunch time by air after landing at Delhi for breakfast and to refuel. An all round trip of about 700 miles or so. I flew the old Dakota nearly all the way from Indore to Delhi (about 3 hours) and thoroughly enjoyed it.*

*Delhi, 4 November. Darling. Yes, the chaps are always jittery when I take over but it is as safe as it can be at 8000 feet! With the pilot at my side with dual controls.*

At Ahmedabad they played Western India on coir matting and, with only Tom Graveney making runs, they were lucky to scramble a two-wicket victory. 'Dusty' Rhodes, the Derbyshire bowler, went down with a septic throat, reducing the party to fourteen fit players. Meanwhile, the captain Nigel Howard was not setting the example for which his manager was hoping.

*Ahmedabad, 9 October. I am sharing a room with Nigel (Niggle to the Indians). Outside, we have vultures, monkeys and parrots and, inside, a constant darting about of lizards catching flies. You cannot imagine the extent to which Nigel worries about his health. He just swallows this, that and the other. Anything that anybody says is good for something.*

*Sialkot, 11 November. Poor Nigel is so scared of illness. The flies are a nuisance up here – worse than anywhere I have been except Alex and Cairo –*

*but he is really stupid about them. Now I have upset him by warning about the dangers of dog bites and hydrophobia.*

*Karachi, 29 November. I was rather unsuccessfully trying last night to persuade Nigel that true civilisation did not depend on plumbing, wireless and motor cars! I am afraid his philosophy has not yet developed, and he thought I was putting on an act.*

Fifty years on, he looks back with a little more understanding. "He was very young, and his upbringing had been so materialistic. In a way, he'd had things too easy in his life. He'd got where he had because of his father."

And the fear of illness? "He didn't like India, and he never really felt well. He was as fit as a flea really, but I'm sure he thought he was going to pick up some awful plague. He was so apprehensive about his health, and the strange thing was that he died at the age of only 54."

For the manager, anxious to make a good impression in the newly independent India, his vice-captain Donald Carr was a better ambassador – but then he had spent some of his early childhood in Northern India and his family often talked about their years there: "I loved India. The people were so delighted to see you. The history was fascinating. I even liked the smell and all the beastliness."

It was not a common attitude among the tour party. The manager was determined to experience India as a modern tourist might – the palaces and mountains beyond the familiar world of the English expatriates – but his charges were mostly suspicious of it all.

George Duckworth had been in India as manager of two unofficial Commonwealth tours, and Tom Graveney still remembers the advice he offered before they left Tilbury. "Three things you've got to do," he said. "Eat egg and chips, because they've got to cook it. Drink as much whisky as you can, because it kills the bugs. And, if you want to score any runs, don't get hit on the pads."

"For breakfast," Geoffrey recalls, "most of them had eggs fried on both sides. They got as near to an English diet as they could – though sometimes, like when the lunch interval in a match was short, it wasn't possible. And they drank Murree Beer in big corked bottles. India was prohibition in those days. So I had to drag it around. Well, I say 'I'. The bearers carried it."

At Ahmedabad the manager went to see Gandhi's bungalow – *and the small community he had formed to educate and improve the lot of the 'untouchables'. A very great man there can have been no doubt.*

At Amritsar they all visited the Golden Temple, where again they were garlanded. *It was wasted on half of our party. Some of them are now waiting outside to get the sharp end of my tongue for ill-mannered behaviour.*

At Dehra Dun there was the chance to climb to Mussoorie, a hill station in the southern Himalayas*: Looking back down the valley and into the plain was wonderful and real enough but on the other side it was breathtaking: a range about 11,000 feet and then towering in the background and covered in the snow lay the 24,000 feet peaks reaching right up into the clouds and 150-200* *miles away. A really awe-inspiring sight. One can well understand the desire to conquer it and to look down on the petty world of man-made marvels. I can't describe the feeling.*

Again the manager proved a more appreciative tourist than his charges: *Only Edgar Turner and I went because it involved a 1000 foot scramble which was far easier than going halfway up Wansfell! The rest – believe it or not – preferred to sit in an hotel, listen to a dance band and drink beer.*

"Donald took to India. And Tom, because he had such a wonderful tour as a player. But I don't think many of them would have gone back there for a holiday.

"I don't suppose I was very popular. I had to get them to go to a lot of functions. Meetings with local dignitaries, cocktail parties with English people. We only had heavy, black dinner jackets, not like the lightweight cotton ones they had in India, and there were always very dull speeches to listen to. But we were there to maintain the reputation of the British in India."

By Dehra Dun, 'Dusty' Rhodes had had enough. Complaining of a rumbling appendix, he was flown home. "Alec Bedser recommended him. 'He's two bowlers,' he said. 'A brilliant spinner and as quick as anybody when you want him to be.' But I don't think his heart was in it. He just wanted the uniform, as they say in the army."

*National Defence Academy Ground, Dehra Dun*

The cricket demanded them to adapt, too. At Bombay they played on turf. At Ahmedabad, coir matting. At Indore, jute matting. At Amritsar, they were back on turf, though here a local protest, that the match had not been allocated to nearby Patiala, led to water being poured over one end of the wicket and the first morning was lost as a fresh pitch was marked.

"A batsman needs to have an acrobatic technique to survive all these changes," Tom Graveney wrote. A front-foot player all his career, he played all tour off the back foot, his driving so good that he scored two centuries and two fifties in his first five innings.

Two weeks into the tour the news broke that the Pakistani premier Liaquat Ali Khan had been assassinated, and for a few days there was doubt whether their scheduled visit to Pakistan in November would take place – though there is a gap in the manager's letters home during these days. "It wasn't unknown for the person who took your letters to peel off the stamps and throw the letters away. I remember Narayan Karmarker advising us to take them to the post office and to make sure they were already franked when you put them under the grille."

With Poole and Rhodes out of action, the party suffered a further blow when Tom Graveney went down with pleurisy on the eve of the first Test at New Delhi. He had been the leading batsman in the warm-up matches. Of the others, only Jack Robertson and Frank Lowson had found much form. So the decision was taken to select the reserve keeper Dick Spooner ahead of Don Brennan, on the grounds that he added strength to the batting.

"Don had been selected the previous summer ahead of Godfrey Evans. I remember Cyril Washbrook coming off after batting in a Roses match: 'There's only one battle going on out there,' he said. 'Alex Coxon is trying to make Don Brennan stand back, but he won't.' Don was a brilliant keeper at his best. It was a bitter blow to him when he didn't play in the Tests."

At New Delhi England struggled on the first day. 'The batsmen failed lamentably against the splendid leg-break bowling of Shinde,' Leslie Smith wrote in *Wisden*. Four of the seven main batsmen were making their Test debuts, but in this rarefied world perhaps not all of them went out to the middle with their minds wholly on the task. "The dressing room was behind where we were sitting," Donald Carr recalls, "and, when the first wicket fell, Don Kenyon got up and, instead of going straight out to bat, he went back into the dressing room and checked that both the exit doors were locked. There must have been a three-minute delay before he emerged."

"His cricket bag was probably full of duty-free cigarettes," Geoffrey jokes.

One of county cricket's most prolific run-scorers, Don Kenyon never showed such dominance in his fitful Test career. He made 35 against the new ball bowlers here at New Delhi but, when he was bowled by Shinde, it started a collapse that saw England slump from 79 for one to 203 all out.

On the second and third days Merchant broke Hazare's record highest score for India with an innings of 154. Then Hazare regained the record with his own 164. "I was alone in the dressing room at one point," Geoffrey recalls. "I was writing some notes, and I looked up and saw this chap wandering about. I thought, 'He looks very familiar.' Then I realised it was Pandit Nehru. He'd lost his way."

Were Merchant and Hazare focused too much on breaking individual records, as Tom Graveney thinks? Or were they, as the England manager suspects, more concerned to put India in a position where they could not lose than to press for victory? Whatever the explanation, their progress was so slow that England did not have to bat again until after the rest day, and a long and determined innings by the senior professional Allan Watkins, supported by Donald Carr, enabled the tourists to escape with a draw. "Allan batted for nine hours. He simply determined not to get out."

Watkins had bowled 31 overs in the Indian innings and, according to *Wisden*, 'he was so tired that once his knees literally buckled.'

**England 203 and 368 for six**
**India 418 for six, declared**
**Match drawn**

What a contrast they would discover in the cricket when they reached Pakistan! "They weren't interested in drawing. They wanted to become a Test-playing country. And they knew they'd advance their cause if they beat us."

First, though, there was the task of transporting the baggage across the border. The Indian bearers had to be left behind and, with the players flying from Delhi to Lahore, it fell to the manager to make the more arduous journey.

*Sialkot, 11 November. I am now the baggage man as well. I went by train from Delhi to Amritsar and from Amritsar to the border – 15 miles – by jeep with the heavy baggage (38 pieces) in convoy in an Army three-ton truck. The border was very elaborately protected, and I had to pass through Indian customs and passport officials, cross 'no man's land' and fall into the hands of the Pakistani officials. It was rather amusing to stand alone between two sets of armies on a small piece of land on which no one else could stand! Tom Tiddler's Ground! We then proceeded to Lahore. I really am working hard.*

At Sialkot, on coir matting, they were lucky to save the follow-on against the Punjab Cricket Association. At Lahore, they played the full Pakistan side: *They are calling it a Test, but the other cricketing countries do not neither does M.C.C. So I hope we do well.* They conceded a first innings lead of 174 but, with several of the team suffering from upset stomachs – *The trouble is water, I think. Not bad water but completely different.* – they were grateful for centuries from Dick Spooner and Tom Graveney.

"That was the first time we'd seen Hanif bat," Tom remembers. "He was only sixteen, and he played against Brian Statham and Derek Shackleton and never missed the middle of the bat. He didn't have any power, but he was a fantastic player for a young man."

Hanif made only 26 in that game, but he made 71 for Bahawalpur the next week, and in the final innings of the second unofficial Test at Karachi he scored 64 in four hours. According to *Wisden*, 'his concentration for a boy of 16 was astonishing.'

In Lahore only the manager and the journalist Edgar Turner took the opportunity to visit the zoo: *To crown a fascinating afternoon, we saw Lion and Lioness in all the stages of their courtship. The boys were really upset to hear what they had missed!!*

Then they all took the train to Bahawalpur. *We departed in an air-conditioned coach at 8.30 last night and arrived at 4.30 a.m. and were shunted into a siding where we continued our sleep till about 6.45. There we were met by the Prime Minister of Bahawalpur, an Englishman called Colonel Dring.*

It sounds from the letter like a civilised and comfortable journey but, when we met with Donald Carr, his memory told a different story.

"It was only the amateurs who travelled in the air-conditioned coach. We went across the Sind desert and, when we arrived, we had quite a decent sleep, had a wash and put our blazers on. Then I said to you, Geoffrey, 'Shall I let the troops out?' I went along to their carriage and, when I opened the door, they all came out, coated in red sand and gasping. I can still see Allan Watkins at the front of them, his face all red, and I couldn't help myself. I just burst out laughing."

It was while they were in Pakistan that Geoffrey Howard was approached by the President of the Pakistan Board, Mr Justice Cornelius, to act as their agent when they came to tour England in 1954. He clearly recognised in the M.C.C. manager a man who was sympathetic to the aspirations of the newly independent nations of India and Pakistan.

Just before the New Delhi Test, news had reached them that the general election back home had brought Winston Churchill back to power, and the England manager was not pleased: *Churchill's views on foreign policy will find no friend here. They know full well that their independence would only have been gained by some sort of physical struggle had old Winston been at the helm. There is nothing but praise here for the way in which it was handled by the Labour Government.*

"They wanted to be rid of the Army," he says now, "but they were quite upset that they lost all the civil servants as well. They weren't ready for that."

Here was a forward-looking Englishman, in the tradition of his visionary grandfather. In India, he wrote: *It is a fascinating country of immense possibilities: what it could be like with our rainfall one just cannot imagine.* In Pakistan: *It is a very interesting country and is being extremely progressive. Their cricket is forging ahead, and I am making many good friends. They are very kind, generous and likeable people.*

"I remember an English woman in Madras. 'Are you telling me you like Indians?' she said. She was shocked."

At Bahawalpur the English cricketers went out shooting birds. *I am afraid I am not a very keen shot as my sympathies are all with the poor birds. It is horrible to see them flop lifeless to the ground in the midst of joyous flight.*

*The State Guest House, Bahawalpur*

The manager and the three amateurs – Nigel Howard, Donald Carr and Don Brennan – stayed in a tent in Colonel John Dring's garden while the professionals were put up by the Maharajah in the State Guest House.

The second unofficial Test against Pakistan was held at the Karachi Gymkhana ground, a very different venue from any they had encountered in India. "The square was not a lot bigger than a tennis court, with a coconut mat nailed down. It was a very dry, dusty place." The mat was unusual in extending to the ends of the bowlers' run-ups, there was a drop of two feet from the mat to the boundary, and the outfield was rolled sand. Yet again the English tourists had to adjust to unfamiliar playing conditions.

"It was a tour of infinite variety," Geoffrey Howard reflects.

"It's easily the most interesting tour," Douglas Jardine had told him before he left. "Geographically and socially."

*Karachi, 30 November. Once again we are struggling. We failed badly as batsmen yesterday against some really good bowling, and then, having got three out for 15, let things slip to 73 for three. I am beginning to fear that we shall do badly on this tour.*

They were staying in pairs with English people in Karachi, and there was no time at the end of each day to reflect as a group on the play. But the second and third days saw an improvement in their fortunes. They restricted Pakistan to a first innings lead of just seven runs – *Brian Statham bowled like a Trojan* – and another century from Tom Graveney – "The pitch had lost some of its bad temper," he recalls – left Pakistan a challenging 285 to win. *We have a great chance of winning the game, and I do hope we do. It really could be a tonic. But poor Nigel can't get going. I am afraid he is just not good enough for Test cricket.*

It was not a Test match, but the Pakistanis were desperate for success and, on the fourth and final day, led by the young Hanif, their wish came true as, with 35 minutes to spare, they won by four wickets. 'The Pakistan authorities were delighted with their success,' Leslie Smith wrote in *Wisden*, 'and regarded it as a great help towards their inclusion in the Imperial Cricket Conference. M.C.C. were below their best, but it must be said that they were very surprised at some of the umpiring decisions in the match, not one of over thirty l.b.w. appeals being granted in their favour.'

"Statham grew nearly hoarse shouting appeals," Tom Graveney recalls.

"Hanif played back with both pads together," Geoffrey remembers, "and was still being given not out. There was no need for that sort of thing. They had so many good players."

*Karachi, 3 December. Of course the Pakistanis were elated and the papers are full of it. Headlines like 'Pakistan's Titanic Test Triumph'. It was a blow, but they played well up to their best and we were below ours. And the umpiring was appalling!! Not just bad but terribly partial – and NOT partial to us.*

Their three weeks in Pakistan were over. The manager put his disquiet about the umpiring in a written report and left the matter behind. Little did he know that four years later he would find himself at the centre of a much greater storm about Pakistani umpiring.

The next stop was Bombay, where they had landed initially, and again the manager travelled separately with the baggage, this time by boat. "It was wonderful weather and, for the first twelve hours, I was one of only two first-class passengers. Then we hoved to off the Rann of Kutch, and we saw a whole fleet of little white sails approaching from the shore, all with passengers for the boat. After that, I couldn't even walk round the deck, it was so crowded. But it was still bliss: nobody wanting to talk cricket, no players' problems to sort out."

It did not last. Within the week they were selecting the team for the second Test, and their deliberations would come back to haunt him twelve years later.

They had been lucky to escape with a draw at New Delhi, they had played badly in Pakistan. So, when the four of them sat down – Nigel Howard, Donald Carr, the senior professional Allan Watkins and their manager – there were some difficult decisions to be taken.

First there was the wicket-keeper. With Tom Graveney to add to the first Test line-up, the need to pick the keeper with the better batting was less strong, but the manager's view was not shared by the others.

*Bombay, 13 December. Poor old Don Brennan is as miserable as sin. We have left him out of the Test match – against my vote. I am convinced that a mistake has been made, apart from my view that the best wicket-keeper should be played regardless of his batting. And there is no doubt in my mind who is the best.*

Then there was the newcomer, Yorkshire's leg-spinner Eddie Leadbeater, who had arrived in place of 'Dusty' Rhodes. He had only played one match, but "he was such a cheerful chap" and the decision was made to include him and to reduce the number of seam bowlers.

Poor Eddie. His first day in Test cricket was a nightmare: in the morning he dropped two slip catches, then after lunch he pulled a thigh muscle and left the field. For all his good humour, he took just two wickets in his two Test appearances and became the only cricketer in the modern game to have played for England and never won a county cap.

But which of the batsmen should give up their place to Tom Graveney? Not Allan Watkins whose nine-hour century had saved the match at New Delhi. Nor Donald Carr whose 76 had kept him company for five hours. Not Robertson and Lowson who had formed an understanding at the top of the order. Nor Don Kenyon who had finally found his touch with 95 in the warm-up match here in Bombay.

It was left to the one professional at the meeting, Allan Watkins, to say what both the manager and the vice-captain were thinking. "Well, I think the skipper is the natural person to leave out."

*Bombay, 13 December. I am afraid that Nigel will not have the courage to stand down. Everyone feels that he should, but it is a hard decision to make and, if he does not do so, then I cannot really blame him.*

"He spoke to me about it in a roundabout sort of way," Donald Carr remembers. "He was not going to let himself be left out. He'd been advised back home that he was not to stand down under any circumstances."

We sit in Donald Carr's living room, and I digest what he has just said.

"What you're saying is that, even before the tour started, he was anticipating being in this situation."

"Nigel wasn't a self-confident chap," Geoffrey says. "Not in cricket terms, anyway. He was well aware of the pressure in Lancashire that he should stand down and let Cyril Washbrook take over."

The decision was taken. Donald Carr would not play. But inevitably in due course this meeting got back to Nigel's father at Old Trafford, and the manager's part in it was noted. "Rupert wasn't one to forget a thing like that."

The Test was played at the Brabourne Stadium before a crowd of more than 40,000. The three-storey stucco pavilion, coloured light blue, dark blue and gold, contained accommodation for the players. With a swimming pool and tennis courts, it was India's best-appointed ground, but the land had been reclaimed from the Arabian Sea and the pitches tended to be slow and to produce high-scoring draws.

Roy and Hazare made centuries in India's first innings of 485. Tom Graveney scored 175 in 8¼ hours 'in trying heat' in England's reply of 456. "I took a drink and a salt tablet every twenty minutes," he remembers. India's batting performed less well the second time, but the match faded into an uneventful draw.

"Uneventful on the pitch," Geoffrey says. "But the crowds were such a demonstration of so many aspects of Indian life. The women, with their colourful dresses and the jasmine in their hair. All the noise and the firecrackers. I know Nigel had a struggle to make himself heard in the field. And, at the end of the day, they all just disappeared. No litter, no newspapers. Just a few mango pips and nut shells. It was a wonderful occasion, a Test match at the Cricket Club of India in Bombay."

| | |
|---|---|
| **India** | **485 for nine, declared, and 208** |
| **England** | **456 and 55 for two** |
| **Match drawn** | |

For the players, accommodation on the ground was wonderfully convenient – "You could fall out of bed, put on your ducks and walk straight down to the dressing room," Tom Graveney recalls – but, for the manager, there were disadvantages.

*Poona, 20 December. I was not sorry to leave Bombay. Quite fun – but very tiring indeed. No peace at all. Constant flow of people through my room from morn to late evening.*

Christmas was spent at the Calcutta Cricket Club, a match that all the tour party played, even the manager. "You walked out to bat with a lighted Christmas tree at the side of you." The Private Banks amateur of the 1930s was back in action, and his approach reflected his pre-war attitude. "Bert Wensley, the old Sussex all-rounder, was the coach there, and he umpired. He was very pleased with me because I kept advancing down the pitch and hitting Malcolm Hilton over his head."

On Boxing Day Nigel Howard and Don Brennan went off to the Calcutta Races, brushing aside the advice of their manager. *I said for goodness sake don't listen to tips from jockeys and owners but they turned a deaf ear – and so lost about £15.*

In Calcutta the contrast between rich and poor was sharper than anywhere. The All-India Tennis Tournament was in progress – *We had to go out to a long and boring tennis dinner last night* – but in the streets there was another India: *Calcutta is an awful place. The squalor of the poor is unbelievable, and the beggars throng the streets in thousands.*

The third Test took place at Eden Gardens. "It's a huge concrete stadium now, but in those days they put up temporary stands, made of bamboo poles and wood, with canvas to go over the top. So many people in India work in the construction industry – women as well as men – and they came in and put these things up in no time. They're called shamiyanas. They did sway when the wind got up."

"It was terrifying," Tom Graveney remembers. "There were so many people in them. I think they sold a second set of tickets, didn't they? And you could see them swaying in the breeze."

The cricket, alas, left fewer memories as a third draw was played out, this one duller than the previous two. 'The pitch was mainly responsible,' Leslie Smith wrote in *Wisden*. 'It was entirely lifeless, and the batsmen were not prepared to take chances.'

**England** **342 and 252 for five, declared**
**India** **344 and 103 for no wicket**
**Match drawn**

Only at Kanpur did the series finally come to life. It was the first Test ever to be played at the ground, and the pitch was a newly laid grass one that took prodigious spin even in the first hour. "It was brown in colour," Tom Graveney recalls, "and, when you tapped it, it made a strange, hollow sound."

The Indians wrongly opted for two leg-spinners, but England dropped their one, Eddie Leadbeater, in favour of the slow-left-arm of Malcolm Hilton and the off-spin of Roy Tattersall. Between them they took seventeen wickets for 218 runs, and England's victory by eight wickets was achieved before the end of the third day.

Buck Divecha, the Indian twelfth man, had played the previous two summers at Oxford, with Donald Carr, and at the end of the match he appeared in the England dressing room. "There had been rumours that the local students were going to hold an anti-British demonstration, but in the end they were so upset by their own team's performance that they demonstrated against them. 'Can I come back in your coach?' Buck asked. 'Ours is being stoned.'"

"The authorities got on to the Indian Air Force," Tom Graveney adds. "They arranged a bit of a show of air diving to quieten things down."

**India 121 and 157**
**England 203 and 76 for 2 wickets**
**England won by 8 wickets**

They had two extra days, and on one of them they went for a boat trip on the River Ganges. They set out from the holy city of Benares, where the Hindus purified themselves by bathing. "We were on a small steamer, and somebody noticed a body floating in the water. 'Oh bluddy 'ell, look at that.' The whole of the team rushed across the deck and nearly capsized the boat."

A week earlier, the manager had been at his most irritable in his letter home: *I am getting a bit fed up with cricket and cricketers. I miss sensible conversation so much. I long for home and family and an end to all this.*

Now his spirits were high – and not just because of their victory in the Test: *We are all delighted and just about to celebrate. Really the lads did well, and we are very pleased with them. Simultaneously came a letter from the President of the Indian Board of Control, saying what a good lot of chaps we were and so much better behaved and gentlemanly than any other touring team that he had experienced. Shabash! That being Hindi for "Well done!" I must tell the boys. They must have their halfpence as well as the kicks!!*

"I think the comparison was with the Commonwealth sides that George Duckworth had taken out there."

Fifty years have passed, and Tom Graveney can look back with greater understanding on the days they declined to visit one of the great sights of India or the groans they let out when another evening function had to be attended.

"It was the first English team to go to India after the war, and everybody wanted to lay on tea parties and musical evenings – which, of course, we didn't appreciate. We used to moan at the manager, but he did such a terrific PR job. All the different places we had to stay. And all the travelling, getting up before the heat of the day so the plane wouldn't bounce too much. It was so well organised. And it was all down to the manager. It's a tour that I wouldn't have missed for anything. It was a wonderful experience."

"Tom was bound to enjoy it," Geoffrey says. "He scored so many runs."

At Nagpur their good spirits continued, with a convincing win on jute matting against Central Zone – "A cobra wriggled across the ground before start of play." – and some memorable entertainment away from the cricket: *Football played on stilts – what will they think of next! It was performed by a troupe of boys from jungle villages about 200 miles away. Some of them had never before left their villages, and none had ever seen electric light. They ran and kicked on their stilts as though the wretched things were part of them, and it was all done in the greatest good humour. We all thoroughly enjoyed it.*

At Hyderabad they were entertained by the Nizam. A Muslim, he had ruled the largely Hindu state before Independence, but his army had been overwhelmed by Indian forces and now his lands were effectively nationalised. His wealth, however, survived: *His fortune is estimated at £1000 millions at least!! As the Yanks would say, 'That ain't half!'* "The richest man in the world, and he was wearing a pair of cheap cotton socks."

A sofa and two armchairs were set out for a formal photograph. Then, when it was developed, the Nizam discovered two members of staff in the back row who were not supposed to be there. "You can see the markings where they've been blacked out," Geoffrey says, showing me his copy.

*Seated, left to right: Geoffrey Howard, the Hon. M.K. Vellodi, H.E.H. the Nizam of Hyderabad, Shrimati Vellodi, Donald Carr.*

"Mine is signed," Donald Carr tells him.

"By his Highness?"

"I think I pinched it. It was meant to go to you."

"His Exalted Highness. He had so many wives we called him His Exhausted Highness. Everything I said, he replied, 'I see.' It became a great saying at home. 'I see, said the Nizam.'"

Don Brennan's tour finally came to life. For weeks he had been grumbling about not playing in the Tests – *Now his theme is that the Tests are not England v India but only M.C.C.!* – but here in Hyderabad he went out on a shoot and, with some assistance, he killed a panther with his first shot. "He was trembling with excitement. It was the high spot of his whole tour."

After surviving four months of health hazards, both real and imagined, Nigel Howard finally went down with a temperature, and the manager decided to put him in a nursing home rather than force him to travel to Bangalore. Even this, though, seemed to alarm the young captain. With the manager and Don Brennan both practising Catholics, he started to imagine a hidden motive. *He is under the care of some Italian Nurse. I think he is terrified that they will attempt to convert him.*

At Bangalore, with Donald Carr leading the team to an exciting victory over South Zone, the manager and a more cheerful Don Brennan took a day off. *We went on a picnic to Seringapatam and Mysore. How I wish you had all been there. It was fascinating, and I enjoyed it more than anything I have seen and done in India. Mysore is a lovely little city, and at night looks like fairy-land with all the lights on. And we had a lovely picnic on the banks of the crocodile-infested River Cauvrey. Very beautiful. It was there that the artillery fired to breach the walls of the fort of the arch-enemy Tippoo Sultan. Then, like the true British, we gave him a wonderful burial place and a magnificent tomb!! May we always have the same magnanimity in victory.*

In Madras, as in Karachi, they stayed with English families. "I remember arriving at the house where Donald and Don Brennan were being put up, and the only person there was this boy who was doing the dusting. I asked him to help us take in the bags. But he was a hammal, not a coolie. 'That's not my job, sahib,' he said. And we had to take them in ourselves."

Indian society was built on such distinctions, and their English hosts were quick to impress upon them the fine details of such customs as tipping. "Be careful," they said. "You mustn't spoil things for us. Don't give too much."

The fifth and final Test began on February the sixth. According to Leslie Smith, the only English journalist left now that Edgar Turner had gone home, 'So great was the interest that queues started to form at 4 a.m. and the ground was almost full two hours before play.'

Donald Carr returned to the team as captain, but events on the field were overshadowed at tea time by the news that King George VI had died. "It was the only time in the whole tour that I received a telephone call from Lord's. It was Rait Kerr telling us to wear black arm bands and suggesting that we didn't play the next day."

When they did finally resume, India showed much greater urgency than in the previous Tests. They bowled England out for 266, with Vinoo Mankad becoming the first Indian to take eight wickets in a Test innings, and Pankaj Roy and Polly Umrigar scored centuries fast enough to have England batting again before the end of the third day, with a deficit of 191. The pitch was worn by this stage, England made only 183 and, at their 25th attempt, the Indians had finally won a Test match.

Unlike the triumphant Pakistanis, however, the celebrations were muted. "They were all very polite to us," Donald Carr remembers. "They said that the reason we had lost was because we were so upset that the King had died."

"What was significant," Geoffrey Howard reckons, "was that the two matches we lost in India and Pakistan were on the two occasions that we were all split up and staying with different families. We didn't come together as a group at the end of the day's play."

**England 266 and 183**
**India 457 for nine wickets, declared**
**India won by an innings and eight runs**

Five Tests had been played, with the series drawn at one match each. Nigel Howard had ended his Test career unbeaten while Donald Carr's one game in charge had brought their only defeat.

'Over the whole series England seem rather lucky to have shared the honours,' was Leslie Smith's verdict in *The Times*. 'India looked the stronger side on their type of pitch.'

It only remained to spend three weeks in Ceylon before making the long journey home. Their visit had been planned to coincide with the arrival of Princess Elizabeth and Prince Philip for the Colombo Grand Exhibition, but the King's death had changed all that.

Once more the M.C.C. manager set off alone with the baggage, meeting up with the players at Colombo airport after two days of train and boat journeys. There they stepped back into the world of British colonialism, staying in a well-appointed hotel and mixing with sportsmen like the golfer Max Faulkner and the tennis player Tony Mottram.

"It was lovely to get there," Tom Graveney says, "after some of the hardships in India and Pakistan."

Their relaxed end to the tour was somewhat shattered when they discovered that their first opponents, a Commonwealth XI, contained Keith Miller and Neil Harvey, but they were able to dominate the following fixture against Ceylon itself.

Then they travelled to Kandy and to Galle where they finished the tour with two two-day matches, which provided the manager with his own moment of glory.

"I played in both of them, and at Kandy I put on a hundred with Tom Graveney – or should I say, he put on a hundred with me?"

Leslie Smith's report in the *Daily Telegraph* is still proudly retained. 'Graveney scored 103 not out here to-day when M.C.C. hit 201 for three in reply to 165 by Central Province. Taking advantage of the small ground, Graveney reached his century with a six in the last over of the day. Mr Geoffrey Howard, manager of the M.C.C. team, proved an able partner for Graveney, after three wickets had fallen for 88. Though short of practice, Howard scored 30.'

"Short of practice? I'd hardly played since 1939."

*Kandy, 28 February. I am a little handicapped this morning as I got a crack on the hand batting yesterday. I was so pleased because Nigel said all the boys wanted me to play. I think they all wanted a good laugh at 'Grandpa'! However, you may have seen, I put on over 100 with Tom Graveney. Now my store stands high with the lads. The old man not only can talk about the game but he can play! Amazing!! They even thought I could run. But how stiff I am today and how bruised.*

In the final match at Galle he recovered sufficiently to grab the headline:

**Manager Howard rallies M.C.C.**

GALLE (Ceylon), Monday.—M.C.C. ended their tour with a six-wicket win, with 15 minutes to spare, against Galle here today.

Captain Alan Watkins and manager Geoffrey Howard figured in a stand of 52 after M.C.C. had lost their first three second-innings wickets for 10 runs.

**M.C.C. — First innings: 187** (R Wijesinghe 5—72). **Second innings: 106 for 4** (A Watkins 42 not out; Ludowyke 2—31, Wijesinghe 2—40).

**GALLE—First innings: 75** (M Hilton 6—28). **Second innings: 217** (B Heyn 61, C Schoorman 49; Robertson 4—52, Tattersall 4—58. Hilton 2—47).—Reuter.

At the end of their stay in Ceylon, Nigel Howard, Donald Carr and Geoffrey sat together in the hotel. *We tried to piece the tour together, but we just couldn't do so. We live entirely in the present and future, and the immediate past is like a strange dream. I am sure that, when we get on the boat, we shall find the door opens and the memories come crowding in.*

Soon enough they were passing Port Said, and the letters home came to an end. Did the tour take any shape as they sailed through the Mediterranean? Or did their minds start to fill once more with the concerns of the country they had not seen for six months?

"I can remember standing on the deck with Jack Robertson – what a lovely man he was, such a reliable tourist – and we were playing London Underground. Making the noises of the motors and the doors shutting, and making each other laugh. Then we listened to the Budget. The last item reported was that petrol was going up to three shillings and sixpence a gallon. And Jack said, 'I can't wait to get home and sell the car. I'm not paying three and sixpence a gallon for petrol."

England had a new Prime Minister and a new Queen, but nothing had changed at Old Trafford. Geoffrey rang the chairman, Dr Bowling Holmes, and he still remembers the response. "There was no 'Well done' or 'Did you enjoy it?' Just 'See you in harness tomorrow.'"

*

Only Tom Graveney and Brian Statham of 'Howard's willow-wielding ambassadors' advanced their Test careers in the sub-continent, but the tour provided a welcome boost for Indian and Pakistani cricket and, in the years that followed, the boards of both countries often turned to the M.C.C. manager for help.

"When we sailed for home, I thought that I'd probably never see India again. But I was so lucky. I went back four times."

The first time was with an Invitation XI he had been asked to form by the Bengal Cricket Association, to celebrate their Silver Jubilee in New Year 1957. The last time was with another side that he raised for their Golden Jubilee. "It was six years after I'd retired, and I took it on at short notice. I shouldn't have done it really, but I felt I owed it to them."

By then the Eden Gardens ground in Calcutta had been transformed into a great concrete stadium, with a seating capacity of 70,000 and no sign of the swaying shamiyanas. India was no longer on a level with England's second team; they had players like Sunil Gavaskar, Kapil Dev and Bishen Bedi.

"You've got to be impressed by what they've achieved – and even more with the progress Pakistan has made. They are up there with the best now."

As his invitation team, led by Mike Brearley, made its way to the Golden Jubilee match at Calcutta, they changed planes at Bombay – and, for one last time, he met his old friend Narayan Karmarker. It was a brief, fond reunion, but there was time for them to do once more what they had done together thirty years earlier.

"I was in charge of all the bags, and he stopped and helped me."

*

The letters are returned to their box in the back room. The photographs are back in their albums. We sit together in his front room in the Cotswolds and, when I finish reading him this chapter, he sighs.

"So many pictures crossed my mind as you were reading. I didn't find it difficult to fall in love with India, even with all its problems. If I was younger and fitter, I'd love to go there again."

# CHAPTER NINE

# A CHANGING WORLD

# OLD TRAFFORD

# 1952 – 64

Geoffrey Howard was the secretary of Lancashire County Cricket Club for sixteen years. He arrived when the ground was in disarray from its wartime damage, working out of the President's Room till the secretary's office was rebuilt. The chairman had been on the committee since 1900, the minutes were hand-written and on match days the scorecards were printed away from the ground. "They were never available on the first morning. For big occasions, like the Roses match, when they did finally arrive, the seller had to stand behind railings to save himself from being crushed."

Old Trafford was one of the great cricket grounds of England, with its rich history and its clear, soft light, and the committee longed to see the county once more at the pinnacle of the English domestic game. "I soon came to see that there were an awful lot of people who were thinking backwards rather than forwards, hoping to restore the club to the status quo before the war."

By the end of his sixteen-year tenure, the world had changed beyond the imagination of his first committee. Austerity had given way to affluence, with television sets and washing machines, motor cars and foreign holidays. The club's income in 1949 came almost entirely from gate receipts and members' subscriptions. By 1964 the balance depended on television and radio fees, catering profits, a football pool scheme, the hiring of the ground for outside functions, car parking charges for Manchester United football club.

In 1949 the committee would not countenance a professional as captain. By 1964 there were no amateurs and professionals, only cricketers.

In 1949 the objective was to win the county championship. In 1964 there were no great crowds for championship matches. But there was a full house for the semi-final of the one-day Knock-Out competition.

In 1949 Geoffrey and Nora Howard were settling into their house in Altrincham, with their four girls all to be educated at the local convent school. He bought the house with a loan but so rare were the pay rises and so great his outgoings that long before he left in 1964 the ownership of the house had passed to Lancashire County Cricket Club.

He was 40 years old in 1949. He had left school at 16, he had spent years of no great distinction in Martins Bank and, though he had reached the rank of Acting Squadron Leader, his war-time service had not been remarkable. Just two years as Brian Castor's assistant had led to his appointment at Old Trafford. Yet, by the time he left, he was one of cricket's finest administrators. A man who could be trusted to manage an M.C.C. tour of Australia without an assistant. A man who served on all the important committees that looked at the future of the game. A man who made sure that Lancashire County Cricket Club did not become becalmed by sentimental traditionalism but cherished and developed its inheritance.

When he returned from India in the Spring of 1952, there was much to do. His assistant Leonard Abel had kept things ticking over, but he was not a great lover of the game. "He was happier tinkering around with his motor car or his radio set." And the club captain, Nigel Howard, was low from his unhappy trip. "He told me quite late in the tour that he was thinking of resigning the

Lancashire captaincy. I had to talk him out of it. It would have left the club in a terrible position."

By early June Nigel Howard had scored 53 runs at an average of 6.63, and he stood down for a fortnight in favour of his senior professional, Cyril Washbrook. The older players knew Nigel when he was a boy, when his father brought him to Old Trafford for coaching, and, though he led Lancashire to a share of the title in 1950 and to third place in each of the next three summers, he never quite acquired the leadership skills or the batting ability to command the full respect of the professionals or to fulfil his father's aspirations. According to *Wisden*, Lancashire were a good enough side to be champions but they lacked *'that little fighting spirit so necessary in the winning of the championship'*.

"We should have won the championship two or three times in the fifties," Geoff Edrich thinks. "We had a good enough side. But we never had the right leadership."

At the end of the summer of 1953 Nigel Howard left the game to enter full-time into his father's textile business. "He wasn't a natural cricketer," Geoffrey Howard says. "His brother Barry, who captained the second eleven, was a better player."

In the summer of 1954 they took the field under the captaincy of Cyril Washbrook. By now there were four other counties with professional captains – Jack Crapp at Gloucestershire, Doug Wright at Kent, Dennis Brookes at Northamptonshire, Tom Dollery at Warwickshire – and the decision passed through committee without dissent.

But, though Washbrook commanded a respect that had always eluded his predecessor, he was not an ideal captain, either.

He was nearly 40, a no-nonsense disciplinarian whose career with Lancashire had started before some of the emerging players had been born: men like Peter Marner, Jack Dyson, Geoff Clayton the happy-go-lucky lad from Mossley. "Cyril never referred to Geoff by name. He always called him The Wicket Keeper."

Did Washbrook's aloof leadership get the best out of them?

"Cyril was too stiff. He didn't understand young people. He was one of those men, you can't imagine him ever being a boy."

Peter Marner had played two matches as a precocious 16-year-old at the end of 1952. The second was against Middlesex at Lord's, where *Wisden* records that he *'distinguished himself by a spectacular catch in the deep from a big hit by Young. He finished a long fast run with a successful leap at the swiftly falling ball.'* "He caught it right in front of the Committee Room," Geoffrey remembers, "and threw the ball up with joy. He was sent for by Sir Pelham to explain himself: 'This sort of behaviour will not do at Lord's.' He probably thought, 'Silly old bugger, what's he know about the game? Warner? Never heard of him.'"

This was a new generation, with a new outlook on life, still boys when the war was over. Not like Geoff Edrich, who had spent nearly four years as a prisoner of the Japanese, going down to six-and-a-half stone and returning home to a wife and son who had long assumed him dead. "They're still together now. It's a wonderful story. But, after all that he'd been through, he wasn't a laughing boy."

In those first years after the war, when Australia and South Africa had all the fast bowlers, Hutton and Washbrook had opened the innings for England, two northern men with great reserves of determination. "Cyril wasn't quite in the same class as Len. He was somewhere near the top, but he wasn't a great player of leg-spin. I can see him at Blackpool, struggling for about three quarters of an hour to get off the mark against George Tribe. He had no idea which way the ball was going to turn."

A poor tour of Australia in 1950/51 brought an end to his Test career, but in 1956 he was recruited as a selector and, with the Australians one up after the second Test, he found himself on the team sheet for the match at Headingley. A 41-year-old who had not scored a century that summer. There were many in the Press who questioned the backwardness of the thinking.

"I was up at St Bees School with an M.C.C. side," Geoffrey Howard recalls, "and I had several of the young pros making up numbers. A wicket had fallen, we were gathered together in the middle, and the news came through from Headingley that England were 17 for three. And one of the young pros said, 'We'll be all right now. The skipper's coming in.'"

He scored 98, and his partnership of 187 with Peter May was the highest for England against Australia since the war. It was the turning-point of the rubber.

"I told Cyril what they'd said at St Bees. He was very touched; it nearly brought tears to his eyes. He knew he frightened the young players, but he didn't realise how much they respected him."

That summer of 1956 was the closest Lancashire came to winning the championship during his six-year captaincy, but their second place owed as much to his deputy, Geoff Edrich, whose ten games in charge yielded as many victories as the captain's eighteen. "Geoff was a much more aggressive captain. He always played to win; Cyril played not to lose."

While England were winning at Headingley, Lancashire entertained Leicestershire at Old Trafford in a match reduced to two days by rain. With the Midland county all out for 108, Geoff Edrich instructed his openers, Alan Wharton and Jack Dyson, to score quick runs, declaring when they had reached 166 for no wicket. They bowled Leicestershire out again, this time for 122, leaving his openers to knock off 65 runs in 50 minutes, the only instance in first-class cricket of a side winning without losing a wicket.

"Geoff could have been a fine captain. He had a great feeling for the game, and he understood the young players. But there was a time towards the end of each summer when his wartime memories got the better of him."

Washbrook and Edrich. They never saw eye to eye. But between them, if you could have constructed one man out of their respective strengths, you would have had a great leader.

For the secretary, though, the most important match of the year was the Old Trafford Test – and in 1956, after Washbrook's triumphant return at Headingley, the series was level at one game all as the fourth Test approached.

Lancashire were playing Gloucestershire at Blackpool the previous weekend, leaving Old Trafford free for the final preparations. The policy of not watering or rolling the pitch had been long abandoned. "Bert Flack was the groundsman by then. He'd come from Cambridge, and he wouldn't have been prepared to accept that."

The previous summer the South Africans had been the visitors, and the Old Trafford Test had provided a feast of run-making that ended in a thrilling finish, three minutes from time, with the visitors victorious by three wickets. "Paul Winslow scored a magnificent hundred, his driving was unbelievable, but the shot I remember best was by Denis Compton. He shaped to hook one of their quick bowlers and, halfway into the shot, he realised it was too close to him and he turned right round and hit it through the covers. It was an incredible stroke."

During that match the Lancashire secretary sat for a while at the Stretford End with Wally Hammond, Wilfred Rhodes and Reggie Spooner. "What a trio that was! Wilfred Rhodes was blind, but he recognised my voice each year. 'They've taken new ball,' he said. 'How do you know that?' 'It makes different sound on bat.'"

For that match in 1955 Bert Flack used a new liquid dressing, and the plan in 1956 was to prepare another surface like it. "I was up at Blackpool, and on the Tuesday he phoned me. I can't remember what about but in passing he said, 'The wicket's a bit dry. I think I ought to give it a bit of water.'"

Geoffrey was busy, hiring a plane from the Lancashire Aircraft Corporation to fly the two teams to Bristol and Bournemouth. It was an unprecedented arrangement, and it cost the two clubs a total of £160. "I can remember the criticism. We'd exposed the whole playing staff of two counties to the risk of flying. The Lancashire scorer wouldn't go. He followed on by train."

In the middle of his arrangements, the telephone rang again and Peter May, the England captain, came through. "What's the wicket like?" he asked, wanting to think through his final team selection.

"As far as I know, it's exactly the same as last year. Bert Flack's just been on the phone. He said he's going to put a bit of water on it."

"Oh, don't put water on it."

With the benefit of 45 years of hindsight, the secretary knows what his reply should have been. "I should have said, 'That's nothing to do with you.' But, when you're in the middle of doing something else, you don't think things through. So I rang back to Bert Flack. I didn't tell him not to water it, but I told him what Peter May had said."

The pitch needed another watering, but it never took place.

On Wednesday, with the two Test teams assembled, the new Lancashire chairman – Tommy Burrows, a Manchester wine merchant – joined his secretary and Gubby Allen, the chairman of selectors, in an inspection of the pitch. "Of course he'll take a bit of grass off in the morning," Tommy Burrows said, and Gubby Allen looked pensive. "Oh, I don't think I'd do that," he said.

"Tommy Burrows was like his predecessor Bowling Holmes. He wasn't really knowledgeable about the game so he never used his own judgement. He went to Bert Flack, and he told him not to cut it."

Unwatered at the request of the England captain. Uncut at the request of the chairman of selectors. When the controversy raged during the match, the Lancashire secretary resolved to stay silent. "The remarks weren't improper, but they would have seemed to have been. I came under a lot of pressure, but I said, 'I'm not going to say anything at all on the subject.'"

He never did – till now.

Once more the wicket at Old Trafford was to be the subject of argument, though it would produce the most memorable match of Geoffrey Howard's sixteen years there. A match as remarkable as any in the history of Ashes cricket.

*

Thursday the 26th of July 1956. The selectors had produced another rabbit from the hat in recalling the Reverend David Sheppard, now working at St Mary's Church in Islington and having played only four first-class innings all summer. The *Daily Sketch* arranged for a coach-load of boys from his parish to come and watch him – "I remember him settling down this gaggle of small boys on the grass, then going off to get changed" – and in mid-afternoon, with the sun bright and the score 174 for one, they watched their curate step out of the pavilion and bat with such assurance that by lunch the next day he had completed a fairy-tale hundred. *'He drove magnificently,'* *Wisden* recorded, *'and he gave not the lightest suggestion of lack of match practice.'*

There were runs a-plenty, but it was not a pitch like the one for the South African Test the previous summer. "It was obvious from the very first ball of Keith Miller's first over that it was a pudding. It had no bounce, no pace in it." Then, just before the close, Richie Benaud dismissed Peter May with a leg-break that turned and lifted steeply, catching the shoulder of the bat. "It was not totally depressing," May wrote, "for it suggested that we had already had the best of the pitch."

*'Mutterings about the pitch could be heard that evening,'* Leslie Smith wrote in *Wisden*, *'but they rose to full fury the next day.'*

By the end of Friday, Australia were 51 for one in their second innings, having being bowled out for 84 in little more than two hours. Jim Laker took nine for 37 from the Stretford End, and *'accusations were made that the pitch had been specially prepared for England's spin bowlers.'*

"The Aussies were no great players of off-spin bowling. The ball turned, and they batted badly. It wasn't just the pitch. Neil Harvey was caught off a full-toss."

After that, it was a story of Manchester rain, with little play on Saturday or Monday, then a bright sun on Tuesday that made a sticky wicket ideal for

Jim Laker, who took all ten wickets to finish with nineteen in the match. The greatest bowling performance in the whole history of cricket.

The weather had played its hand in England's favour and Australia's captain Ian Johnson, gesturing towards the Reverend David Sheppard, complained. "It's not fair. You've got a professional on your side."

That night the rain returned. There was not a ball bowled anywhere in England the next day.

"It wasn't Bert Flack's fault. Or Tommy Burrows. The last cut would have made little difference. If the mower had gone up and down, you wouldn't have got a boxful. No, if anybody was to blame, it was me – for passing on Peter May's message. The pitch should have been watered."

*

Each year, on the Sunday of the Test match, the secretary turned out for E.W. Swanton's XI at Didsbury, and he recalls one occasion when Richie Benaud was on his side. "A young Pakistani, with no batting gloves, hit him out of the ground again and again. I doubt if he'd ever heard of Richie. He just had a wonderful eye. He probably thought, 'This is a nice, easy pace.'"

*

In *Wisden*'s newly created Index of Summer Weather, there are no five-year periods with a worse point score than the summers from 1954 to 1958. Changes in leisure patterns were gaining pace – "People had other things to do than watch other people doing it" – and the financial statements of Lancashire County Cricket Club made grim reading. In Geoffrey Howard's first five years, there was an average annual surplus of £3,181. In his next five years, there was an average loss of £5,853. With a turnover under £50,000, there was clearly a need for change.

For Rupert Howard, still active behind the scenes, the answer lay in reducing expenditure. "He was forever doing little sums to show how much the reserves had dwindled away. He had no interest in the maintenance of the ground and the buildings. Only the cricket itself – and money. He thought I was spending money that ought not to be spent."

For the secretary, though, the focus was on raising income. "I had a real struggle to get them to raise the turnstile charge from one and sixpence to two shillings. But the main thing I did was to make them realise that they had assets which were usable all the year round. We installed central heating in the pavilion, curtained the Long Room and started to run dinner dances through the winter. I can still remember the first one. I was standing in my dinner jacket, the licensee for music and dancing. The first couple came in, and I heard the woman saying, 'This isn't a cricket pavilion. Cricket pavilions are little wooden huts.' The Long Room was a dance floor, and there was a bar next door to it. We took something like £10,000 in our first year."

They were following the example of Edgbaston, and Warwickshire's caterers offered their services. "The catering had been in the hands of one of the committee, and we'd had deficits every year. It had been run in a very amateurish way. He vigorously opposed the change – I found out why in due course – but the proposal was carried. Suddenly we had a professional caterer and we were making a profit."

The secretary proposed that they should experiment with Sunday play, arranging with Derbyshire that their Old Trafford fixture in July 1959 should take place on Saturday, Sunday and Monday. "It would have been a great step forward, but at committee Leonard Green said, 'What about the Non-Conformists of Oldham?' and people said, 'We hadn't thought of that.' And they withdrew the idea. It was another seven years before Surrey staged Sunday play at The Oval."

Warwickshire had had great success with a football pool scheme, and other counties – Gloucestershire, Glamorgan and Hampshire – took up the idea. So Lancashire created their own Auxiliary Association, and by the early '60s it was generating several thousand pounds a year for building works – "though nothing like the sums they collected at Edgbaston. We were too late. The climate for that sort of thing was starting to go."

By 1959 the county's income was once more greater than its expenditure, and in 1961 – blessed with a dry summer and another Australian tour – the surplus was a record £8,199. And that was despite a drop of 45,000 in county attendances.

What a pity that these financial improvements should have been accompanied by a slump in the playing fortunes of the county! The summer of 1960 saw them rise to second place in the championship, recording their first double over Yorkshire since 1893, but in the next four years they finished 13th, 16th, 15th and 14th, depths to which they had never before sunk in all their proud history.

In the immediate post-war years Lancashire had been happy to recruit players from farther afield – Geoff Edrich from Norfolk, Jack Ikin from Staffordshire, the Australian Ken Grieves – but by the 1950s the committee was pursuing a 'Lancastrians only' policy. Cyril Washbrook spotted Ted Dexter at Fenner's – "He watched him in the nets and he came back, saying he'd seen the next Keith Miller" – but the minute is clear: *'After discussion it was resolved that the policy of playing only Lancashire-born cricketers should be followed and no approach should be made to Dexter.'* Geoff Edrich received the same response when he recommended his young cousin John. And overseas players completing residential qualifications in the Lancashire Leagues – Bill Alley, Roy Gilchrist, Basil d'Oliveira – all had their approaches rebuffed.

Just think! In 1962, when Lancashire won two and lost 16 of their championship matches, they could have boasted a batting line-up of Edrich, Pullar, Dexter, Barber, Alley, d'Oliveira.

From 1959 to 1968, Yorkshire won seven championships with their Yorkshire-born eleven, but Lancashire's attempt to emulate them ended in humiliating failure.

"They are very different counties. Yorkshire is far bigger, and it's much more unified. In Lancashire there was a divide between east and west.

Liverpool and Manchester had practically nothing in common; culturally or commercially. So the people thought of themselves as from Manchester, Liverpool, Bolton, much more than they thought of themselves as from Lancashire. But Yorkshire people – whether they came from Sheffield, York, Bradford, Leeds – they were first and foremost from Yorkshire.

"I remember in the bar at The Oval a chap beating his chest and saying, 'I come from Yorkshire and I'm proud of it.' Well, you don't get people from Berkshire doing that, do you?

"There's no county in England where the county spirit is stronger than in Yorkshire – except perhaps Northumberland and Durham."

League cricket in the two counties reflected this difference. "The Lancashire leagues were not nearly as supportive of their county cricket club as the Yorkshire leagues were of theirs. The professionals in the Yorkshire Leagues were all Yorkshiremen – but they weren't Lancastrians in the Lancashire leagues, particularly not in the Lancashire League itself."

Whatever the distinctions, Geoffrey remembers the cricketing people of both counties for their warmth and their ability to entertain. "Wonderful hospitality was always being dished out. Mostly drinks, at close of play in the committee room. At The Oval any drinking was at the individual's expense. At Old Trafford the club bore the cost. And if no committee member was present, I had to do it – until the last guest left. I remember having to take Lindsay Hassett home in order to get him away from Old Trafford, and he was still going strong at one o'clock."

As a result of managing the M.C.C. tour of 1951/52, the Lancashire secretary acquired the role of liaison agent for the Pakistan Cricket Board in England. He supervised their travel and hotel arrangements – "I delegated it to a chap from Thomas Cook." – and acted as a friendly point of contact for their cricketers. In time he came to do the same for the Indians.

"You had several of the Indian players come back to stay with us," his daughter Frances reminds him. "Mum cooked this wonderful curry. The cooking correspondent of the *Guardian* rang up for the recipe."

His secretary at Old Trafford, Rose FitzGibbon, remembers the telephone calls.

"Can I speak to Mister Howard?"

"Who is speaking, please?"

"I am speaking. Asgar. Mr Howard, he is my father. I must speak to him."

Geoffrey smiles. "He used to ring me at home. 'You are my father and my mother,' he used to say. I got him a job in the Lancashire League. I got Fazal a job, too, at East Lancashire. And Pankaj Roy at Blackpool. And Hanif."

"They used to write copious letters," Rose remembers, "with a list of things that you were to send to them: a suit length, a fridge, a frying pan. 'Are you really going to buy all these things?' I said. And you did. I don't know if you ever got paid, though."

"Somebody came into my office when I was back at The Oval. He'd been sent by the secretary of the Indian Board of Control for an advance of £50. I certainly never got that back."

*The Pakistani tourists outside the Queen's Hotel, Manchester.*

The Lancashire committee never appreciated its secretary's involvement in cricket matters beyond the county. There was a lengthy discussion before they agreed to his taking on this liaison function, and they rarely showed any delight when he was chosen to manage overseas tours.

He was also a member of several important M.C.C. sub-committees during his stay at Old Trafford. In 1957 a committee, chaired by the Duke of Norfolk, examined the status of the amateurs. "It was set up in response to pressure from the amateurs to be paid more liberal expenses."

By this time there were few cricketers who could afford to play the four-month summer without any remuneration, yet the world of cricket remained wedded to the existence of a stratum of amateurs.

> *Distinction between Amateur and Professional*
>
> *The committee accepted as basic to the problem that, whereas some fifty years ago many Amateurs could afford to, and did, play first-class cricket entirely at their own expense, this was no longer the case.*
>
> *The committee rejected any solution of the problem on the lines of abolishing the distinction between Amateur and Professional and regarding them all alike as "cricketers". They considered that the distinctive status of the amateur cricketer was not obsolete, was of great value to the game and should be preserved.*
>
> *The Professionals whom they had consulted supported these views. They did, however, emphasise the urgency of resolving certain anomalies existing in present practice.*

The anomalies were becoming plentiful. Several amateur captains were employed as assistant secretaries, with no particular duties; others had nominal positions found for them. Often, on overseas tours, the amateurs received more generous payments – in lieu of lost earnings – than the professionals received in wages. And increasingly there were the grey areas of journalism and sponsorship. "The Surrey professionals didn't like it that Peter May was being paid to endorse Surridge bats."

"I can remember Bernard Norfolk hearing some evidence and saying, 'Well, as far as I can see, if the professionals are not satisfied with their earnings, they can always turn amateur.'" With the emphasis of the word 'amateur' firmly on the final syllable.

The Duke was the Earl Marshal of England, and Geoffrey recalls his arriving late to one meeting. "I must apologise," the Duke said. "I've been putting the finishing touches to the arrangements for Winston Churchill's funeral." It would be another seven years before the ceremony would take place – seven years that would see changes that this Norfolk committee did not recommend.

In 1959 M.C.C. awarded honorary membership to 26 retired professionals, among them Lancashire's own Ernest Tyldesley, a modest man who, in Cardus's words, 'never exceeded the privileges of class and manners.' He had scored 102 first-class centuries and was chairman of cricket at Old Trafford, but "he couldn't really reconcile himself to being a member of M.C.C. He was so pleased, but I had to go out and buy the tie for him. He'd never have done it himself, and I had to persuade him to wear it."

Then at the end of 1962, M.C.C. tore up their previous conclusions and abolished the amateur/professional distinction completely. *'We live in a changing world,'* Norman Preston, the *Wisden* editor, wrote. *'Conditions are vastly different from the days of our grandparents; but is it wise to throw everything overboard?'*

Yet Lancashire, who had appointed Cyril Washbrook as captain in 1954, had reverted to tradition in that last amateur summer of 1962. With Bob Barber stepping down after two unhappy years as captain, the committee turned to a club cricketer, Joe Blackledge, an Old Reptonian whose family ran a textile business in Chorley and who had never played a game of first-class cricket.

They say that one morning, when they chased the ball to all parts of Old Trafford, the amateur captain turned to Brian Statham.

"What do you think we should do now, Brian?"

"I think we should have an early lunch, skipper."

It was not a success, and in 1963 the county turned back to the professional ranks, recalling the Australian Ken Grieves whose first year in charge saw them finish 15th rather than 16th, with *Wisden* seeing *'grounds for optimism that Lancashire would soon begin to climb to a more worthy position in the table.'*

That summer of 1963 was historic not only for the absence of amateurs but for the introduction of one-day cricket. After years of toying with the idea

– "I believe Lancashire proposed it before the war" – the counties set up the Knock-Out competition, with a final scheduled at Lord's. The matches were to be 65 overs a-side, with a maximum of 13 overs for each bowler.

The Lancashire secretary had served on the committee that had developed this idea, and he and Cyril Washbrook had put forward some alternatives to the format that was finally agreed:

> *That a limitation of the number of overs a bowler may bowl was contrary to the interests of the game in any form.*
>
> *That it was vitally important to keep the game moving quickly; two suggestions were offered for consideration.*
>
> *(i) that the fielding side should be compelled to bowl a minimum of 20 overs per hour.*
>
> *(ii) that it should be ruled that the wicket-keeper must return the ball direct to the bowler.*

Lancashire reached the semi-final. "I remember driving down to Worcester. We stopped for some strawberries on the way and, by the time we arrived, the match was almost over." They had been bowled out for 59, and the home side needed just ten overs to knock off the runs. It was a disaster – but not the disaster that the semi-final the following year turned out to be.

*

"Old Trafford has changed so much since I left. I attended Brian Statham's funeral and, when we went back to the pavilion, I had to ask the way. But everybody was there, and they were all so hospitable – and, by the time it came for me to go, I felt I'd never left."

But leave he did at the end of 1964. And, like so many in those years, his leaving was not a happy one. "I don't want to give the wrong impression. I had sixteen years at Old Trafford, and I haven't many unhappy memories. I remember looking out of the french windows at the house in Altrincham, thinking 'I don't want to leave here.' The family were all settled, and I only had ten years left before I drew my pension."

Rose FitzGibbon recalls how the staff heard the news that he was going. "Everybody was up in arms. Some were in tears. He'd built up such a family atmosphere among the staff, and at Test matches his daughters used to help in the ticket office. I went to see the chairman and the president. I can see them now, staring out at the cricket as I spoke to them. 'Can you not tell Mr Howard that you want him to stay?' They said, 'We've done all we can, my dear.'"

"They hadn't done anything," Geoffrey says.

"You know what you've got to do," Rose told them. "You've got to stop Rupert Howard interfering in everything, allow Mr Howard to do his job."

"You said that?"

"I did."

"When I got back to The Oval, I had a letter from Nigel Howard, saying 'I hope your leaving Old Trafford has got nothing to do with any member of my family.' Of course he knew it had."

His brother Barry struck a different note. "At least we've got rid of the secretary," he was overheard to say.

A couple of the staff followed him to The Oval. One of them – Harry Dyderski, a former German prisoner-of-war – was "a magnificent sign-writer. He used to do all our hand-bills."

Harry Dyderski, Rose FitzGibbon, Bert Flack, Alf Wilkinson. These people – "and so many more" – were for Geoffrey the lifeblood of the club.

"One or two of the committee members thought, as soon as I'd gone, that they'd start cutting the staff down. But they didn't. They soon realised what a good job everybody was doing."

*

The summer of 1964 brought the centenary of the Lancashire County Cricket Club. There was a celebration Victorian fancy-dress evening in the pavilion, with a penny-farthing bicycle and Peter Lever and Harry Pilling dressed up as the Lancashire immortals Hornby and Barlow. It glows still in Geoffrey's memory, along with the evening for Brian Statham's benefit when Harry Secombe joked and sang and Roy Castle tap-danced up and down the Long Room.

*The audience as Harry Secombe performed.*
*Nora Howard is seated, bottom right. To the left of her are Frances, then Rose FitzGibbon. Geoff Pullar is standing at the back, to the left of the nearer door frame.*

One hundred years of a great club. A booklet, compiled by the secretary, celebrated its history, with pictures of some of its greatest sons: Hornby and Barlow, MacLaren and Briggs, the Tyldesley brothers, Paynter and Washbrook and now Brian Statham.

How sad that their largest crowd that summer should have witnessed such an unpleasant match as the Gillette Cup semi-final against Warwickshire. "The ground was full. I was on the gate myself, helping to take the money."

Limited-over cricket was still in its infancy, and Lancashire bowled with normal fields through Warwickshire's innings of 294. Their former captain Bob Barber opened the batting for the visitors, making a *'splendid'* 76 but, when Lancashire's reply reached 60 for no wicket after ten overs, they found themselves facing a different challenge. *'M.J.K. Smith brought on Ibadulla and Cartwright,'* Denys Rowbotham wrote in the *Manchester Guardian*. *'Both pitched just short of a length, with six deep fielders equally spaced round the ring. The effect was immediately and comprehensively blanketing. Lancashire's cause was doomed from this point onwards.'*

The later batsmen grew frustrated and, after Pilling and Marner had got out, Geoff Clayton decided to *'underline their frustration by refusing obstinately further contest.'* He appealed against the light, then batted the final 45 minutes for 19 not out. The crowd barracked, one man ran on the field to remonstrate with him, and at the end of the season he, Marner and the captain Ken Grieves all had their contracts terminated.

The committee issued a statement, saying, "We intend to build up a new team, who can be relied upon to conduct themselves well and pay a proper respect to the captain at all times." They left it to the secretary to meet the press over tea and biscuits and to deal with their questioning which, according to Denys Rowbotham, *'he rode with typical courtesy, frankness and, where necessary, evasion.'* But it was not enough to calm the anger of the members, still seething after the fiasco of the semi-final.

One hundred of them petitioned for a Special General Meeting and, at the Houldsworth Hall on the 24th of September, a motion was proposed, expressing 'dissatisfaction with the cricketing affairs of the Lancashire County Cricket Club'.

Denys Rowbotham wrote at length in the *Guardian* on *'the personal prejudices and repeated disagreements'* which bedevilled the committee's work, adding that, for more than a decade, confidential decisions and differences of opinion had been *'leaked by one or more members of the responsible committee.'* As Cedric Rhoades, the leading rebel, put it at the Special Meeting, "If the committee can't discipline itself, how can it discipline the team?"

Before the turmoil of that meeting, the secretary had tendered his resignation. His differences with his predecessor had reached a head, and he had accepted the vacant secretaryship at The Oval. While he worked out his notice, he made one last effort to solve the problem of the Lancashire captaincy. "Alan Smith wants to be a county captain," he told the committee, "and he won't be one at Warwickshire while Mike Smith is there. With your approval, I'd like to approach Warwickshire about speaking to him."

It was all agreed: by the committee, by Warwickshire and by Alan Smith himself. "His only concern was that Geoff Pullar and Brian Statham would resent his arrival. But I sorted that out. Brian knew he wasn't going to be captain, anyway. Nobody on the committee thought he was the right man for it."

But events overtook the arrangement. The motion of dissatisfaction was passed by 656 votes to 48, with members venting their rage about a whole catalogue of failures. "You've lost the best secretary the club has ever had," one member declared. A new committee was formed, a new secretary arrived – Jack Wood of Wigan Rugby League Club – and the new regime decided to do things differently. The offer to Alan Smith was withdrawn, and Brian Statham began a three-year spell in charge, years in which Lancashire finished 13th, 12th and 11th. In his first year, *Wisden* thought that he *'led a largely experimental side remarkably well'*, but by the third year the verdict was less flattering: *'Statham's captaincy often puzzled.'*

Leadership. No other game places as much importance on the skills of captaincy as cricket, and at Old Trafford the absence of an amateur who commanded respect was never offset by the emergence of a professional with the right qualities, like Don Kenyon at Worcester or Dennis Brookes at Northampton.

"Geoff Edrich had it in him to do it. And if you looked at the team in the early '60s, the chap who had recognisable leadership qualities was Geoff Clayton. But he had such a poor background, with so little education. He might have led them well – a sort of poacher turned game-keeper – but he might just as easily have misled them."

Geoff Edrich and Geoff Clayton. Perhaps, under the secretary's more benevolent and perceptive guidance, they might have prospered. But both finished their association with Lancashire by being sacked: Geoff Edrich in 1959, carrying the can for some late-night indiscipline among his young second-team charges in a Birmingham hotel, Geoff Clayton in 1964 after his ill-considered protest in the knock-out semi-final.

Clayton spent three years with Somerset before drifting through a succession of jobs outside cricket.

Geoff Edrich became groundsman and coach at Cheltenham College. "I recommended him. I said to them, 'Treat him like a master. Don't just use him as a groundsman.' But they didn't take any notice. He wasn't given the status he needed to restore his self-esteem."

I bumped into him at the Cheltenham Cricket Festival.

"They've made me a vice-president at Lancashire," he told me, his pride mingled with a little bitterness, "After all this time. And I've had my prisoner-of-war compensation – though not from the right people, not from the Japs."

For several years he has struggled with the after-effects of a cancer, unable to digest solid food, but his fighting spirit is still there.

"Geoff Edrich was a very fine cricketer. He never let anybody down on the cricket field."

So many cricketers left Lancashire in those years, and their revival only began when Jack Bond became captain in 1968. "He was going to leave at the end of 1964, Nottingham were interested in him, and I talked him out of it."

Geoffrey Howard was well-settled at The Oval by the time Jack Bond's Lancashire side, with the West Indian Clive Lloyd and the Indian Farokh Engineer, became masters of the fast-expanding world of one-day cricket.

*

In 1963 Rupert Howard was appointed chairman of the match committee, and the fault line that had opened up in 1949, when he had been co-opted on to all the other committees, created a fresh tremor.

It was the responsibility of the secretary to speak to staff about contracts of employment, and Geoffrey remembers how hard it could be when he had to tell long-established players that they were being released.

Like Winston Place, who had given so many years of cheerful service. "On the last day of his first season, they were all talking about where they were going for their holidays, and somebody said, 'What about you, Winston?' He said, 'This is the last day of my holiday.'" At the end of 1955 he reported to the secretary's office, and "he was in tears when I told him."

It was not a pleasant task, but it was the secretary's duty to carry it out. Geoffrey Howard placed the highest premium on doing such things properly. So he was not happy to arrive one morning and discover that, during his absence from the office, Rupert Howard had summoned Brian Booth to his house in Sale and told him that he was not required the following summer. Brian Booth had been at the club since he was a boy, his benefit year was approaching, and Rose FitzGibbon, who chauffered him that day, recalls how shattered he was when he came out of the house.

Rupert Howard was 74 years old. Fifteen years had passed since he had retired as secretary, and he was still treading on the toes of his successor.

In 1964, at the instigation of the chairman, the two men met for a clear-the-air talk, and all the long-held grievances spilled out.

"Under no circumstances must what I say go beyond these four walls," Geoffrey insisted and, having got this agreement to total confidentiality, he unburdened himself of all his frustrations: the hostility he had always felt from his predecessor, the refusal to let him get on and do things his own way, the inappropriateness of a past secretary accepting the chairmanship of the match committee. "Rupert had many good qualities, not least a sense of humour, and everything he did, he did for the good of Lancashire cricket. But he was such a mischief-maker. He made my life there very difficult."

On Rupert's side, there was still the smart of his son's being asked to stand down in India in early 1952. "He even brought up that phone call I'd made to Rait Kerr at Lord's during my first summer."

The next day the chairman, Tommy Burrows, summoned his secretary. Rupert Howard had left their confidential meeting, called a gathering at his home and repeated everything that Geoffrey had said to him. "I'm very surprised," Burrows said, "that you should have spoken in these terms to a senior vice-president."

"Tommy, if you're reprimanding me, I simply don't accept it."

The secretaryship at The Oval had been advertised, and Geoffrey had recommended his deputy Bob Warburton. But, when the message came back, "He won't get the job but, if you apply, you will", the timing made the offer irresistible.

His years at Old Trafford were over, and he returned with his family to London. "They promised me that they would transfer my pension, but in the end it turned out that they couldn't."

Fifty-five years old, and he was starting again. No home to sell, no pension accrued. "I really didn't want to go. I was so settled, and I had such a wonderful workforce. But they put me in an impossible position."

Even Brian Sellers, the Yorkshire chairman, pleaded with him to stay. "Lancashire needs you," he told him.

At the special meeting that threw out the committee, the secretary stood up to speak, and the members cheered him mightily.

"Booger Londoners," they might have said when he first arrived, but, according to Sheila Delve, whose father looked after Geoffrey's motor car and who herself worked in the office, "He won them all over."

"He reduced me to tears a few times," Rose FitzGibbon remembers. "I was a very timid person when I arrived, and he did seem rather awe-inspiring, very strict. He went off to India for a short tour in my first winter there, and I can't tell you how glad I was to see the back of him. But in time he brought the best out of me and I learnt so much from him. In the end I came to look upon him and his family as almost my family.

"He worked so hard – the jobs he did that they have so many people doing now – and he would never ask anybody to do anything that he wouldn't do himself. And it wasn't just him. His daughters would help in the office when we were busy, and Nora was always so hospitable to everybody. During Test matches she would be open house, cooking wonderful meals for so many people. In the early years of the Gillette Cup, we used to put up the opposing sides in family homes, to save their clubs some money, and Geoffrey would take several home with him for the night.

"They were wonderful days. Everybody on the staff was devoted to him."

Rose stayed for forty years, and she has witnessed other leadership styles.

"It all seems to be textbook management now. You certainly never see the chief executive cycling round the ground like Geoffrey used to do every day."

*

"They knew how to be generous at Old Trafford," Geoffrey recalls. "At Christmas, we'd get large boxes of chocolates, bottles of wine from Tommy Burrows, even a crate of whisky from one of the vice-presidents, Stanley Holt.

And everybody was so very fond of Nora. I don't want anything I say to give the impression that I didn't enjoy my years in the north. Far from it."

*

Thirty-six years later he was in the Old Trafford pavilion after Brian Statham's funeral, meeting again some of the players from his days in Lancashire.

There was Bob Berry, who had started his working life as a painter-decorator and finished it as a successful publican. "I reminded him of the time he came round to our house in Altrincham to do some decorating, and we upset a bucket of distemper all over the pair of us."

There was Jack Dyson, a professional footballer who never quite fulfilled his cricketing talent. "I reminded him of the overs he bowled at Blackpool when Jim Stewart of Warwickshire hit 17 sixes. He didn't know what to do. Nobody did when Jim was in that mind."

And Jack Bond, who became one of Lancashire's great captains. "A wonderful chap. A real son of Bolton. Almost the last thing I did at Old Trafford was to persuade him not to leave. 'Stay on, Jack,' I said. 'You won't regret it.'"

"They were all so pleased to see him," Rose FitzGibbon says. "They had such great respect for him. And they said to me, 'Fancy Mr Howard remembering that.'"

"How can one forget?" Geoffrey asks. "It was all so much part of my life."

*

"When you get back to The Oval," Jim Kilburn, the cricket correspondent of the *Yorkshire Post*, told Geoffrey, "you'll be shocked. It's an awful mess."

Surrey had won seven championships in succession in the fifties, "but they never cashed in on their success. There was no perceptible change in the surroundings from when I'd left in 1948. Certainly they hadn't raised money from things like football pools. They would never have stooped to such a thing."

"We're looking forward to having some of your ideas," Alf Gover told him.

The challenge beckoned.

# CHAPTER TEN

# THE ASHES

# ADELAIDE AND AFTER

# JANUARY – MARCH 1955

Friday the 28th of January 1955.

After three weeks away from the Test series, the England cricketers assembled at the Adelaide Oval. Their four-month-old tour had reached another critical point and, having lost the toss, they took the field on the first morning in humid heat.

'As one looks from the pavilion,' Jim Swanton described, 'the eye takes in tents and a belt of trees, with the fine Anglican cathedral of St Peter's slightly obscured by the scoreboard on the hill. Behind, on the skyline, stretch the Mount Lofties, burnt dappled shades of brown by the summer heat.'

It was a beautiful scene, but the English players' hearts sank when the first balls from Frank Tyson bounced gently off the pitch and reached Godfrey Evans knee-high. 'There seemed no reason,' Alan Ross wrote, 'why Australia should not score enough to make the difference between batting first and second a crucial one.' They had reached 51 for no wicket at lunch and, in the view of *The Times*, 'with all the afternoon and evening to stroke the ball for runs on this most gentle wicket', there was no reason why they should not be 300 for one or two at the close.

Alan Ross's report was second-hand as he was lying in Calvary Hospital, recovering from the removal of his appendix, while *The Times* writer was Stuart Harris, not John Woodcock who had suffered a burst ulcer in Hobart.

The M.C.C. party were staying at the Pier Hotel in the little seaside resort of Glenelg, with the journalists' hotel round the corner. John Woodcock did not arrive there till the evening of that first day – and then against medical advice.

Tyson captured Morris's wicket soon after lunch. At this point the England manager settled down to write home.

*Adelaide, 28 January. Denis has just dropped Colin McDonald – a fairly easy catch – oh dear. The Press will be after him, I suppose – especially if he should fail with the bat.*

'McDonald,' Swanton wrote, 'was batting well enough to make this seem an ominous miss.'

"I went to Denis's memorial service at Westminster Abbey,' Geoffrey says. 'I remember John Warr reading out his statistics. 38,000 runs, 600 wickets, and finally he said, 'He took 416 catches – when he happened to be looking.' He was so easily distracted."

*A great piece of luck – Peter May has just caught Colin McDonald after he made only another 4!! 'Orfa Appleyard', as old Alec Bedser would say.*

A light breeze eased the heat, and Hutton, using all his five bowlers in two- and three-over spells, strangled the Australian scoring rate to the point that they reached close of play at 161 for four. The largest Adelaide crowd for over twenty years – some 30,500 – 'had little to admire but the confining efforts of the English bowlers, subtly managed and directed by Hutton.'

*

"I was thinking in bed last night," Geoffrey rang to tell me. "A six-month cricket tour has so many likenesses with six months of soldiering. For one thing, you have these short periods of action and, just like in war, people have to deal with all the time in between. Some go and have a few beers, others fall to philosophising."

The England party had its drinkers and its philosophers. It had its veterans, travelling with the scars of previous defeats, and its young men, expecting victory. It had its loners, thinking of home and family, and its socialisers. There were the key performers and the men on the fringes.

They all had to be looked after, and it was not going to be Len Hutton who would look after them. Peter Loader recalls going to the toilet near the end of the tour and standing next to his captain. "Did you have a good trip?" Hutton asked. "It was almost the only time that he spoke to me off the field." To Keith Andrew, a mechanical engineer by qualification, the captain's greeting was always the same. "Now, don't forget you've just got married." The manager remembers Keith's complaint to him: "I think he thinks I'm simple."

The team might not have been made up of the most compatible of characters, but somehow the relationships were formed.

"We used to have a Saturday night club, to let off a bit of steam. One time Bill Edrich and Godfrey Evans arrived late. They'd been to the Races, and they were full of grog. We were in the middle of the fines. Bill got up to speak, and he couldn't utter. The words wouldn't come out. He was smiling away, talking nonsense, and young Colin was sitting there, looking at him, thinking 'What's wrong with him? This isn't the man I know.'"

Today one might call it bonding. For Geoffrey Howard, he was only doing what he had done for his squadron in Alexandria, the thousand men 'not all of them capable of looking after themselves'. It was his responsibility to make sure that they were fed, accommodated, in good health and good spirits.

"Of all the tours I went on," Trevor Bailey says, "that one of Australia was easily the happiest."

For the manager, one suspects, there was always a vision of a harmonious group, their physical and emotional needs met as his grandfather had sought to meet the needs of turn-of-the-century city dwellers. Sir Ebenezer had built Letchworth with a carefully considered plan, but his grandson was working for an employer with a lesser attention to detail.

"Another similarity with soldiering is the value of reconnaissance. I told the M.C.C. when we returned from India that they should send out somebody in advance to check the accommodation, but they didn't do that sort of thing. For Australia they hadn't even made any financial provisions. We just had to take things as they came."

"I want you all to go out there," Lord Cobham told them at Lord's, "not thinking that you're playing cricket *against* the Australians but that you're playing *with* them."

"I wonder how many of the team remembered that when we were playing for the Ashes at Adelaide. Not Len, I'm certain."

*

It was after tea on Saturday when Len Hutton and Bill Edrich walked out to open England's innings, with a total of 323 to be overtaken. Earlier in the afternoon Australia had been 229 for eight, but Maddocks and Johnson had kept England in the field till the evening session and, according to Jim Swanton, 'in so doing were perhaps going some way towards winning a match that would square the rubber.'

That morning the captain and manager visited John Woodcock in his hotel.

"Where are you spending the day?"

"In the Press box."

"No, you're not. You'll come and spend it with us."

"I wouldn't dream of it."

"Yes, you will."

"In the event I spent the rest of the match in the England dressing room. I was of an age with the players. I'd sailed out with them, so that many of them were close friends by then. It's not a match or a gesture that I shall ever forget. It wouldn't happen now."

Meanwhile, his replacement described the final hour when Hutton and Edrich played out the Australian captain's off-breaks: 'Johnson looked like taking wickets all the time but, of course, he was bowling at two tired men, drawing on their last reserves of concentration.'

Hutton and Edrich survived and, at 57 for no wicket, they had already achieved the best England opening stand of the series. It was not attractive cricket but, with the pitch likely to take increasing turn after the weekend, Hutton had set his mind on building a large first innings lead.

*Len really means business*, his manager had written before the match, *and is determined to make a lot of runs.*

*

Four years earlier on this ground Hutton became the only Englishman since Bobby Abel in 1892 to carry his bat in a Test against Australia. For more than six hours he was at the wicket, scoring 156 runs, but his team's total was just 272 and the match was lost by 274 runs.

If this match in 1955 went the same way, the series would be level, and the Australians would arrive at Sydney rejuvenated and with the Ashes still at stake.

For the first time Len Hutton was in a position to win a Test series in Australia, and he was determined to lead the way there with his own bat.

*

Monday was Australia Day and, before play started, the home team lined up before the members' stand, Ian Johnson raised the national flag, and the crowd sang 'The Song of Australia'.

'And all above is azure bright –
Australia, Australia, Australia.'

Within fifteen minutes Edrich, then May, had been dismissed, and the score was 63 for two. 'A chasm yawned in England's way,' Stuart Harris wrote in *The Times*, 'and it was left to Hutton and Cowdrey, working on the very brink, to build a bridge across.'

*Adelaide, 31 January. Darling, I have decided to come away – watching Test cricket in Australia is not very good for the nerves and very conducive to indigestion. We made a bad start this morning – Bill Edrich bowled in the first over and Peter May brilliantly caught soon after. Colin Cowdrey made a very shaky start but battled on and Len is holding on magnificently. I was rather afraid that Peter would fail today. He was so het up and on edge all the morning. If only he had Colin's temperament. Colin plays every match with equal imperturbability. Temperament is everything in these contests.*

Peter May and Colin Cowdrey. Seven years earlier Geoffrey Howard had sat taking minutes as the Surrey committee had decided to concentrate their attentions for the time being on the older May. Now, as their manager, he was observing them at close quarters, knowing that they were England's brightest batting prospects since the war. But did Colin Cowdrey really have the better temperament?

"He was a much more relaxed person. I can see him, walking between overs and mimicking the way Denis or Peter was walking. He probably wasn't that aware he was doing it. It was just a natural sense of fun. Peter had a sense of humour, too, but he could be quite austere. He wasn't really the born leader of men that you'd have expected him to be with his upbringing, but he was dedicated in everything he turned his hand to. If Colin had a weakness, it was his indecisiveness.

"When Peter retired from cricket, he went into insurance and his commitment was quite beyond the belief of Colin. 'I've just been talking to Peter in his office,' he told me one day. 'That's a serious business. I hope I never have to do anything like that.'"

Twenty years their senior, the England manager watched them as they returned from Australia to become the cornerstones of England's batting for years to come, each in turn progressing to the captaincy. He continued watching them as they made their respective ways after cricket. The easy-going and charming Colin Cowdrey, moving through society with a smile, becoming a successful chairman of the International Cricket Conference and finishing his days in the House of Lords. The quieter, more serious Peter May, retiring early from the game and happier to stay away from the limelight, dedicating himself to his business and his horse-mad family: "I prefer motor cars," he confided to Geoffrey one day. "They've got brakes."

"I can't imagine Peter standing up in the House of Lords, telling anybody what he thought, but I believe Colin took his political responsibilities very seriously. George Duckworth identified him as a potential leader very quickly. He thought Colin would go into the church and become a spiritual leader."

Colin Cowdrey's life was celebrated with a memorial service in Westminster Abbey, Peter May's privately by family and close friends. "They were such different personalities, but I wouldn't like to say that either had a better temperament."

Both were great admirers of Len Hutton, but at Adelaide on that Monday it fell to Cowdrey to partner his captain through the rest of the morning. In *The Times*, 'Hutton's bat became a yeoman's pike to slay the spin of Johnson' while Cowdrey 'was smelling the ball as he met it, bat by pad.' Jim Swanton quoted 'a friend', and it might even have been the M.C.C. manager: 'Len's been preparing for this innings ever since Melbourne.'

At lunch it was 111 for two. Twenty minutes before tea it was 162 for two. Then the England captain hooked hard at Johnston, and the ball hammered into the stomach of short-leg Alan Davidson, who clutched and found he had it in his hand. Hutton's 80 had taken four and a half hours – 'a monastic innings,' Alan Ross called it.

"I went to Len's memorial service at York Minster," Geoffrey recalls. "David Sheppard gave a marvellous address. He told this story of going out to bat with Len."

"After about an hour of silence," the Bishop of Liverpool recalled, "he made overtures for a conversation. 'Are you all right?' he asked, eyes open wide, eyebrows lifted. That was all the conversation. The England team of 1954/55 gave him a silver salver with their signatures engraved all round the edge, and in the middle they had put the words, 'Are you all right?'"

At Adelaide on Australia Day Hutton's wicket was the third and last to fall. Compton joined Cowdrey – 'For the first time in the series,' Swanton wrote, 'Compton went in to bat whole in wind and limb and in good match practice' – and together they raised the total to 230 for three. Within minutes of the close, 'Cowdrey was stretched out on the massage table 'out to the world', not fainted but asleep.' Cowdrey 77, Compton 44.

*The Times* was optimistic. 'England could lead Australia by such a margin on the first innings as would give a chance of victory.'

*

In the event they led them by just 18 runs, and the deficit had already been cleared before tea on Tuesday when Morris cracked a ball into the gully and broke the bridge of Colin Cowdrey's nose. It meant another trip to the hospital for the M.C.C. manager – *I have seen many x-ray photographs in my time but never a more obvious break* – and he missed the excitement as Bob Appleyard reduced Australia to 69 for three. 'On this evidence,' *Wisden* reported, 'most people reckoned Appleyard would be unplayable next day.' As at Melbourne, England were entering the fifth day with their hopes pinned on the strong shoulders of the tall Yorkshireman.

A 26-year-old Bradford League cricketer in 1950, Bob Appleyard had broken into the Yorkshire eleven the following summer and become the only bowler in the history of cricket to take 200 first-class wickets in his first full season. The following May he was diagnosed as having tuberculosis, and he did not bowl again till 1954 when another 154 wickets were sufficient to see him picked for this tour of Australia. It was an extraordinary story – two summers of spectacular success, separated by six months of lying on his side, gripping a cricket ball so that the hard layer of skin on his spinning finger would not soften – and he got up on Wednesday morning at Adelaide, expecting to be given the opportunity to bowl England to victory and the Ashes.

But it was not to be.

On another morning of great heat Hutton turned back to his fast bowlers, Tyson and Statham, looking to assert once more the psychological hold they had gained over the home side's fragile batting. He was not to be disappointed. 'The Australian batting truly went to pieces,' Alan Ross wrote, 'and there was no semblance of a recovery.'

With Tyson and Statham sharing the wickets, Australia reached 103 for nine at lunch. Then, after two maidens by Appleyard, his only spell of the day, Wardle captured the final wicket, and England were left with just 94 for victory. Hutton's finest hour was upon him.

*

Since the Bodyline tour in 1932/33, England had only known defeat in Australia: 2-0 up, they had lost 3-2 under Gubby Allen in 1936/37; still rebuilding after the war and captained by an unfit Wally Hammond, they had lost 3-0 in 1946/47; then, with just a consolation victory in the final Test, they had been crushed 4-1 under Freddie Brown in 1950/51.

Compton and Hutton had played through the defeats of the two post-war series, and now they had the opportunity to taste success on their final tour.

*

Compton remembered the conversation as they left the field.

"Denis, I don't feel like going in again," Len said. "Do you mind going in first?"

'I answered that, of course, I would if he wanted me to, but I had no experience in that position. We went into the dressing-room and I started to get padded up. After a few moments I looked up and, with a good deal of amazement, saw that Len too was getting padded up. I went across to him and asked him if he still wanted me to go in first.'

"Oh, no, no, no … I'll be going in first … I'll be going in first."

Soon Hutton was back. Keith Miller, summoning all his competitive aggression, yorked Edrich for nought, had Hutton caught at second slip for five, then had the wounded Cowdrey caught at first slip for four. It was 18 for three and, as Compton gathered himself to step out, his captain was overcome by anguish.

"The boogers have done us."

"He was inconsolable," Frank Tyson wrote later. "Denis Compton was livid. He grabbed his bat and marched down the pavilion steps, with the words, 'I'll show you who's beaten us.'"

The convalescing John Woodcock was still a guest of the team, watching the game with them, and he recalls Hutton alone and close to despair. "He was sitting in the dressing room. He'd taken his shirt off, and he had a towel round him. He still had his pads on."

The drama was not over. With the score on 49 Peter May hit a fierce drive into the covers, inches off the grass, and Keith Miller, in Alan Ross's words, 'dived to his left and held the ball as he rolled over and over.'

By this time Hutton was watching anxiously, in the company of his team and its manager. It was not obvious to any of them that the catch had been held.

"It clearly bounced out of Miller's hand and hit the ground," Frank Tyson has written.

"It dropped out of his hand," Geoffrey says. "But Peter walked. Denis at the other end was waving his hands and protesting, but it was too late. Peter had given himself out.

"Afterwards, Keith said to Peter, 'I'm sorry, Peter, I thought I'd caught it.' Well, you don't *think* you've caught a ball, you know it."

Frank Tyson's account is much the same: "He admitted he had grassed the chance, but he thought he had held the ball long enough for it to have been a catch."

"Len wanted me, as manager, to make an official protest."

It was 49 for four. In the words of Ian Peebles, 'the battle was still very much on.' Trevor Bailey, the last of the batsmen, 'defended with his usual determination'. Compton 'scored steadily with chops and occasional sweeps'. Keith Miller returned for a last fearsome blast. In a long hour after tea the score moved slowly from 49 to 90, and the tension of the game started to evaporate – in the England dressing room and on the terraces.

"The ground had been full," Geoffrey recalls, "and the cheering was enormous when Keith was running through the top order. But, by the end, there was hardly anybody left to say goodbye to the Ashes."

Bailey was lbw with only four runs still required, but Godfrey Evans – 'trotting out' – was soon hitting the winning boundary. With Denis Compton unbeaten on 34, they left the field together – while the England players, John Woodcock among them, jumped up and clapped. Twenty weeks to the day since they sailed out of Tilbury, they had accomplished their mission.

Compton had been at the wicket at Melbourne four years earlier when England had gained the consolation of victory in the last Test. He had hit the winning runs at The Oval in Coronation Year when the Ashes had been regained. Now he was there as the Ashes were won in Australia for the first time since Douglas Jardine's Bodyline tour.

Just as important – for Geoffrey Howard and for Lord Cobham, the M.C.C. president – they had won them without making enemies.

*Adelaide, 2 February. I feel like the fellow who could not refrain from shouting "Beaten the schoolmaster!" Beaten the Aussies – and what a win. No bodyline, nothing but playing cricket better than they have.*

*At the moment of victory.*
*Left to right: Alec Bedser, Trevor Bailey, Keith Andrew, Bob Appleyard, Unknown (with back turned), Johnny Wardle, Bill Edrich, Frank Tyson (in background), Tom Graveney, John Woodcock, Geoffrey Howard (behind), Colin Cowdrey (with broken nose).*

The next day it was the turn of his two youngest daughters to receive a letter from him.

*From Daddy – Adelaide. On Feb 3rd, the day after we won the great cricket match. My little darlings, It is quite a long time since I wrote to you because I have been very busy helping Len Hutton to win the "Ashes". Very funny things to win, aren't they? I expect you will feel very important little people at school. "My Daddy helped England to win the Ashes." It sounds as though your Daddy is a dustman! It is lovely to think that we are getting near the end of our time in Australia. I am so tired of standing upside down.*

"That was the tour I would have again," John Woodcock says. "We beat Australia in Australia. You can't ask for more than that. To live it over again would be simply marvellous."

The champagne flowed. "I had to sign for 100 bottles," the manager recalls, "at about a guinea each. And I was so busy that I never even had one glass myself." The celebrations lasted into the night, and John Woodcock's replacement on *The Times* was euphoric. 'A man should dip his pen in blood to write about this day. Let no one talk and write about the wicket and explain away the deeds of heroes in terms more fit for gardening notes. Let no one deal in dull statistics – as if men can be measured!'

Hutton and Compton, May and Cowdrey, Evans and Edrich, Wardle and Statham. They are all dead now. Only Appleyard, Bailey and Tyson survive – and their manager. "What a lovely day that was."

*

The Ashes had been won with three of the best games of Test cricket you could hope to watch. After that, the tour was bound to lose its intensity.

Three wives arrived – Dorothy Hutton, Greta Bailey and Jean Evans – and the manager was clear what he thought about that development.

*Melbourne, 16 February. It is NOT a good idea to have wives. From the moment they arrived, the husbands have virtually left the party and I strongly disapprove! It throws a great additional burden on both the baggage man and their manager. It is not right in principle and I shall say so.*

"Peter and I had to run the tour. Len's main interest was in securing Dorothy satisfactory accommodation. 'Best possible terms,' he was after. He only turned up to play the matches."

There was a two-day country match in Yallourn where the manager made up the eleven – *I had an awful match. My left knee came up like a balloon on Saturday, and today I pulled a thigh muscle in my left leg.* – and a rain-ruined match in Melbourne. Then at Sydney they lost to New South Wales, with Len Hutton causing some consternation by leading his players off the field when a light drizzle began. "Both the batsmen and the umpires remained out in the middle." The young Bobby Simpson was on 98, on the verge of only his second century, and *Wisden* records that, on the resumption, 'he made a wild stroke and was stumped.'

The return to Sydney for the final Test was greeted with relentless torrential rain. The match did not start till halfway through the fourth day, losing the M.C.C. side £8,000 in profits – plus the donation the manager made to the Flood Relief appeal – and it did not attract great crowds. *Australian people, being what they are, the edge has gone off their enthusiasm: they don't really give a damn for cricket – only for Australia winning at cricket.*

Tom Graveney had hardly batted since his loose drive in the second Test had incurred his captain's dismay but, when Len Hutton won the toss in this final Test, he came into the dressing room and sought him out. "I'll never forget it. He came in. 'Tom, put your pads on and come in with me.' That was the first I knew that I was playing." Graveney obliged with a free-flowing century, which he followed with an even more fluent one in the next match in Christchurch, New Zealand, but the runs were not enough to dispel the view – held, certainly, by captain, vice-captain and manager – that he was at his best when the going was easy.

*Christchurch, 5 March. Tom Graveney is batting beautifully again as I write: I am so glad. I have always had a very soft spot for him. But I am a bit afraid that he is not quite the chap for the big occasion when the "heat is on". He is just about murdering their bowling at the moment.*

Not quite the chap when the heat is on. It would be the summer of 1966 before Tom Graveney would finally shake off this judgement.

His century in the Sydney Test had left England at 196 for four with only the fifth and sixth days remaining. But there was time enough to force Australia to follow on and to end the match with them six wickets down and still in arrears – the last wicket falling when Benaud became Hutton's first Test victim since 1939. The England captain took his cap and, without a smile, led his men off the field.

At some point in this match Jim Swanton had become exasperated by the lack of urgency in the England play, and this set off the manager in his letter home.

*Sydney, 2 March. Jim Swanton is after Len again. He never misses a chance to take a dig at him! It's all so silly: the Lord Protector of English Cricket. He has not made a great deal of progress out here, and people are beginning to tire a bit of his stuff, I think.*

"That's a little unkind," Geoffrey says now. "I never thought his criticisms were unfair, and his bias was always to uphold the best traditions of English cricket."

Swanton died in January 2000, and Geoffrey made his way to the Memorial Service in Canterbury Cathedral where he sat in front of Doug Insole through an hour and a half of a service that Jim had planned himself. "Well, that's it," Doug said as they stood up to leave. "Swanton's revenge. Made us all sit quiet and listen."

*

Neville Cardus was another English journalist whose enthusiasm for the victory was accompanied by criticism. While he saw May and Cowdrey as harbingers of a welcome revival of the amateur influence, he was less enamoured of the leadership of Len Hutton: 'His idea of the game is not my idea. I see no fun, art or imagination in tactics that handicap free impulses of sport. I am not interested in cricket if it constantly is nothing but competitive and needs perpetual reference to the scoreboard to justify or explain its more or less cataleptic moves and movements.'

They were damning words – but not perhaps as damning as the words the England manager wrote home about him: *Neville Cardus on the Tests should be <u>good</u>! I don't think he saw a ball bowled in any of them – perhaps just a little at Sydney but that is <u>all</u>.*

"Yes, that was Neville," he says now. "I remember sitting on a train with the leader of the Liverpool Philharmonic Orchestra. 'Cardus is a very gifted writer,' I said, 'but he doesn't know anything about cricket.' 'Oh,' he said, 'I thought it was music he didn't know anything about.'

*

While the rain fell on the first days of the final Test, the New South Wales Cricket Association approached the M.C.C. manager to play an extra day.

"I'm sorry. We can't. We're due to play at Christchurch."

"Oh, it doesn't matter about New Zealand."

For Geoffrey, though, it did matter. "Ronnie Aird had been in New Zealand before he joined us, and he told me, 'They're desperately keen to have you. You must give them a good time. And make sure they see Tyson."

*Christchurch, 6 March. It is good to say that life in New Zealand is great. They are very friendly and very hospitable but they do not press everything on you. So far not one person has said, 'How do you like New Zealand?' or 'How do you like our beer?' And thank goodness for that.*

Alec Bedser, the forgotten man of the tour, flew home at the end of the Australian leg, but the New Zealanders had plenty of opportunity to see in action his young successors. At Dunedin, Tyson and Statham bowled them out for 125 and 132. Then at Auckland, where Appleyard came to the fore, the home country managed 200 in their first innings, but in the second they were all out for a new record Test low of 26.

On the Saturday the tourists flew across the Pacific, stopping in San Francisco and New York before arriving home on Tuesday. The United States was in the grip of McCarthyism, and they had had to visit the U.S. Consulate in Sydney for entry visas: *Quite a palaver, I may say. They took the finger prints of each member of the team and a statutory declaration that we were not, never had been and never would be Nazis, Fascists or Communists!!*

It was all over, there was a £55,000 profit to be shared among the counties, and the manager was happy to be home. *I am beginning to be a person like Brian Castor – "Much have I seen!" It is high time I stopped travelling and saw a bit of Cheshire.*

"I can still remember the outfits Mum made for us all," his daughter Ursula says. "Black Watch tartan two-pieces with piqué collars. And the cake with the Ashes on it. We spent weeks looking forward to his homecoming."

*

On Monday the sixth of June, while Lancashire were entertaining the South Africans at Old Trafford, he and George Duckworth flew to Hendon where they changed into dinner jackets and headed for the Dorchester for the dinner that would welcome them home officially. Geoffrey hands me the list of guests and the seating plan.

On table two, where Denis Compton and Colin Cowdrey sat, were the M.C.C. secretary Ronnie Aird, four selectors – Bob Wyatt, Freddie Brown, Walter Robins and Les Ames – the old Surrey captain Errol Holmes and the Rugby Union supremo, Bill Ramsay. "They're all dead now."

On the top table Geoffrey was seated between Lord Cobham and the Earl of Rosebery. There was Len Hutton and Peter May, Jack Hobbs and Gubby Allen, Field Marshal Earl Alexander of Tunis and Viscount Bruce of Melbourne.

"There were twenty of us there on that top table," he points out, "and I'm the only one still alive."

For some there has never been a higher tide in all English cricket, that moment when the great men of one generation – Hutton and Compton, Edrich and Evans – shared the stage with their successors: May and Cowdrey, Statham and Tyson. With the Brisbane Test lost comprehensively, they had fought back in a trio of contests as thrilling as any in Test match history, and they had won the Ashes – in Australia.

At Lord's in the summer of 2001, Geoffrey and I sit with Colin Cowdrey's eldest son Christopher. "Tell me, Geoffrey, what was your management team for that tour?"

"Management team?" he repeats with a smile.

'The management was almost entirely Geoffrey Howard,' Peter May wrote. 'Helpful and unruffled, he made the whole thing work. He had no assistant manager, no accountant, although he did have George Duckworth as baggage master and wise counsellor.'

Before the tour was over, Geoffrey was anticipating the celebrations – *I suppose we shall be a bit "lionised" when we get back – can't be helped.* – but he also knew: *It will soon get back into its proper perspective.*

"After that dinner at the Dorchester, George and I flew back the next day from Croydon – in a DH dragonfly whose normal duties were flying fruit from Liverpool to the Isle of Man. It was a very small aircraft, very few of the instruments were working, and I remember George spending the whole journey looking at the escape hatch. It was far too small for him to get through. Quite another world, isn't it?"

*Wellington, 19 March. At any rate, whatever is said, I know that we have not done anything to damage the good name of M.C.C. overseas.*

The following winter, despite his resolution to stay at home, he would be in Pakistan, and his ability to preserve the good name of M.C.C. overseas would be put to a much sterner test.

# AUSTRALIA v ENGLAND – FOURTH TEST

Adelaide. 28, 29 & 31 January, 1 & 2 February 1955

ENGLAND WON BY 5 WICKETS

## AUSTRALIA

| | | | | |
|---|---|---|---|---|
| C.C. McDonald | c May b Appleyard | 48 | b Statham | 29 |
| A.R. Morris | c Evans b Tyson | 25 | c & b Appleyard | 16 |
| J.W. Burke | c May b Tyson | 18 | b Appleyard | 5 |
| R.N. Harvey | c Edrich b Bailey | 25 | b Appleyard | 7 |
| K.R. Miller | c Bailey b Appleyard | 44 | b Statham | 14 |
| R. Benaud | c May b Appleyard | 15 | (7) lbw b Tyson | 1 |
| L.V. Maddocks + | run out | 69 | (6) lbw b Statham | 2 |
| R.G. Archer | c May b Tyson | 21 | c Evans b Tyson | 3 |
| A.K. Davidson | c Evans b Bailey | 5 | lbw b Wardle | 23 |
| I.W. Johnson * | c Statham b Bailey | 41 | (11) *not out* | 3 |
| W.A. Johnston | *not out* | 0 | (10) c Appleyard b Tyson | 3 |
| *Extras* | *b 3, lb 7, nb 2* | 12 | *b 4, lb 1* | 5 |
| | | **323** | | **111** |

1-59, 2-86, 3-115, 4-129, 5-175, 6-182, 7-212, 8-229, 9-321, 10-323
1-24, 2-40, 3-54, 4-69, 5-76, 6-77, 7-79, 8-83, 9-101, 10-111

| | | | | | | | | |
|---|---|---|---|---|---|---|---|---|
| Tyson | 26.1 | 4 | 85 | 3 | 15 | 2 | 47 | 3 |
| Statham | 19 | 4 | 70 | 0 | 12 | 1 | 38 | 3 |
| Bailey | 12 | 3 | 39 | 3 | | | | |
| Appleyard | 23 | 7 | 58 | 3 | 12 | 7 | 13 | 3 |
| Wardle | 19 | 5 | 59 | 0 | 4.2 | 1 | 8 | 1 |

## ENGLAND

| | | | | |
|---|---|---|---|---|
| L. Hutton * | c Davidson b Johnston | 80 | c Davidson b Miller | 5 |
| W.J. Edrich | b Johnson | 21 | b Miller | 0 |
| P.B.H. May | c Archer b Benaud | 1 | c Miller b Johnston | 26 |
| M.C. Cowdrey | c Maddocks b Johnston | 79 | c Archer b Miller | 4 |
| D.C.S. Compton | lbw b Miller | 44 | *not out* | 34 |
| T.E. Bailey | c Davidson b Johnston | 38 | lbw b Johnston | 15 |
| T.G. Evans + | c Maddocks b Benaud | 37 | *not out* | 6 |
| J.H. Wardle | c & b Johnson | 23 | | |
| F.H. Tyson | c Burke b Benaud | 1 | | |
| R. Appleyard | *not out* | 10 | | |
| J.B. Statham | c Maddocks b Benaud | 0 | | |
| *Extras* | *b 1, lb 2, nb 4* | 7 | *b 3, lb 4* | 7 |
| | | **341** | (5 wkts) | **97** |

1-60, 2-63, 3-162, 4-232, 5-232, 6-283, 7-321, 8-323, 9-336, 10-341
1-3, 2-10, 3-18, 4-49, 5-90

| | | | | | | | | |
|---|---|---|---|---|---|---|---|---|
| Miller | 11 | 4 | 34 | 1 | 10.4 | 2 | 40 | 3 |
| Archer | 3 | 0 | 12 | 0 | 4 | 0 | 13 | 0 |
| Johnson | 36 | 17 | 46 | 2 | | | | |
| Davidson | 25 | 8 | 55 | 1 | 2 | 0 | 7 | 0 |
| Johnston | 27 | 11 | 60 | 2 | 8 | 2 | 20 | 2 |
| Benaud | 36.6 | 6 | 120 | 4 | 6 | 2 | 10 | 0 |
| Burke | 2 | 0 | 7 | 0 | | | | |

Umpires: M.J. McInnes and R. Wright

## AUSTRALIA v ENGLAND – FIFTH TEST

Sydney. 25, 26 & 28 February *(no play on these days)*, 1, 2 & 3 March 1955

MATCH DRAWN

### ENGLAND

| | | |
|---|---|---|
| L. Hutton * | c Burge b Lindwall | 6 |
| T.W. Graveney | c & b Johnson | 111 |
| P.B.H. May | c Davidson b Benaud | 79 |
| M.C. Cowdrey | c Maddocks b Johnson | 0 |
| D.C.S. Compton | c & b Johnson | 84 |
| T.E. Bailey | b Lindwall | 72 |
| T.G. Evans + | c McDonald b Lindwall | 10 |
| J.H. Wardle | *not out* | 5 |
| F.H. Tyson | | |
| R. Appleyard | | |
| J.B. Statham | | |
| *Extras* | *b 1, lb 3* | 4 |
| | (7 wkts, dec) | **371** |

1-6, 2-188, 3-188, 4-196, 5-330, 6-359, 7-371

| | | | | |
|---|---|---|---|---|
| Lindwall | 20.6 | 5 | 77 | 3 |
| Miller | 15 | 1 | 71 | 0 |
| Davidson | 19 | 3 | 72 | 0 |
| Johnson | 20 | 5 | 68 | 3 |
| Benaud | 20 | 4 | 79 | 1 |

### AUSTRALIA

| | | | | |
|---|---|---|---|---|
| W.J. Watson | b Wardle | 18 | c Graveney b Statham | 3 |
| C.C. McDonald | c May b Appleyard | 72 | c Evans b Graveney | 37 |
| L.E. Favell | b Tyson | 1 | c Graveney b Wardle | 9 |
| R.N. Harvey | c & b Tyson | 13 | c & b Wardle | 1 |
| K.R. Miller | run out | 19 | b Wardle | 28 |
| P.J..P. Burge | c Appleyard b Wardle | 17 | *not out* | 18 |
| R. Benaud | b Wardle | 7 | b Hutton | 22 |
| L.V. Maddocks + | c Appleyard b Wardle | 32 | | |
| A.K. Davidson | c Evans b Wardle | 18 | | |
| I.W. Johnson * | run out | 11 | | |
| R.R. Lindwall | *not out* | 2 | | |
| *Extras* | *b 10, lb 1* | 11 | | |
| | | **221** | (6 wkts) | **118** |

1-52, 2-53, 3-85, 4-129, 5-138, 6-147, 7-157, 8-202, 9-217, 10-221
1-14, 2-27, 3-29, 4-67, 5-87, 6-118

| | | | | | | | | |
|---|---|---|---|---|---|---|---|---|
| Tyson | 11 | 1 | 46 | 2 | 5 | 2 | 20 | 0 |
| Statham | 9 | 1 | 31 | 0 | 5 | 0 | 11 | 1 |
| Appleyard | 16 | 2 | 54 | 1 | | | | |
| Wardle | 24.4 | 6 | 79 | 5 | 12 | 1 | 51 | 3 |
| Graveney | | | | | 6 | 0 | 34 | 1 |
| Hutton | | | | | 0.6 | 0 | 2 | 1 |

Umpires: M.J. McInnes and R. Wright

# CHAPTER ELEVEN

# TOO SERIOUS A GAME?

# PAKISTAN

# 1955 – 56

The city of Peshawar is the capital of the North-West Frontier Province. It is an ancient city, eleven miles from the start of the Khyber Pass, in a corner of Pakistan where local tribesmen and invading armies have fought through the ages for supremacy. Persians, Greeks, Huns, Turks, Mongols, Moghals. Their warlike journeys all led through the steep, winding Khyber Pass, and the people of Peshawar reflect this history of combat.

Before the world's attention turned so dramatically to the Afgfhan-Pakistani border, the tour guide books sought to make an attraction out of this history: 'Peshawar is now, as always, a frontier town. There is just that little touch of excitement and drama in the air. Hefty, handsome men in baggy trousers and long, loose shirts wear bullet-studded bandoliers across their chest or pistols at their sides.'

Back in the mid-1950s the city was beginning to expand beyond its ancient walls and sixteen gates. To the west, on the road to the Khyber Pass, the University of Peshawar was growing up. To the east, amid the orchards, factories were being built. In 1955, eight years after the end of British rule, Pakistan announced its intention to become a republic within the Commonwealth.

The winter of 1955/56. Abdul Nasser took full control in Egypt, threatening to nationalise the Suez Canal. A state of emergency was declared in Cyprus, where Archbishop Makarios's EOKA movement pursued independence with a bombing campaign. And in Kenya Jomo Kenyatta was imprisoned, along with thousands of his Mau Mau supporters.

Back in England, when the young M.C.C. 'A' team gathered at Liverpool Docks to sail to Pakistan in December 1955, the best-selling record was 'Rock Around The Clock' by Bill Haley and the Comets.

Change was in the air, and in the world of international cricket a great deal had changed in the four years since the M.C.C. tourists had last visited Pakistan. A 3½-week call in the middle of their 6-month tour of India. Perhaps more had changed than anybody at Lord's had realised.

It certainly seemed that way when they read the bold headlines from Peshawar: 'GUNS GUARD MCC' in the *News Chronicle*, 'Squad-cars rush players from ground as third Test ends in a menacing silence' in the *Daily Mirror*.

*It has been hell fire and pop for me,* Geoffrey Howard wrote to his wife. *These two days have been the hardest I ever remember – I have hardly slept for an hour or two for three nights now.*

Forty-five years later he reflects on the tour. "It seems to have been an awful to-do about such a little incident. When I think about that tour, I must say that it really was the happiest of the three that I managed."

The happiest tour. The high spirits of the young English cricketers bubbled over in the north-west corner of Pakistan, and the tinder was lit. Add an eccentric umpire whose decisions had occasioned much comment, a proud Pakistani captain seeking to uphold the dignity of his now independent people, two English journalists looking for a sensational story, the militant students of the new university, and within days telegrams and telephone messages were passing back and forth between Lord's and Karachi. 'PAKISTAN DECLINE OFFER TO RECALL MCC 'A'' was the *Daily Telegraph* headline.

In the midst of it all, the M.C.C. manager – friend and agent of the Pakistanis when they toured England in 1954 – sought to damp down the flames and to restore good relations. So hard did he work in those few turbulent days that he never dwelt on the full detail of what had occurred.

Forty-five years on, in the summer of 2001, as I try to piece together the story, I drive him to Radlett in Hertfordshire to meet once more with Donald Carr, the captain on that tour, the one who shouldered the full blame in M.C.C.'s final statement on the affair: "The committee consider that the responsibility for the incident rests entirely with the captain, and he has been so informed."

"I'm not clear, Geoffrey," I say as I drive down the A40 on a hot June morning, "who else was involved, apart from Donald Carr." And the reply brings the most surprising revelation of all.

"I never knew," he says. "I was too busy trying to sort out the consequences."

*

"We had a very fine manager in Geoffrey Howard, the Lancashire secretary," Fred Titmus wrote in his book *'Talk of The Double'*. "He was an excellent administrator and a great friend of the boys. You could always go to him if you had a problem, but if you stepped out of line he put you in your place at once in the nicest possible manner. It is a shame that he has not managed more tours, but he is a family man and touring loses some of its attractions when you have domestic ties."

The letters to Nora are handed to me. "The emotions I get from reading them," he sighs. "What on earth was I doing, with a family at home? It was my third tour in five years. Three Christmases away from home, and I'd been away six years during the war, too. Poor old Nora. Wives do suffer, don't they?"

One manager, fifteen players and one reporter, Ron Roberts, gathered at Liverpool Docks in early December 1955. Coming so soon after the long tour of Australia, this 'A' team tour should have been allocated to a different manager. But it had been arranged at relatively short notice and, with his previous experience of the Indian sub-continent and his role as the Pakistanis' representative in England, Geoffrey Howard could not resist offering his services. A rumbling appendix developed in the autumn, but so keen were M.C.C. to take up his offer that they refused his attempt to withdraw. "Have it removed privately," Harry Altham told him. "We'll pay."

In those days the top England players did not generally tour in successive winters and, with Australia in '54/5 and South Africa '56/57, M.C.C. decided to use the opportunity of this extra tour to give experience to some younger players. Pakistan, after all, had been a Test-playing country for just three years and, although they had won a famous victory at The Oval in 1954, many observers thought that that was something of a fluke. One up in the series, England had taken the opportunity to look at some younger cricketers in the match, then on the Monday evening several batsmen had got themselves out needlessly in an attempt to have a free day on the Tuesday. If, four years earlier, a second eleven had held its own in India, then an 'A' team was surely sufficient now in Pakistan.

In any case, there were some fine young cricketers emerging around the counties. Tony Lock, Ken Barrington, Fred Titmus, Jim Parks, Brian Close, Peter Richardson. In time they would all become established in Test cricket. There was the brilliant young reserve wicket-keeper from Surrey, Roy Swetman, and the emerging Middlesex fast bowler, Alan Moss. Allan Watkins the senior pro, Maurice Tompkin the elegant Leicestershire batsman and Harold Stephenson the Somerset keeper added experience, while Hampshire's Peter Sainsbury and the Yorkshire pair of Billy Sutcliffe and Mike Cowan provided enthusiasm and youthful promise.

*Left to right, standing: Roy Swetman, Harold Stephenson, Fred Titmus, Mike Cowan, Alan Moss, Brian Close, Jim Parks, Ken Barrington, Peter Sainsbury. Sitting: Peter Richardson, Allan Watkins, Billy Sutcliffe, Donald Carr, Geoffrey Howard, Tony Lock, Maurice Tompkin.*

"I remember Mike Cowan on the voyage out. I called him into my cabin to settle his travel expenses. 'Oh, I don't expect to be paid,' he said. 'I'm so happy to be on this tour.'"

The letter home confirms the memory: *It is good to see these very keen youngsters. It is all so new to them and they listen wide-eyed to what I tell them.*

The boat took a week to reach Port Said: *We just plod on at our steady 15/16 knots, being passed by everything but rowing boats.* There was P.T. before breakfast: *To the surprise of some, the aged manager turned out.* Then there was a second week reaching Pakistan, with a fancy dress party on the last night. The plan to assemble a Snow White and the Seven Dwarves, with little Roy Swetman as Snow White and the likes of Brian Close and Alan Moss as the dwarves, was abandoned, and it was left to Fred Titmus as a Teddy Boy and the manager as Hitler to steal the show.

A happy party disembarked at Karachi, and their first days were taken up with Christmas celebrations. A children's party saw Father Christmas arrive on a camel, and the day itself was passed at the Sind Club.

*Karachi, 26 December. The lads were splendid and behaved so well. We sang carols very softly and toasted the Queen, the Sind Club, and wives, sweethearts, families and absent friends. It was dignified and sober and a contrast to last year's orgy in Sydney.*

What a happy tour this was shaping to be – and, though the first match against Karachi was left drawn, there were plenty of individual successes: fifties for Close, Richardson, Tompkin, Barrington and Parks, wickets for Moss, Titmus and Sainsbury. Only the captain missed out. *Donald was unluckily run out when playing very well indeed – in fact better than anyone, I should say.*

Forty-five years on, I sit in Donald Carr's living room, and I ask him about the players on that tour.

"Tony Lock was the great success, wasn't he?"

"Poor Peter Sainsbury. He nearly gave up cricket on the spot when he saw what Locky could do with the ball."

"And, of the batsmen, Ken Barrington was the one who went on to achieve most. Did you realise at that time how good he was going to be?"

"He certainly had a great belief in himself. If there was a run out, he wasn't going to be the one who was out."

Karachi, December 1955. Carr, run out, 14. Barrington, not out, 70. The memory remains.

The next match was also in Karachi, but at the new National Stadium – *Amazing. It is a large playing area, surrounded by concrete stands of considerable dimensions, probably capable of holding 50,000. All built in less than 4½ months!* – against the Governor-General's XI, a side that included almost the entire Pakistan Test team, and here perhaps the chain of events that led to the trouble at Peshawar began in earnest.

'A tour so happy in concept, so unhappy in its unfolding,' Ron Roberts called it in his end-of-tour report for the *Daily Telegraph*, and he described how sport and politics were already becoming entwined in the newly-declared republic:

> When Pakistan beat England at The Oval in 1954, a ray of sunshine cast its smile upon that watery summer. The most junior member of the Imperial Board of Control thus received tremendous moral impetus.
>
> So it was that the Pakistan Government came to recognise their cricketers as good for export value. Liberal aids were made to help in the progress of the game, and the majority of players not already in the armed forces were given jobs under the State auspices.
>
> They were granted extensive periods of leave for playing cricket. New stadia were built or are in the course of construction in most of the main cities – and mostly on Government loans.
>
> The Pakistan Test players assembled a month before M.C.C. arrived. They practised, trained and lived, under canvas, together at the National Stadium at Karachi.
>
> In this atmosphere the original motives of the tour, those of encouraging the development of Pakistan cricket and of providing overseas experience for young English cricketers, began to merge into obscurity.

In October the New Zealand team visited, making themselves popular by losing a three-match series 2-0. "Pakistan had already beaten us at The Oval," Geoffrey Howard says. "They wanted a full M.C.C. tour of their country. There was no way that they were going to allow themselves to be beaten by our 'A' team."

But in that Governor-General's match at Karachi, on *a very strange matting wicket on which we have not been allowed any practice at all*, the young M.C.C. cricketers inflicted defeat on Pakistan's almost full-strength side. The batting failed, apart from two spirited knocks by Fred Titmus, but the bowling of Tony Lock proved decisive. Five for 31 in 38 overs in the first innings, six for 57 in 40.4 in the second.

*Karachi, 1 January. Tony Lock bowled superbly yesterday – we must keep him fit. He has already established a reputation which is likely to keep the opposition on tenterhooks. He is splendidly enthusiastic and hostile.*

So wary of him were the Pakistani batsmen at Karachi that at one stage he sent down 17 successive maidens. The impish Roy Swetman sat alongside his manager. The young keeper was selected for this tour after just ten matches in the Surrey first team, but he had seen enough of Tony Lock in that time to know what to expect. "Just wait till he starts bending his arm."

"I don't think he was bowling properly on that tour," Donald Carr says, "but it wasn't an issue. Some of the locals bent their arms even more – though not so successfully."

Already Tony Lock was acquiring the god-like status that would see him feted wherever M.C.C. went – 'We want Tony Lock, we want Tony Lock' – but, in the Pakistani camp, the match provided an early warning of the strength of the young English side.

The captain of Pakistan was Abdul Hafeez Kardar who, before Independence and Partition, had toured England with the 1946 Indian team. He had stayed on to study philosophy at Oxford University, playing in his final year in the same team as Donald Carr. He was not an easy-going character like Ramesh 'Buck' Divecha, the Indian Test cricketer who followed him into the Oxford eleven: "He was a bit of a loner. We never really understood him or what he was thinking."

In three years in the Oxford side Kardar scored over 1100 runs and took 130 wickets with his left-arm flight bowling. In his first two years Oxford dominated Cambridge at Lord's, forcing the follow-on in '47 and winning by an innings in '48. But Donald Carr played with him mainly in '49 when Kardar's mind was on other matters.

"Our final game before playing Cambridge was against M.C.C. at Lord's, and he spoke to our captain Clive van Ryneveld the day before the game. 'I will not be available, Clive, but I think I will probably be back for the Varsity match. I have to go to Coventry.' It turned out that he had a girl friend in the Folies Bergères, and he was going up to see her. The night before the Varsity match, we still had no idea if he was coming back. John Bartlett was called to the colours in case. Then Hafeez rolled up. He didn't play very well, and we lost the match."

Hafeez Kardar played a full season for Warwickshire in 1950 but, though he scored a fast hundred at Lord's in May and married the chairman's daughter, the relentless schedule of county cricket brought out his temperamental side. His penultimate appearance was at Old Trafford, where Geoffrey Howard was secretary. "Tom Dollery sent him off the field. 'If that's the best you can do,' he told him, 'you might as well go off.' And the twelfth man came on." Then the Warwickshire team went down to Swansea, where Hafeez laid on a party in the hotel with alcohol a-plenty that would certainly not have been acceptable in his home country.

"When we went to Pakistan in 1951," Donald Carr tells, "somebody asked me if Hafeez had any nicknames at Oxford, and I remembered that some people called him The Mystic of the East. When I got back for the second tour, one of the Pakistan players said that this had been translated as The Mistake of the East, which I thought was rather funny."

At a dinner after the Governor-General's match at Karachi, when the M.C.C. captain was asked to say a few words, he recounted the story of The Mystic and The Mistake. "I got a very good hand for it, and everybody went their separate ways after the dinner."

The Mystic of the East. The Mistake of the East. It was a harmless joke between old team mates, and Donald Carr left Karachi with only the after-glow of the audience's applause.

But the Mistake was his. He had not realised that times had changed, that Hafeez was a man of importance now, the captain of cricket in the proud republic of Pakistan. While M.C.C. went north to play two minor matches, Hafeez had time to play over in his mind the insult.

Rare rain washed out most of the cricket at Hyderabad, but there was further triumph, including a hat-trick, for Tony Lock in Bahawalpur where they beat the Amir's XI by an innings, their first match on grass.

The manager's letters home, though, were preoccupied with the country around him, its history and its development.

At the dhobi's

*Hyderabad, 5 January. Hyderabad is an incredibly dirty city. It has a really magnificent old fort and is interesting because it was in a battle just outside the city that General Charles Napier defeated the local armies and captured Sind for the British. Did he not send back the famous 'PECCAVI' – 'I have sinned'? I think so.*

*Bahawalpur, 11 January. The Sind desert spreads itself in a thick coat over everything, and I woke with large lumps of it in my teeth.*

*In the train from Bahawalpur, 14 January. We are rocking all over the place, but I will do my best. We all went out to the Amir's palace yesterday. He has lost nearly all his lands and all or nearly all his private income in consequence. He still has a bodyguard of 600 men but they are insignificant compared with the 10,000 he formerly employed! He manages to struggle along with a mere 80 motor cars. ... The state of Bahawalpur has made tremendous strides. In 1929 the Indus was dammed. At the time Bahawalpur was 4/5ths desert. It is now 2/3rds cultivated! They can grow everything: wheat, cotton, oranges, dates, nuts, apples – the lot! And it also carries a very big animal population: camels, cows, horses, bullocks, buffalo, goats and sheep everywhere. A fine example of science being used to benefit mankind.*

There were fewer Europeans around, fewer functions to attend, and the young tourists started to develop their own amusements, with their manager at the heart of the fun.

At Bahawalpur the *aged manager* beat all-comers at squash – except the captain: *I lost the first game fairly comfortably but was holding my own in the second when Don tested his racquet on my nose. He then proceeded to give it a more serious test and smashed it against the wall. End of our squash as there were no more racquets.*

In the street

At table tennis, Donald Carr worked his way through to the knock-out final, but here he came up against the indomitable competitiveness of Brian Close. It was the same when, for a moment, the manager threatened to beat Close at tennis. "He got his head down and made sure he beat me. He was just the same when we played football. You could be knocking a ball about and, within minutes, he'd have turned it into some three-a-side hostility. And, of course, he had to win."

The train took them further north to Lahore, where a game against Combined Universities was to be followed by the first of the four representative matches. They were not to be called Tests, for this was not a full England side, but even Ron Roberts in the *Daily Telegraph* recognised their ambiguous status, calling them Tests but placing the word in inverted commas.

The University match was dull, with the students batting seven hours for a total of 256: *They have no idea how to hit the ball. They concentrate all the time on staying in!*

On the second evening Mike Cowan developed sciatica and, with no masseur on hand, it fell to the manager to find help. But how do you locate the best medical help in an unfamiliar city? He remembered an Australian doctor they had consulted four years earlier, and he rang him from the hotel. The phone was out of order so he took a taxi to the doctor's residence, only to be told that he was at a dinner at the hotel from which he had come. Later, with a prescription in his hand, he toured several chemists, all of them shut, only to discover that the first chemist he had tried was also at the dinner. The hotel had no hot water bottle or thermos flask so he set out a third time, this time arriving near midnight at the home of the UK High Commissioner, David Hunt. It was all in an evening's work for a manager without an assistant.

There was a pleasure, too, in discovering that David Hunt's wife was a niece of Brian Castor. *All the family it seems have a quiet giggle about Brian and his irritability! Very amused to know that Peter May and I know him as the irascible Colonel of Kennington.*

Against Combined Universities M.C.C. conceded first innings lead, and the match petered out into a draw. *Poor Donald was run out again* – once more by Ken Barrington – *and Bill Sutcliffe had a bad decision against him. But we are a happy band.*

A happy band. Unbeaten in their five warm-up matches, the off-the-field fun was starting to become quite boisterous. "I remember Billy Sutcliffe had a water pistol."

On the night before the first representative match both teams were staying at Faletti's Hotel, and Donald Carr and Tony Lock sat for dinner at a table by the dining room door. "Hafeez came in with some of his mates," Donald Carr recalls. "He walked straight past and sat as far away as possible. I thought, 'What the hell's up with him?' So after dinner I went up to his table. 'I don't think you saw me when you came in, Hafeez. How are you? Nice to see you.' But he was very curt and turned back to his friends."

"I had the same response," Geoffrey remembers. "He was wearing a finger splint. 'What's the matter with you?' I asked him, and all he said was 'Finger trouble' and went back to eating his dinner."

The following morning, as the two captains walked out for the toss, the source of the problem was revealed.

"Donald, I would like to have a word with you."

"Yes, Hafeez. I know something's wrong, but I don't know what it is."

"That speech you made in Karachi. I've never heard anything so disgusting in my life."

"What did I say? … Oh that story about The Mystic of the East. You can't be being serious."

"Disgraceful."

"Well, if you want to take it that way, you'll have to take it that way."

The coin spun into the air. Rain had delayed the start, and Hafeez Kardar invited M.C.C. to bat first.

The early batting by Close and Richardson was bright but at 56 Kardar bowled Close and soon afterwards had Tompkin lbw. "Poor Maurice," Geoffrey says. "He had some dreadful decisions to put up with, but he took them all so well." After tea Fazal Mahmood bowled Richardson and had Barrington caught behind. Then in the last twist of the day Allan Watkins was given out, also caught behind off Fazal, and M.C.C. closed on 109 for five. Ron Roberts was the only English reporter on the ground and, filing reports for several papers, he used the pseudonym John Warner for his piece in the *Daily Herald*: 'The last decision, alas, left a nasty taste in the mouth. Watkins did not appear to touch the ball and was given out to an appeal which was started half-heartedly by one of the close-in fielders.' It was a view of events shared by the manager: *Lahore, 20 January. In spite of a bad day today (two bad decisions against us) the boys are cheerful and happy.*

With five days allocated to the match, the final M.C.C. total of 204 left Pakistan the opportunity to build a big lead and to press for victory. But, after their defeat in the Governor-General's XI match in Karachi, they preferred to ensure that they could not lose. On the third day, in five and a half hours, they progressed from 66 for no wicket to 173 for one.

*Lahore, 22 January. They are being very slow, ridiculously slow: they scored 28 in two hours before lunch when they should be pressing home the advantage they won on the first two days.*

The newly-arrived Englishman in their midst was not impressed, as 'John Warner' reported: 'George Duckworth, the former Lancashire and England wicket-keeper, who has just arrived here on a lecture tour for the British Council, said that the Wars of the Roses matches were whirlwinds against this stuff.'

*Lahore, 24 January. George makes me laugh. He has now made four trips to India and he only knows one word of Urdu: Char! A cup of Char!! Not a great effort. Typical – it's up to the natives to get to know English – or be shouted at! Poor chaps who can't read or write their own language must learn to understand another.*

The cricket drew a massive crowd – *far more than the ground can contain, with fights going on all over the place and a general free for all* – and during lunch the spectators spread themselves over the playing area. *In consequence the scavenging crows and kite hawks are blackening the sky, swooping down all over the place to carry off the titbits. And there are thousands of vultures wheeling overhead.*

'Pakistan, zindabad,' the crowd chanted. 'Pakistan, zindabad.'

Tony Lock bowled 77 overs, taking three for 99, Peter Sainsbury 41 overs for 52 runs, as Hanif – "Oh god, the tedium of it."– took 8¾ hours to complete his century. "That wasn't his nature. He must have been under orders." Waqar Hassan took 6½ hours over 62, and Pakistan's first innings lead of 159 left too little time for a result to be achieved. Peter Richardson hit a three-hour century – 'PAKISTAN COULD NOT BEAT FARMER PETER' triumphed the News Chronicle – and the game ended in a sterile draw.

| | |
|---|---|
| **M.C.C.** | **204 and 322 for seven** |
| **Pakistan** | **363 for nine, declared** |

**Match drawn**

The next journey took them across India to East Pakistan, to Chittagong where they stayed in the homes of British people: *I am with some people called Macauley and am living almost in splendour.* In a match on jute matting M.C.C. beat East Pakistan by an innings, with Tony Lock returning figures of 11 for 17 in 27.3 overs, and at the local club they secured another easy victory, taking on all-comers in a rugby match, M.C.C. versus The Rest, with a cushion for a ball. *A sport rather too young for the ageing manager who nevertheless did his best, suffering only minor cuts and abrasions.*

From Chittagong they flew to Dacca, the chief city in the East where the second representative match was to be played. Their unhappiness at some of the decisions at Lahore had led them to request that the umpire Idris Begh not stand again in the series. It was a convention of tours that the visiting side should be entitled to such a request, and the secretary of the Pakistan Board of Control, Group-Captain Cheema, nodded his consent. "Yes, all right," he said. "Idris Begh will not umpire."

The M.C.C. party was accompanied throughout the tour by a representative of the Pakistan Board, Daud Khan, *a kindly, genial, gentle character, a great friend to us all.* It was he who had, in fact, umpired four years earlier when Hanif's wide bat and great pads had seen Pakistan to their historic victory over M.C.C., and he was on hand to offer his translation of Cheema's reply: "You can expect Idris

*with Daud Khan*

Begh in Dacca." Forty-five years later, Geoffrey Howard laughs: "I think it's true to say that Idris was almost the first person to greet us at the airport."

Some say that the best umpires are the ones who are barely noticed. On that basis, Idris Begh was not one of the best. "He was such a silly chap in many ways. So vain. He used to go and address the crowd if they weren't behaving properly. He said to me one day, 'You must understand, Mr Howard, that a lot of the crowd come to watch me umpire.'"

"My recollection," Donald Carr says, "is that Idris was rather on our side at Dacca. It was the other fellow who was appalling."

On a matting wicket that provided plenty of lift for pace bowlers, M.C.C. were immediately handicapped by the unavailability of Mike Cowan.

*Dacca, 1 February. I am so sorry for poor Mike Cowan. He was so keen and enthusiastic, and he has had one bit of bad luck after another. Now it looks as though he may have a disc lesion of some sort, and he must go off to Karachi.*

Rain on the first two days made batting hard on the mat, and M.C.C.'s eventual total of 172 owed much to a four-hour innings of 43 by Ken Barrington – 'a defensive batting effort of considerable merit,' Ron Roberts called it. Jim Parks and Harold Stephenson suffered 'a couple of odd lbw decisions', but at the end of the third day, with Pakistan's reply at only 13 for no wicket, the headline was hard to dispute: 'DRAW LIKELY TEST RESULT – FEW HOPES OF MCC FORCING VICTORY'.

The sun returned after the rest day, and the match finally came to life. Alan Moss, bowling 'with great heart', took two quick wickets before lunch as Pakistan subsided from 88 for no wicket to 109 for four. But the absence of a second quick bowler and a less accurate spell from Tony Lock allowed the Pakistanis to press on in the afternoon heat. Hafeez Kardar joined Wazir Mohammad on the mat, 'his first two scoring shots were bold sweeps off Lock off balls that must have been pitched on the middle stump', and in less than two hours they added 134 enterprising runs.

Then, after tea, the wickets fell, with Idris giving the Pakistani captain lbw to Tony Lock. "He hit the ball," Donald Carr remembers. "And it was missing the stumps, anyway." At the end of the day Idris laughed about it: "Did you not think it was funny when I gave Hafeez Kardar out?"

Pakistan took a first innings lead of 115, and in the closing minutes they removed Brian Close first ball. "He said, 'I tried to hit him off his length,'" Geoffrey remembers. "What a bad shot! To try to hit a fast bowler off a length at the end of the day." With the sun shining, though, and nine wickets in hand, the letter home was confident of the outcome: *This match looks doomed to be another draw.*

Back in the hotel Billy Sutcliffe's water pistol had set off more extensive water games and now there were full buckets in play. The visiting George Duckworth, dressed immaculately in his dinner jacket, suffered a soaking. As he sat on his bed, and the laughter pealed out of the room, who should have passed by the open door but Idris Begh? "He chuckled away," Donald Carr recalls, "and I said to him, 'We'll get you, too, before the end of the tour, Idris.' 'Oh no,' he said. 'You'll never get me.'"

Would it all have worked out differently if he had not walked past the door at that moment? If he had not been so conscious of himself as a character? "You'll never get me," he said and, to the boyish tourists, it must have seemed more like a challenge than an assertion of dignity and authority. "Oh yes, we will," they called out. "Just you wait."

The letter home the next night told of much lower spirits.

*Dacca, 8 February. Darling, I'm a bit gloomy like! We really got an awful hiding today – and what is more we really deserved to. They outplayed us in all departments. Our batting was terrible – to lose by an innings against a total of only 287. One mistake we have made is to underrate them, and the other is to rely on Tony Lock's ability to get them out easily. They have been very quick at learning how to play Tony, and he has to work much harder for his successes.*

**M.C.C. 172 and 105**
**Pakistan 287 for nine, declared**
**Pakistan won by an innings and 10 runs**

At the game's conclusion, according to Ron Roberts, 'a colourful human wave spilled out from the concrete terraces and engulfed the Pakistan and M.C.C. players. This was the spontaneous gesture of almost delirious enthusiasm with which Pakistan's most deserved victory was greeted.'

Even in this acknowledgement of the home side's superiority, though, there was a note of reservation. 'One must in all conscience observe they received the benefit of one or two rather unusual umpiring decisions, but these facts must not be allowed to distract from an estimable piece of team bowling.'

*Poor old Donald is very disappointed. He himself was out for 0 and so he feels worser and worser. The worst feature is that the British residents think we have let them down. Of course they want us to win but we want to beat the Pakistanis to please ourselves and the folks at home. Not to make life easier for the Pukka Sahib out here.*

Pakistan were one up, with only two representative matches remaining.

*I believe that we shall find it very hard to win the next two tests. If by chance we do win at Peshawar and go to Karachi all square, we really shall have a struggle for we shall be up against more than eleven players – verb. sap.*

Verbum sapienti satis est. A word to the wise is enough.

At Peshawar they were to discover what it was like to be up against more than eleven.

*

After Dacca, there were four days free from cricket, and Donald Carr arranged to visit friends in Calcutta, taking several of the party with him. But, when the manager arrived to escort them to the airport, he was not pleased by what he found.

*Dacca, 9 February. They were over at the club playing snooker – five minutes before they were due at the airport. Not packed, not lunched, in fact not ready. I pitched into Donald and told him he was utterly irresponsible and worse than all of them put together. He got them onto the plane so of course they said all was well!!*

We sit in Donald Carr's living room, and I read out the letter.

"I do apologise."

"No ill feelings."

Donald Carr turns to me. "Geoffrey was so unfussed but, when he had to, he could make it known that he was displeased."

And the manager's verdict on the captain? *Donald sometimes wants a lot of reminding or pushing along or he doesn't get things done. Better than Len tho' and much better than Nigel.*

In Dacca Geoffrey Howard went off for a flying lesson – *I did enjoy it, but I would have done better if I had been able to follow the instructor more easily.* Then in the evening there was *a jolly reception at the local club. They produced an enormous silver cup full of champagne as a loving cup. Brian Close, sipping rather gingerly, had it a little tipped for him and responded by nearly spilling the whole lot over poor Maurice Tompkin.*

Was it just horse play, or was there a little too much aggression in it? Perhaps the exuberant tourists were finding it hard to tell the difference.

The following morning, at 5.30, they were airborne again, heading back to West Pakistan and refuelling in Calcutta and Delhi. They were still in the air at four in the afternoon: *The Bristol freighter does not dash along, I must say! It also gives you an awful ear bashing.*

At Calcutta they were rejoined by the others, with several copies of the Kama Sutra coming aboard. "I was sitting next to Brian Close, and he sat and read it from cover to cover without a word. Then he put it down. 'Well,' he said, 'I've learnt nowt from that.'"

Brian Close always liked to appear worldly wise. "We went out shooting samba, and you should have seen the way he was waving his rifle about. 'I know what I'm doing,' he said. 'I've done this a lot.' He frightened the life out of everybody."

At Sialkot, where Ian Thomson arrived in place of Mike Cowan, M.C.C. proved much too strong for a Combined XI, with Tony Lock taking ten more wickets in an innings victory. The setting of the ground was well-described in the letter home: *Sialkot, 13 February. Brown and dusty and partially surrounded by gum trees. A railway runs beside it at one end and in the distance one can see the minarets and domes of the mosque and further off still the spire of the now locked and disused Garrison Church of England.*

The hotel evoked no such pleasant description:

*Dark, dingy and dirty. The 3D Hotel, in fact. The plumbing is the old Thunder Box system: "Takes a pride in all he carries out." You know what I mean. The electric light in my bedroom is so dim that one almost needs a box of matches to find the bulb when it is switched on. There is a bath and a hand basin, both with taps, but in neither case does any water come out. Water for the hand basin comes in a teapot, for the bath in a bucket or two. The best of all however is the drainage system from the bath. One removes the plug and the water gushes through the orifice on to the floor. The floor is ingeniously sloped so that the water eventually runs out of the door into the garden – and the floor dries on its own.*

"In no time at all," Brian Close told in his book *'I Don't Bruise Easily'*, "everyone was roaming the gardens with supplies of water in whatever receptacle he could find, stalking everyone else. Tony Lock had gone to bed, but he was dragged out with the ultimatum: 'Either you come out or you get soaked there.' He got soaked anyway, and pretty soon the only two who had escaped were Jim Parks and myself. I'm not sure how Jim kept clear, but I climbed a tree and sat there for an hour and a half, watching everyone else stalking through the gardens down below, with water being splattered everywhere."

The water treatment. Improvised football. Rugby with a cushion. The M.C.C. tourists were enjoying themselves – and so was their manager, 47 years old on February the 14th. *I had a very jolly if hectic birthday evening. I am afraid the tour has set the clock back for me, and there have been times when I have led the horse play and ragging. Today we have had a great soccer match and I more than held my own and scored a goal too!*

*

Sialkot to Lyallpur is little more than 100 miles but, with a night spent in sidings at Wazirabad junction and the morning train stopping at every station, it was a long and arduous journey.

*Lyallpur, 16 February. Whilst we were waiting in one station, our early tea came in one window on a tray: through the door on the other side suddenly appeared a beggar. The train started and he did not move: Daud, who was sharing with me, realised at once the boy was blind and called on him to*

*stand whilst we shut the door. We took him to the next station and I helped him onto the platform: I hope he got back. He just crouched in the corner of the train like a beaten animal and felt all round him. I don't suppose he had ever been in a train before, and he was terrified: he kept beating the floor with his hands and whimpering. He pathetically clutched the bottom of a circular tin which was probably his only possession and which served as the tray he used to beg a few coins. His eyes were quite sightless, only the whites were visible. And quite possibly he was deliberately blinded at birth to equip him for begging. Man's inhumanity to man. Awful, darling.*

At Lyallpur, where they were housed in new bungalows in the compound of a large cotton mill, they beat the Punjab side by an innings. Tony Lock took another ten wickets to bring his tally to 57 in six appearances, there were fifties for Barrington and Titmus, but the manager's letter home was more concerned with the frustrations of the plumbing.

*Lyallpur, 19 February. Taps marked hot are usually cold, but there is always a chance that the cold will produce a trickle of hot. Only a chance and it has not come off this evening. The mystery of the East certainly extends to everything mechanical – they look good but they rarely work and they never bother to mend things. Inshallah – it is the will of Allah that it should not work – so not to worry.*

After four days in Lyallpur they were back on the train, this time a 24-hour journey to cover the 200 miles up into the North-West Frontier to Peshawar.

*Peshawar, 22 February. It really was quite a fascinating journey; for the first time we saw some mountains and they were capped with snow – an odd sight when one is travelling in shirt sleeves and feeling the heat a bit. It is an odd country; the plains are dry and dusty and the rivers all dried up; in the distance one sees the hills and the snow and gets a feeling that things must be very different up there; then the train begins to climb and one ascends slowly up through the passes and begins to look for the changes. And how slight they are! The rains of countless centuries have washed all the soil from the hills and filled the valleys with it; so again one is in hot and dusty country with very little vegetation of any sort except scrub and one is, at 1600 feet, no nearer, or apparently no nearer, the snow than one was in the valleys.*

The letters home grew ever fuller of the world in which they were immersed: the blind beggar boy in the carriage, the cave dwellers on the sides of the hills as the train climbed slowly towards Peshawar, the cricket fans who garlanded them at each railway station. But there was still a home-sickness, a desire as always to be back with his family. *Three weeks today. The last match will be over, and we will be on our merry way. We all think and dream of home now.*

*

There was a coach trip to the Khyber Pass on the day before the third representative match.

*Peshawar, 23 February. A fascinating place. Very wild and rugged, dry and dusty – and ideal territory for soldiering. An infantry man's delight, I should say, plenty of cover all over the place but of course that goes for both sides. All the lads enjoyed the experience – in a way quite frightening. At times there is a sheer drop of thousands of feet on either side and of course there is no sort of wall or safety fence – if anything goes wrong, over you go.*

Some of them very nearly did go over. Two journalists, Crawford White of the *News Chronicle* and Brian Chapman of *the Daily Mirror*, joined up with the party at Peshawar, and Crawford White, quick to file his first story, reported the drama of the day:

> The M.C.C. team rescued the Pakistan opening batsman, Hanif Mohammad, and both Test umpires when their car crashed within two yards of a 100-foot precipice in the Khyber Pass today.
>
> We had all gone in a convoy of two cars and a coach on a sight-seeing tour which took us over tortuous mountain pass roads.
>
> Hanif and the two umpires were in a car ahead of us on the way back when they were hit by a truck as they took the outside edge of a steep hair-pin.
>
> The car was badly damaged and had to be abandoned, but its passengers escaped injury.

I show the newspaper reports of those days to Geoffrey Howard. Forty-five years have passed since he found himself at the centre of the scandal of Peshawar, and it is the first time he has read what was written. 'MCC RESCUE UMPIRES' was the headline from the Khyber Pass outing. "I have no memory of that at all." And I am left wondering if the real accident was rather less dramatic than this report. "I think Crawford White and Brian Chapman were only there because they scented trouble. They were news-hounds. Not like Ron Roberts, who was covering the cricket. They were looking for trouble and, if they couldn't find it, they tended to invent it. I remember George Duckworth saying, 'Chapman's a bastard.'"

Back at the hotel the team for the third representative match was chosen. The grass wicket looked as if it would take spin so the plan was to pick three spinners – Lock, Titmus and Sainsbury – and only one pace man, Alan Moss. Jim Parks made way for Billy Sutcliffe. The young Parks had been the second highest run-scorer in England in 1955, but he was a batsman who liked to play on the front foot with his pad beside his bat and he had already suffered six lbw decisions on the tour. "I remember Billy Griffith writing from Lord's saying, 'Whatever's happened to Jimmy Parks? He's not getting a run.'"

The final change involved the wicket-keeper, with Harold Stephenson making way for Roy Swetman. 'Five feet of fun and fire,' Crawford White called him in the *News Chronicle*. 'But there is nothing small about the impact he has made both as a player and as a cricket ambassador out here. He commands quite a lot of the cheerful, galvanising fire of Godfrey Evans.'

Fred Titmus went further: "I have never seen keeping bettered by anyone, not even Godfrey Evans. If he could have kept up this form he would have become the greatest wicket-keeper in the world."

"He was so young," Geoffrey Howard says, "and he had such a mischievous sense of fun."

On the field, though, he had a 'level-headed' temperament, and on the first day of this match at Peshawar he needed it, coming in to bat with the scoreboard reading 88 for six. 'Looking as ever like a proud boyish winner of his school colours,' Brian Chapman wrote, 'he notched top score of 40 and scored them well.'

M.C.C. were all out for 188. Hafeez Kardar, six for 40. 'M.C.C. hearts are heavy this sultry evening on the North-West frontier,' Ron Roberts wrote. 'There are insufficient runs in the bank on a pitch of calm and serene behaviour.' Brian Chapman was quicker to the same point: 'A golden chance had turned to husks.' As was Crawford White: 'We are in a tough spot.'

All three reporters, however, led their reports with the same angle:

'LBW DECISIONS SHAKE MCC BATTING'

'LBW DECISIONS SHATTER SHAKY YOUNG ENGLAND'

'CAN LOCK DO SAME AS KARDAR? – It depends on umpires'

The Pakistani captain Hafeez Kardar bowled slow left-arm round-the-wicket from the end where Idris Begh was umpiring, and he secured four lbw decisions. 'Pakistani spectators, as well as M.C.C. fans,' Crawford White wrote, 'seemed surprised at such prompt dismissals against men like Barrington, Tompkin and Swetman – who were at full stretch down the pitch when the ball hit them. If they were between wicket and wicket at that point, it would need a tremendous amount of spin, from a bowler bowling round the wicket as wide as Kardar, to bring the ball back to hit the wicket. And on this wicket the ball was hardly turning at all.'

Ron Roberts was as frank: 'While the umpire is the one person able to judge these things, and while it is a betrayal of the British-and-proud-of-it characteristic to question these things, the fact is that three men were given out playing well forward to left-arm bowling delivered from round the wicket.' Franker still in his 'John Warner' report in the Daily Herald: 'A cloud hangs over the series and much thin ice has been skated upon.'

In the last minutes of the day Tony Lock bowled to the Pakistani opener Alim-ud-Din, and 'pinned him right back on his stumps.' According to Brian Chapman, 'The English 'howzat' echoed down the rocky defiles of the Khyber Pass. But Idris preserved an aloof calm in face of one of the most explosive appeals that have ever assaulted an umpire's eardrums.'

Close of play. M.C.C. 188. Pakistan, 24 for no wicket.

*Peshawar, 24 February. Darling, forgive a short one today. We have had a very bad day. Our batsmen were the victims of some, to say the least, surprising decisions and, in the circumstances, which I will not now relate, I believe that we have done quite well to make 188. It is not nearly enough, and I expect that we shall probably lose – but since that is what everybody wishes, then we shall at once become the most popular tourists ever and all will be well.*

If only the outcome had been this!

At tea time on the second day the game was back in M.C.C.'s favour. With Tony Lock taking five for 44 in 33 overs, they had bowled out Pakistan for 144. They had a first innings lead of 36 runs and, with Pakistan's Fazal unable to bowl, they had every prospect of setting a target that would be beyond the hosts on a pitch showing early signs of wear and tear.

By close M.C.C. were 66 for six, 'most of them out to strokes best left undescribed,' according to Ron Roberts. Brian Chapman called the batting 'pale, puerile and pusillanimous', though Crawford White was more willing to offer excuses: 'A batsman in constant fear of a leg-before decision can lose both footwork and confidence and become a shadow of his true self.'

M.C.C. fared little better on the third day. Donald Carr and Billy Sutcliffe stayed almost the whole morning, adding just 39 runs. 'A salvaging operation,' Ron Roberts called it, but Brian Chapman had a story of England incompetence to tell and he was in no mood to let go: 'This meagre pile: it was like building the pyramids with pebbles.'

Carr sliced Kardar's quicker ball to slip, and the final three wickets fell for just six more runs. M.C.C. 111 all out. Pakistan needed just 148 for their coveted series victory.

Hanif and Alim-ud-Din tucked into Fred Titmus's new-ball spell, and by tea Pakistan were halfway to victory, with just one wicket down, Hanif's first lofted shot landing in Brian Close's hands at mid-wicket. 'Lock was a dervish of waving palms and catlike leaps,' Brian Chapman wrote, 'but there was no real devil in his bowling.'

*Peshawar, 26 February. We are in the process of losing this Test and with it the rubber, I am afraid. They really deserve to win for they are a stronger side. But things have been made far too easy for them by some really shocking umpiring. It is such a pity that they allow these incompetents to do it – they are without doubt there to help the home side – because they are quite strong enough to at least avoid being beaten by us without this aid. Unfortunately we are not in a good position to protest because one simply cannot do so when one has lost. I am afraid that we shall have to in the case of one, and they will agree that he does not stand again. But by then the damage will have been done – and he will have done it!*

By close of play the match was almost over. Pakistan, 130 for two. Eighteen runs away from victory. 'Tomorrow is the rest day,' Crawford White wrote, 'or perhaps, it would be better to call it a think-it-over day.'

Little did he know, as he dictated those words back to London, how much they would all have to think over.

*

Sunday night at Dean's Hotel in Peshawar. A rest day ahead of the disappointed M.C.C. players. They sat through a formal dinner for the two teams. Then they relaxed.

Geoffrey Howard sat and shared a drink with Douglas Carr, Donald's brother, who was over from Malaya on a short holiday. The manager's letters were written, his day's work had been done. The hotel was spread out so he did not expect to see everything that was going on. But he became aware of its going quiet, and he thought he saw a tonga, a pony and trap, setting off down the road. Was that Donald in it? And who was with him? "I remember thinking, 'What are they up to?'"

It was a happy tour and, though he was quietly dismayed at the umpiring, the success on the field of the cricketers was not his principal concern. 'The old country couldn't have had a better ambassador,' they told him when he got back from India four years earlier, and that was still his chief objective.

It was a happy tour, and the players were a good bunch of lads. Sometimes they were a little churlish when the fans tried to garland them at the railway stations. Most of them were too suspicious of the local food, a little too unappreciative of the hospitality. But Donald had been a good captain – 'better than Len, much better than Nigel' – and they had made a good impression on the whole. Quietly he drank his whisky and soda with Douglas Carr, and he did not worry unduly where they had gone in the tonga.

By the time he found out, Idris Begh was sitting in a chair in their hotel, drenched with two buckets of water. "You'll never get me," he had chuckled at Dacca, and now they had been across to the Pakistanis' hotel and brought him back in the tonga, sat him in the chair and given him the full water treatment. By the time the M.C.C. manager arrived, Idris Begh was enjoying the attention of the laughter. "He was taking it all in good spirits, really. What changed everything was that two of their players came along and started laughing at him as well."

Horseplay and humour had kept this M.C.C. tour party in good spirits, even when the cricket had disappointed, but, as Donald Carr had found at that dinner in Karachi, humour does not translate easily across cultures.

"You're one of us now," the laughing M.C.C. players told Idris as he departed for his own hotel, but that was not how Hafeez Kardar – in some reports, sharing a room with the umpire – saw it. "He pointed out to Idris that he'd lost face, he'd been made to look ridiculous, and before long the whole situation had got out of hand."

By the following morning the M.C.C. manager was at the squash court, looking for his captain. "I'm afraid we've got a problem," he said, never one to inflame a situation with rash words.

Idris Begh was briefing reporters, back from the hospital with his arm in a sling: "They gagged me, twisted my arm up my back and sat on me. At their hotel water was poured all over me. I thought my shoulder had been put out in the struggle, but the hospital said it was only strain and bruising."

One local newspaper published a quotation from Hafeez Kardar that the tourists should be sent home, though he later denied saying this. As a result, the atmosphere in the 'frontier town' of Peshawar grew increasingly unpleasant, with university students organising demonstrations.

Meanwhile Group-Captain Cheema, secretary of Pakistan's Board of Control, flew to Karachi, where he briefed the Board President, Governor-General Iskander Mirza. A telegram was sent to Lord's, and troops were sent north to protect the M.C.C. party.

In the midst of it all, Geoffrey Howard worked all hours to calm the situation, and at the end of the day he issued a statement:

> I have offered Idris Begh my apologies on behalf of all persons concerned, which he has accepted in the best possible spirit. He has told me that he regards the incident as closed and joins me in the hope that friendly relations between the cricketers of both sides will be continued throughout the remainder of the tour.

How lucky M.C.C. were to have a manager on hand who had built up so much goodwill among the Pakistani officials. Another manager might have struggled in his situation, as a letter home earlier in the tour confirmed: *I had an amazing letter from Brian Castor. Glad to see Len Hutton go, thought we should sever diplomatic relations with India and Pakistan because of the way they play their cricket! It gets worse and worse, I am afraid. Good job he's not in my shoes!!*

'His tact and quiet strength have never been put to better use,' Ron Roberts concluded.

On Tuesday morning rain fell, forcing a delay till 2.30 in the resumption of the cricket. Even then, according to Ron Roberts, 'the square was as liberally sawdusted as a four-ale bar.' Pakistan hit off the remaining runs for the loss of one wicket, and many in authority must have wished that the game had been concluded on Sunday evening. A hundred students stood outside the ground, shouting 'Go home, MCC', and sections of the crowd chanted 'Shame, shame' in unison.

Crawford White, 'the man on the spot', was enjoying the news scoop:

'Scenes at the ground today made the bodyline trouble in Australia look like a garden party. ... There were armed, khaki-clad police everywhere. ... Every man who entered the ground today was "frisked" for arms. Two who somehow escaped the net were spotted by police as they leaned on the rails just outside the M.C.C. dressing-room. They were quietly disarmed as I watched from two yards away."

"We were just watching the cricket," Geoffrey recalls, "with the chief of police in front of us. This chap walked past, and the policeman tapped him on the shoulder. He immediately took off his belt, with all its weapons attached, and handed it to the policeman. Crawford took that to mean that there was trouble about; he'd have liked to have disappeared. But the policeman turned to us: 'He wears that as you would carry an umbrella. No more serious than that.' My job was to minimise the seriousness of the whole business. Crawford was trying to blow it up."

Or, as he put it some days later, after Nora had relayed Crawford White's *News Chronicle* report to him, *Mr C.W. is a real stinker. He can whistle for information from me in future.*

**M.C.C. 188 and 111**
**Pakistan 152 and 149 for three**
**Pakistan won by seven wickets**

Back at the hotel, where they had returned late, to allow the demonstrations to simmer down, and with an armed guard, the manager finally found time to pour his thoughts and feelings on paper.

*Peshawar, 28 February. Darling, I am afraid that I have not written for two days. I have in fact had an awful time as I suppose you can imagine. I don't know what has been written at home but out here it has been hell. It was all very foolish and must look terrible in print. It was only a piece of ragging but was not taken as such and the Press did the rest. It has been hell fire and pop for me, but the boys have stuck it well in a pretty hostile atmosphere. We shall be glad indeed to leave here and I only hope that our reception in the next three places will be reasonable. It is not likely to be very friendly. Bother it all, darling – it really has been a desperate worry and will be for a while – I don't know what M.C.C. will have to say.*

*I can understand and forgive the Press out here for an outburst agin us, but I can neither understand nor can I forgive the representatives – other than Ron Roberts – who have placed their own interests and those of their papers above National feelings and loyalties, and that is a thing I shall never understand. They could have done so and they didn't, and I shall not easily forgive.*

*'The match mercifully is over – not without some demonstrations and noise. Great security precautions were made – a sad reflection on the power of the Press and mob rule. These two days have been the hardest I ever remember – I have hardly slept for more than an hour or two for three nights now.*

The following day the M.C.C. tourists left the frontier. No longer garlanded at every stop, they arrived three hundred miles away in Sargodha, a rural backwater where they stayed at the Royal Pakistan Air Force College. All their social functions were cancelled, but they played their cricket positively and, though at first the crowd took pleasure in leaving the fielders to run to the boundary to collect the ball, gradually they won back some affection, not least when Tony Lock followed four wickets in seven balls with a spectacular 62 not out. 'He was the apple of the crowd's eye,' Crawford White wrote.

"It was at Sargodha," Geoffrey remembers, "that Peter Richardson and I got hold of two burkhas, the long garments that Pakistani women wear over them, with just the holes for the eyes and for breathing. We put them on, walked into the visiting team's quarters and watched the faces of the men. I can remember how confined and airless I felt inside the dress."

After the match they hurried away to catch the plane to the next venue, Multan, an ancient city with a fort where Alexander the Great, in a siege, received the wounds from which he died.

*Multan, 3 March. It was very hot today, and Daud and I had an awful struggle with the baggage. We had to get all the boys and their cricket bags from the ground to the airfield in 40 minutes. Having lost our popularity to some extent we have lost our V.I.P. status so had to travel by an R.P.A.F. Freighter – very noisy and pretty uncomfortable.*

At Multan they beat the Railways XI by an innings, with Tony Lock capturing his second hat-trick of the tour. Then, with the match over by lunchtime on the third day, they took on the challenge of a football match against a strong local side.

Back in Sargodha they had warmed up with a 7-0 win against the Royal Pakistan Air Force College. But this match in Multan was a tougher contest altogether and, when goals by Carr and Swetman gave them a 2-0 victory, they were elated. 'They could do themselves credit in competitive soccer of a reasonable amateur standard,' wrote Ron Roberts.

Donald Carr had played two Amateur Cup Finals at Wembley with Pegasus, and 45 years on he can still recite the M.C.C. team. "Barrington, Parks, Thomson, Stephenson, Close, Watkins, Lock, Tompkin, Swetman, Carr, Titmus. I think we were a better football team than we were at cricket. The only weakness really was Tony Lock at right wing, but he had to play because he'd arranged the ball."

"The only chap disappointed to be left out," his manager adds, "was me. I'd loved to have played."

The crowd for the cricket at Multan – 12,000 on the first day – was the largest for any at the minor matches, but there were nearly twice as many at the football and they roared with laughter when at half-time Alan Moss and Billy Sutcliffe appeared with buckets of water and drenched their team mates. *We were cheered all the way through the town and everybody thoroughly enjoyed it all. ... We shall be able to tell of the good we have done to offset this one silly blunder.'* In a footnote to the letter, he replied to an enquiry from his daughters: *I am afraid that I don't know a thing about Davy Crockett – never heard of him in fact!*

Davy Crockett, king of the wild frontier. After ten weeks in Pakistan, the M.C.C. tourists had had their own wild frontier to negotiate and were out of touch with the latest songs back home. They were not even up to date with developments in the negotiations between Lord's and Karachi, as they discovered during the second day of the match at Multan, a full nine days after the drenching of Idris Begh.

*Multan, 6 March. By the purest chance Bill Sutcliffe switched on the radio, and there was a BBC announcer's voice telling us of messages passing between Lord Alexander, the President of M.C.C., and the Governor-General of Pakistan, quoting exchanges of telegrams and telling us of decisions reached about which neither Donald nor I know a thing. Even now I have not even had a telegram, not a word. I am afraid that we are the victims of intrigue and are now helplessly in the hands of the Politicians and the Press. To say that I am sick and tired of it all is to grossly understate the case. The plain fact is that we have been jockeyed into all sorts of embarrassing situations throughout the piece and have got through the tour or would have done thanks almost entirely to Daud Khan. Now as the result of a prank that I agree got out of hand and which I agree was foolish we are branded almost as assassins. ... I was amazed that Tommy Trinder should have used it to raise a laugh on T.V.*

Earl Alexander, the last British soldier to evacuate Dunkirk, had offered to bring home the tourists and to compensate the Pakistanis for resulting loss of revenue, but Governor-General Mirza, who as a senior Indian civil servant had known Alexander in the 1930s when they had both been stationed in the North-West Frontier, had declined, calling on his people 'to show a sporting spirit and ensure that M.C.C. get a friendly reception for the rest of their tour.' Or, as the *Daily Mirror* put it, 'PAKISTAN DON'T WANT ALEXANDER'S RAG TEAM BANNED'.

From Multan they flew back to Karachi, where the tour had started with such high hopes. There was one last game of cricket to be played, the fourth of the representative matches, then they would all be going home.

*

For the fourth time in the series Idris Begh was to umpire. According to Brian Chapman, 'Pakistani officials feared the mood of the crowd if his absence were wrongly linked with the incident at Peshawar.' He was the centre of attention on the first morning as he walked around the boundary, addressing the banks of spectators; "We want no howls, no shouting, no trouble. We want a nice game with by-gones forgotten. I will do my duty out there, and so will the players. So you leave it to us." Crawford White reported the reaction: 'As if hypnotised by this neat, theatrical, white-coated figure in his brown topee, the crowd were as good as gold.'

With the start delayed by an hour, because of the arrival in the city of the Shah of Persia, the game proceeded keenly but quietly. Hafeez Kardar was absent, with an injured arm, and the series was already decided. Pakistan, put in to bat, made 178, and at the close of the second day M.C.C. had reached 133 for five in reply.

The last letters home revealed no improvement in the manager's spirits.

*Karachi, 8 March. I am afraid that we shall go down as the most unpopular side ever to leave England – such a rank injustice for it is certainly the best team I have ever had experience of and I shall say so if I am allowed to do so. ... I hope M.C.C. will make their measures swift and soon over for some of these lads are going to be very good cricketers and badly needed. ... I must say that I am glad that I have plenty to do; I am too sensitive to find it pleasant to be thought of as a hooligan.*

*Karachi, 10 March. Every letter I get makes me feel worse about the way this business has been handled. To try to deal with it is like trying to stem the ocean. Whenever I make a move here to improve things, back I get set by hearing of some other awful Press stunt. I really could go for Mr C. White – he really is an outsize in so and so's.*

On the third day, two further incidents on the field put the tour back in the headlines. First, Jim Parks was given out caught by the wicket-keeper Imtiaz when, according to Ron Roberts, 'it appeared the ball might have been taken on the half-volley.' Nobody bore the disappointments better on that tour than

Parks, and his return to the pavilion was prompt and sporting, though his partner at the wicket Fred Titmus gave vent to frustration. "It was palpably not out," Geoffrey says. "I can see Fred Titmus advancing down the pitch, with his bat in the air, protesting, but obviously it wasn't going to have any effect."

When, later in the day, Imtiaz survived a loud appeal for lbw from Brian Close, Allan Watkins started to mutter at short-leg and Imtiaz pulled away, appealing to the umpire to stop the bad language. 'TEST FLARE-UP!' was Brian Chapman's headline in the *Daily Mirror*. 'The sooner this wretched tour finishes the better,' wrote Crawford White, adding 'I have been loth to write this, for it does not make pleasant reading. But it happened before 30,000 people and the facts must be faced.'

There were more calls from the Pakistani press for the M.C.C. team to go home, another round of apologies, more troops on hand in case of disturbances.

At close of play Governor-General Iskander Mirza summoned Geoffrey Howard and Hafeez Kardar to talks, and he listened carefully to what the two parties had to say. From the England perspective, there had been a catalogue of bad umpiring decisions in each of the representative matches, almost all at their expense, and their request to have Idris Begh replaced after the first Test had not been granted. The ragging of Idris that occurred in Peshawar was not malicious and was not in any way related to his umpiring. The claim by Imtiaz to have caught the ball that morning was unacceptable. From the Pakistan side, the umpires had done their best and the tourists had shown insufficient respect, both in querying decisions and in subjecting Idris Begh to a soaking. It was important that the honour of officials be upheld at all times.

Iskander Mirza paused before drawing his conclusion. He was an old cricketer himself, a friend of the British, and, forty-five years on, his words remain clear in the England manager's memory: "Having listened to what you have had to say, Mr Howard, and to you, Abdul Hafeez, I have to say that I form the view that Idris Begh, as an umpire, is a cheat."

"But he's the best we've got," Hafeez protested.

"The best umpire? Or the best cheat?"

A public statement on the day's incidents was agreed: 'An inquiry has revealed that both sides were equally at fault.'

*

Pakistan set M.C.C. only 125 for victory, but wickets were soon falling again. Ron Roberts yearned for 'the swinging bat' but, as partners came and went, Ken Barrington 'showed no propensity for frolics'. By close of play, with the score on 71 for six, he was running out of partners.

"When are you going to play a few shots?" his manager tackled him.

"I'm holding myself in readiness for tomorrow," he replied.

"But you might get out tomorrow." And, of course, he did, leaving M.C.C. 75 for seven and on the verge of a third defeat.

'I thought it was all up with them,' Brian Chapman wrote, 'but those two lads of London Town, Titch Titmus and Swagger Swetman, had other views. Then when Fazal Mahmood – and Idris Begh – disposed of Titmus, Tony Lock carried on the good work.' According to Ron Roberts, 'Swetman was as poised as a seasoned campaigner and the remaining runs came quickly.'

Victory by two wickets. Pakistan's first ever defeat on home soil. 'A grand finale to an unhappy tour,' Crawford White called it.

**Pakistan 178 and 130**
**M.C.C. 184 and 126 for eight**
**M.C.C. won by two wickets**

★ It wasn't all bickering during the M.C.C. "A" team's tour of Pakistan. Here Donald Carr, captain of the tour team, puts a friendly arm round the shoulders of Idris Begh, the Pakistan umpire who was ragged after the third Test, as they walk off the pitch.

*from the Daily Mirror*

It was a tour unlike any before it – but the issues which it raised would return in time.

The winter of 1955/56. Archbishop Makarios in exile, Jomo Kenyatta in gaol, Abdul Nasser with his eyes on the Suez Canal. Now Pakistan was becoming an Islamic republic, with Iskander Mirza – President of the Pakistan Cricket Board – set within days of M.C.C.'s departure to become the first President of Pakistan itself.

'Touring conditions in places such as India, Pakistan and the West Indies are not what they were before the war,' Crawford White suggested. 'However much M.C.C. might feel that racialism, nationalism and politics are "not cricket", the hard fact is that they are at the core of these new problems.'

'WHY CRICKET BECAME TOO SERIOUS A GAME,' ran the headline in Ron Roberts' concluding despatch. 'When governments and sport are intermingled, sport usually becomes a matter of international prestige rather than national enjoyment.'

Pakistan, Zindabad! Pakistan, Zindabad!

At a farewell dinner, Hafeez Kardar proposed that in future neutral umpires should officiate in representative matches.

*

Even the journey home was difficult. A late departure from Karachi. A dust storm, engine trouble, civil disturbances. They flew from Bahrein to Basra to Bhagdad, ending up in Beirut. "All we want is an earthquake," Billy Sutcliffe joked.

"We were up at the top of the building," the manager remembers. "Having a quiet drink and waiting. We could see the lights of these two aircraft approaching. Then suddenly there was this rushing and shaking, and I thought the aircraft had hit the building. In fact, it was an earthquake, up in the hills. Quite a bad one. A lot of people were killed. We ran as fast as we could down the stairs. I remember Ken Barrington going past me."

By the time they arrived in London, nineteen hours late, they had to go straight to Lord's for the post-mortem on the tour.

Earl Alexander took the chair, and he showed no amusement when told the full story of the soaking of Idris Begh. Gubby Allen and Walter Robins were quicker to see the funny side of it, as was the M.C.C. secretary Ronnie Aird. "He could hardly contain himself for laughing," Donald Carr recalls. "I told it just as I'd seen it. It was one of the funniest things I've ever seen in my life. But it didn't raise a smile from Lord Alexander."

Geoffrey's memory is of Walter Robins turning to Maurice Tompkin. "'You're an experienced cricketer, Maurice,' Robbie said to him. 'What would you like to say about the tour? And Maurice said, 'I enjoyed every minute of it, except the cricket.'"

The stylish Leicestershire batsman had scored 1000 runs in every post-war summer, 2000 in 1955 with an attractive hundred for the Players at Lord's securing him a place on this tour. "He was the sort of player who, if he'd played for Middlesex or Surrey, would have played for England." But in Pakistan he never found form, and his team mates took to sympathising with him. "Hard luck," they would say, but his reply was philosophical. "Ah well, never mind. There are plenty of English summers to come."

The summer of 1956. Peter Richardson and Tony Lock, buoyed by their successes on this 'A' tour, became vital members of the England team that beat the Australians 2-1, but Maurice Tompkin struggled in vain to find form in the county game. Complaining of pains in the back and abdomen, he reached the end of August with an average of just 16 runs an innings. Then at the start of September, at the Torquay Festival, he found his touch with a powerful 64 not out before rain swept in from the Atlantic and washed away the last of the summer. A fortnight later he was in hospital in Leicester, cancer diagnosed in his stomach. By the end of the month he was dead.

"Dear Maurice. He was such a lovely chap."

*

The statement released from Lord's placed full responsibility for the incident on the captain and 'hoped that the publicity that has attended this affair may now be discontinued, both in the best interests of cricket relations between the two countries and for the sake of a team of young cricketers, who up to that time had proved themselves loyal, conscientious and well-mannered tourists.'

'Carr has paid severely for a thoughtless mistake,' Michael Melford concluded in the *Daily Telegraph*, 'but his reputation as a captain is such that he is better fitted than most to bear the blame. One has frequently heard players of other counties say how much they enjoyed playing against Derbyshire, a peculiarly striking tribute. Carr has been one of the outstanding post-war captains in English cricket and will no doubt continue to be so.'

*

"Geoffrey hasn't been able to tell me who, apart from you, Donald, was involved in the incident."

"I think it has appeared in print."

"Geoffrey thinks it was fairly unlikely that Roy Swetman wasn't involved."

"He was a great thrower around of water," Geoffrey adds.

"He was."

"He was there, was he?" Geoffrey presses.

"I mean, he was a great thrower around of water," Donald replies cagily.

I persist. "Geoffrey's other suspect was Peter Richardson, but I think that might not be right."

"Might have been Sutcliffe," Geoffrey guesses.

It seems extraordinary that so many years have passed, and he has never been told.

"Now, do you want the official answer?" Donald says. "Mind you, I shall probably get it wrong. My memory isn't as good as yours, Geoffrey."

"Go on then," I suggest.

"It was Swetman and Close."

"Brian Close," Geoffrey repeats, with a smile. "Just the three of you?"

"No, there were seven or eight in the room."

"That's interesting. Brian Close. That's typical Brian. Typical Swetman, too."

"The problem was that Idris took a bit of fright when Closey grabbed him and put him in the tonga. Brian can be a bit intimidating. He's tremendously strong.

"When we got back to our hotel, we invited him to sit in a certain chair so that Closey and Swetman could go round the back and hide behind the wall. 'Idris, would you like a drink?' I said. 'No,' he said, 'I do not drink.'

"There were two holes in the wall, and they each had a bucket. 'I will have nothing but water.' So I said, 'Well, here it comes.' And I must say, it was a marvellous bit of shooting. It plummeted down right on top of him, and he spluttered away.

"Then we rubbed him down, got a towel, and in quite a short time he saw the funny side of it. And it was all fine. He'd done his hair and was looking more respectable.

"Then two of their boys – one was Khan Mohammad – came in and roared with laughter. 'Oh, it's about time that happened to you, Idris.' And because he was being laughed at by his own people, he disappeared out of the room. Went back to his own hotel and reported it to Hafeez."

*

At the end of his playing career Donald Carr became assistant secretary of M.C.C., then secretary of the Test and County Cricket Board and of the Cricket Council. A respected administrator who himself managed three overseas tours, including one in 1972/73 to India and Pakistan. "I gave them a talk before we set out. 'Although winning is important,' I said, 'I would like to think that, when we leave India, they will be sorry to see us go.'" In the *Wisden* report of the tour, he was 'imperturbable, efficient, and popular', epithets that undoubtedly applied to his role model, Geoffrey Howard.

Hafeez Kardar was by that time President of the Pakistan Board of Control, soon to become a minister in Zulfikar Ali Bhutto's government. At a function he called for the headquarters of the International Cricket Council to be moved to Karachi or Lahore, and it fell to Donald Carr to get up and reply. By now he knew better that to try his hand at joking.

"I must give him his dues. He did a lot of work for Pakistan cricket."

Perhaps a better ending to the story of Peshawar took place in Karachi two years before this. A typhoon and tidal waves had killed 150,000 people in East Pakistan, and Donald Carr assembled an international side for an exhibition match to raise money for the relief fund.

"We got out there. One day for practice, then straight into the match. We went down to the ground for our practice, the boys started getting changed, and there was a knock on the door. The dressing room was very dark and, as the door opened, this immaculate figure appeared in the light. A lovely hat, nice jacket. 'Is the manager here?' he said, and I realised it was Idris Begh. 'I'm in charge of everything to do with this match.' He put his arms around me. Then he started telling me the playing conditions and the hours of play.

"As we went out together, I could see Kanhai and Gibbs rolling around the floor, laughing. Then I felt a tap on the shoulder. It was big Dave Brown. 'Would this help, manager?' he asked. And there he was with a great bucket of water.

"Idris laughed. It was fine."

*

The journey back from Donald Carr's house passes quickly. It has been a long day, but Geoffrey remains alert and conversational.

"I learnt a lot today," he says, "but nothing that surprised me. It all seems to have been a great fuss about such a little thing. It really was the happiest of the tours I managed."

# CHAPTER TWELVE

# POP GOES THE OVAL

# THE OVAL

# 1965 – 74

At the Vauxhall end, a temporary stage had been erected, with matting laid across the cricket square and amplifiers filling the Kennington air with the sound of The Faces.

*I had nothing to do on this hot afternoon*
*But to settle down and write you a line.*

It was September 1972. Surrey's cricket season was over, with Micky Stewart retiring after twenty years on the staff. In his first summer the county had won the second of its seven-in-a-row championships, yet for all the glory of those years the attendances fell and fell – and, for his final appearance in late August, there were fewer than 400 paying spectators per day in the ground, each contributing five shillings.

For this pop concert, with an admission charge of one pound, there were 40,000 present, and the Stewart who drew them was not Micky but Rod, top of the charts with a song whose lyrics could almost have been written about the elderly cricket ground and its efforts to move with the times.

*You wear it well –*
*A little old fashioned but that's all right.*

*Early in the day, long before the ground was full.*
*The audience covered the playing area before filling the seats.*

It was the second of Surrey's excursions into staging pop concerts, the first the previous year featuring The Who. The county had been approached by Ricky Farr, son of the boxer Tommy and organiser of the Isle of Wight pop festivals, and the annual accounts for 1971 show clearly why the proposal was so attractive:

| | | |
|---|---|---|
| 1971 | Income from pop festival | £4,210 |
| | Excess of income over expenditure for year | £561 |

In the late 1950s, when Warwickshire was redeveloping Edgbaston on the back of a Supporters' Club football pool, the suggestion was made that Surrey should launch a similar venture. 'Over my dead body,' said Errol Holmes, and a veto also greeted the proposal for greyhound racing around the perimeter.

By the time the Lancashire secretary returned to Surrey on the first of January 1965, it was clear that changes had to be made.

"You must be mad," the *Yorkshire Post* writer Jim Kilburn told him before he left Manchester. "Have you been to The Oval lately?"

"I hadn't been back since I left at the start of 1949, and it was staggering. All the work we'd done at Old Trafford to improve the ground, and there was no perceptible change at all at The Oval. The only difference was the attendance. Where we'd had thousands in 1948, there were only hundreds in 1965. I remember the Gillette Cup semi-final against Middlesex that year I got back. The previous year at Old Trafford, when Lancashire had played Warwickshire, the ground had been full, and we were expecting the same at The Oval. But it wasn't even half full."

The annual loss in his first year was £17,559.

Derek Newton, a club cricketer in the insurance business, joined the committee at this time. "If we'd been a PLC," he says, "we'd have had to go into liquidation."

Micky Stewart, as captain, attended committee meetings. "I played professional football," he says, "and even in those days, if you went into the boardroom of a football club, the talk was all about revenue, income, expenditure, break-even. If you came into the committee room of a cricket club, you never ever heard money mentioned. I was aware that the club was broke, but nobody wanted to talk about it."

Nobody, that is, till the new secretary arrived.

For the 1966 Surrey year book, he commissioned an article by Charles Bray: *'The outlook is dismal, of that there can be no doubt. ... Cricket, to survive, must move with the times. What was good enough in the thirties is not good enough in the sixties.'* Then, from 1967, the year book contained the annual accounts, with a detailed discussion of the club's finances.

Geoffrey's predecessor had been Lieutenant-Commander Brian Babb, who had served as Assistant to Brian Castor. His number two was Lieutenant-Colonel Nigel Romer. "They were known as 'The Army and Navy Club' by the staff," Geoffrey recalls. "I don't think either of them ever wanted anything to change."

"When I was captain," Micky says, "the side used to travel by car. But two or three times a year the fixture was so far away that we went by rail. Each time I used to ask Nigel Romer to look up the times of suitable trains. We hadn't needed to worry when Tom Clark was playing, because he was a walking Bradshaw, but I could never get an answer out of Nigel. I don't think he could work out the guide. I came off the field at tea time one day, flew up to his office in a bit of a rage, and he wasn't there. So I started looking for the guide and, when I opened his drawer, a glass of pink gin fell out."

"Everybody called him Sweetie," Geoffrey says. "Even his wife. He was a lovely chap, but he wasn't somebody you could look to for ideas."

Ideas were certainly what Surrey were looking for by 1965. That was what Alf Gover told the new secretary before he left Old Trafford: "We are looking forward to having some of your ideas."

"They wanted a chap who would not be trotting away on horseback," Geoffrey says, "but using the spurs."

Lancashire had begun to raise income from utilising its facilities out of season, and this was a development that the new secretary instigated at The Oval. Back in the 1940s there was a Theatrical Garden Party, with Richard Dimbleby as compère, but now there were bonfire nights, Sunday markets, Christmas funfairs, donkey derbies.

"There was one occasion," Micky recalls, "when I turned up in winter to have my photograph taken between two camels. Oh, the smell of them! I'd just bought a beautiful new overcoat, and they spat all over it."

Then came the pop concerts.

*Well I suppose you're thinking I bet he's sinking,*
*Or he wouldn't get in touch with me.*

"The police wouldn't come into the ground," Geoffrey remembers. "'If you want us,' they said, 'we'll be outside.' The people who made it run smoothly were the Hell's Angels. When they trooped in, I thought, 'This is the end.' But they kept the peace. A stall was selling bacon and eggs at an extortionate price, and the Hell's Angels went over. 'Either you take that price down or you're out of business.' The stall refused so they tipped the whole lot over.

"The concert went on far too late into the night. The cars were parked all haphazard, and the police lifted them all and turned them round so that, when everybody left, they all went straight out. It was the most magical thing.

"The lavatories and a lot of the seating were practically ruined, but the backers paid for everything to be repaired."

"I had just taken over as manager of the Corinthian Casuals football club," Micky recalls. "I negotiated with Geoffrey to play our home games at The Oval, and the first match was the weekend after the concert. I looked in during the week, and everything seemed fine. We had new white nets, and my wife had made some new corner flags. But on the morning the sun was out, and I could see all these little things glistening on the pitch. Crushed plastic glasses. I was scratching my hand to see if I could cut myself on them. Fortunately, before everybody arrived, the sun went in."

"One of the groundsmen," Geoffrey adds, "saw a bottle top and, when he went to pick it up, there was another underneath, and another, and another. There were fifteen of them, one on top of the other."

"It was all a very considerable departure for a staid old cricket club like Surrey. Ian Wooldridge wrote an article headed 'POP GOES THE OVAL'. His final sentence was, 'Surrey County Cricket Club lifted up its mini-skirts and tripped into the twentieth century.'"

*A little out of time but I don't mind.*

Unfortunately, this source of funds dried up. A concert at Crystal Palace ended in the death of an audience member, Lambeth Council introduced a regulation that tickets must be limited to the number of available seats, and the enterprise became unviable financially.

*

"Surrey was stuffed full of loyal workers," Geoffrey says. "People who had given their lives to the club. But nothing had been moving forward.

"When I was at The Oval in 1947, a great character in the dressing room was the masseur, Sandy Tait. He'd been there since 1929, and he was there when I got back in 1965. By no means could you describe him as a physiotherapist. He was just a good rubber. 'Where do you feel the pain?' he'd ask and he'd lay his hands upon it. 'No, not that leg, Sandy, the other one.'"

He belonged in a lost world, where he could be loyal servant to gentlemen masters, making cups of tea for committee members and teasing the players with his practical jokes. "I caught out Len Hutton with the Fly in the Bottle right in the middle of a Test match," he loved to tell. But, when Sandy Tait died in early 1966, his replacement David Montague, who had been at Lord's and had learnt his trade at the London School for Injuries, required a specialist room with all sorts of equipment. Another item of expenditure that was not in the budget.

In 1958 the old Surrey keeper Herbert Strudwick had retired at the age of 78 from his position as scorer, to be succeeded by the ex-coach Andrew Sandham who stayed till 1970 when he was 80 years old – though even that was young compared with Northamptonshire's Jack Mercer, who went on to the age of 86. "I remember Andrew and Jack in the box at The Oval. I doubt if either of them could see even halfway to the middle, but they had a wonderful time together."

Sandham played for Surrey before the Great War, and his presence in the scorebox as late as 1970 certainly kept alive the county's past.

"I interviewed him," Geoffrey remembers, and he produces a shorthand note pad with his scribbled notes. "Among his duties as twelfth man was to go to the Members' Bar and buy a large whisky when Tom Hayward was out. 'I don't think I remember him ever paying me.'"

Sixty years later Andrew Sandham was keeping the score – just the simple book, not the coloured pens, the run charts, the computer link-ups of his present-day successors. "It's developed into an art form now, though I think sometimes it tends to overvalue figures in assessing achievement."

Each year Herbert Strudwick came up to Kennington from his home in Shoreham. "The Oval was his whole life. Whenever he came, he would first look into my office, to present his compliments, then he would go down to the scorebox to give Andy a bag of sweets. One time he got to Victoria Station and he realised he'd forgotten to buy the sweets – and, in his agitation, he got knocked over by a bus."

Alas, it fell to the secretary to tell Andrew Sandham that it was time to retire. "I knew that he was struggling. We introduced fielder number lights. The scorer had to turn on the light against the fielder's number to familiarise the crowd with the different fielders. But it was beyond him. He simply couldn't see.

"His wife had died. Surrey County Cricket Club was his life. And I was pensioning him off. 'You can't do that,' people told me. 'It will kill him.'

"But when I told him, he looked so relieved. 'Thank goodness,' he said. 'I didn't know how to tell you myself.'"

Then there was John Carter, the book-keeper and accountant, who in 1965 was doing as he had done in 1947, standing the weekly wage packets in a box and leaving everybody to come in and help themselves, so that anybody could read what was in any of the other packets. "Poor old John. He was horrified when I suggested it wasn't a very good way to do things."

Nothing had evolved as it should have done, and now the changes had to be made against a background of rising losses.

They were hard years for cricket. The crowds had deserted the county game, and the large television monies had not yet arrived. Somerset were considering the sale of their Taunton ground, Essex were down to a playing staff of twelve and a 1966 Advisory sub-committee on County Cricket, which included the Surrey secretary, spelled out the gravity of the situation:

*'If no action is taken, the sub-committee believes the trend will continue and ultimately result in some counties being forced to leave the county championship.'*

"If the worst had come to the worst, we could have finished up with four counties: Lancashire, Yorkshire, Glamorgan and Kent."

The committee recommended the immediate reduction of the championship to 16 three-day games, with an additional 16-match one-day league, but the counties were in no mood for such a radical change. "What a load of tommy rot!" Glamorgan's secretary Wilf Wooller declared as they voted overwhelmingly to retain the status quo.

*

At Surrey the committee started to change, with new sub-committees formed for Public Relations and Sales Promotion. The former was chaired by Raman Subba Row, who had retired from cricket at the age of 29 to develop his own PR company, the latter by Bernie Coleman, landlord of the Dog and Fox at Wimbledon and an enthusiastic generator of marketing ideas.

Back in 1965, when the clock at the Vauxhall end had gone beyond economical repair, a committee man who worked for Guinness had said that his company could replace it. "It was always hard with the old Roman numerals to know whether it was 6.29 or 6.30, and Guinness were offering to put in a digital clock. The committee opposed it – because it was advertising. But if you looked out of the window, at all the bars around the ground, you could see Watneys signs everywhere. But 'NO! to Guinness time' was their decision."

Within two or three years, the old amateurs' dressing room had been redecorated and offered for hospitality to Excess Insurance, who displayed an advertising board and paid £500.

"Our problem," Bernie Coleman recalls, "was that we had to keep our members' subscription rate below that of the M.C.C., and they would never put theirs up."

"I suppose we *could* have raised ours above theirs," Geoffrey says, "but there was much more cricket to watch at Lord's and infinitely more privileges. You could practise in the nets. You could play tennis. And of course you had free entry to the Lord's Test."

At the time Gubby Allen was the M.C.C. Treasurer, and Bernie remembers him arriving in the Committee Room for the Oval Test.

"He sat in the doorway, with his cigarette, like the Lord Almighty. Then suddenly he saw this blue Excess Insurance sign. 'What the devil's that?' he said. 'Mr Allen,' I said. 'We're broke, and that's £500. If you'd put your subs up two guineas, we might be solvent.' 'We couldn't possibly do that,' he said. He just couldn't understand that times were changing."

By 1974 there were seven companies sponsoring matches, another fifteen with advertising on the ground and a tent where Ladbrokes established betting facilities. Taken all together, their contributions were greater than the receipts from the county's paying spectators.

*

Sunday play was tried. Despite the objections of the Lord's Day Observance Society, the three-day match against Kent in June 1966 was staged on the Saturday, Sunday and Monday, with play on the second day running from two o'clock to seven. "We weren't allowed to charge an entrance fee so we sold the scorecards at half a crown each. Unfortunately, when people realised that they didn't have to pay, a lot of them went in for nothing."

Nevertheless, a crowd of 8,000 gathered, and they watched fidgety and frustrated as, according to *The Times*, *'Play seemed to lose momentum altogether.'* Colin Cowdrey set a defensive field – *'It left little leeway for stroke-making.'* – and a self-absorbed Ken Barrington scored 42 in nearly three hours. "I can see him offering his bat to the crowd. They were playing for Monday. It was a disaster. It was the best Sunday gate in all my time at The Oval, better than we ever got for the Sunday League, and in the end they were going out faster than they'd come in."

"It's indelibly printed on my memory," Bernie says.

"I can remember how busy I was getting people into the ground," Geoffrey says, and Micky laughs: "And Kenny was busy getting them out."

*

Overseas players were introduced to stimulate interest. In 1965 Dennis Marriott, a Jamaican who had settled in England, and Younis Ahmed, younger brother of the Pakistani Test cricketer Saeed Ahmed, qualified by playing second eleven cricket, though not without some opposition in committee – "Just colour prejudice. 'We don't want foreigners ... We don't want coloured players.' Just that." – and, when the residential qualification was removed, the immensely popular Intikhab Alam joined them in 1969.

But their arrival did not bring back the crowds quite as all the counties had hoped. "I remember when Nottingham came down with Gary Sobers for the first time in 1968. The crowd came along in some numbers from Brixton. He didn't make many runs and, as soon as he was out, they all departed. The introduction of overseas players was no great success in terms of crowds."

*

Surrey's success in the 1950s had been built on a great bowling attack – Laker, Lock, Loader and the Bedsers – and pitches that produced results. By the 1960s all that had changed. The Oval pitch had become unrewardingly slow for the bowler, and Surrey spent several years in mid-table with its strength more in the batting of Edrich, Barrington and Stewart.

There was a flicker of a revival in 1964, when the 17-year-old off-spinner Pat Pocock joined left-armer Roger Harman to provide hope of a revival in the slow bowling. "George Duckworth said to me at Old Trafford that he'd just seen Laker and Lock's successors." But Harman's star soon faded. "He had a very fine action, but he was a quiet, easy-going chap, not at all a combatant like Tony Lock."

Pat Pocock was an England player by the age of 21, Robin Jackman and Geoff Arnold developed into a new-ball pair of some distinction, and in 1969 the bowling attack gained the leg-spin of Intikhab Alam and the raw pace of the young Bob Willis. They beat Yorkshire at Scarborough on August the 22nd, 1969 – *'after Yorkshire seemed to have the game in hand'* – and suddenly they were the best-placed county to overhaul the championship leaders Glamorgan.

"On the way home," Micky Stewart recalls, "the lads were speculating as to the size of the crowd for our next home match. Eight to ten thousand was the most popular figure."

It was not to be. Not their championship – and not eight to ten thousand spectators at The Oval when they played Hampshire. 3,868 paying spectators spread themselves over the three days while news came back from Swansea that, on the Monday alone, Glamorgan were playing in front of 12,000.

Cricket was not catching the imagination of Londoners, and at close of play on the Saturday even Bob Willis was heading for the Isle of Wight, where his idol Bob Dylan was playing to a crowd of 100,000.

*You'd better start swimming or you'll sink like a stone*
*For the times they are a'changing.*

"It is time for Surrey to play around the county," Micky wrote in the year book. "I am sure that members would far sooner spend their cricket-watching hours in a more country-type atmosphere than The Oval. We have to face the fact that we are called Surrey and represent a county where we hardly ever play."

"A lot of members complained about that article," he remembers.

*

"When Geoffrey came," Micky says, "it was the first time we as players could communicate with the secretary's office. We found it difficult to have a conversation with Brian Babb or Brian Castor, or they with us. But with Geoffrey you could knock on his door and discuss anything with him. You knew, too, that he wasn't a mug about the game."

"In all my years in cricket," Derek Newton adds, "I'd say that Geoffrey is the only older person I've ever met who, if you put up an idea, would say, 'Marvellous, we're looking for new ideas.' That was very rewarding for a young committee man."

"Leslie Ames and Geoffrey were two of the greatest administrators in the game," Bernie Coleman says, "because they were looking ahead. I've always felt that, if Geoffrey had been in charge of the whole of cricket, the game would have been running well."

"I do remember one committee meeting," Derek says, "when Geoffrey arrived in a yellow shirt. He said, 'Why don't we wear these for our Sunday matches?"

"I got the idea from you, Micky. You told me that Chelsea were devising a special strip for their cup matches, and I thought, 'Why don't we do that?' I think I gave it to Robin Jackman, who wore it in the dressing room and said, 'What do you think of this?'"

"I thought it would be fun," Bernie adds, "if we got the players wearing coloured cummerbunds, like they did long ago. But the Board turned it down."

*

"There wasn't the pressure to win the championship in Surrey like there was in Yorkshire," Micky Stewart says. "I wish there had been."

In 1970 he led Surrey to the head of the table in early August, only for them to finish fifth. The following year, though, they went to Southampton in mid-September, and the four Hampshire wickets that they took earned them just enough bonus points to take the title.

It should have been Micky's last match before retirement, but pressure was put on him to stay after his triumph. *'He would be well advised to stand by his original decision,'* John Woodcock wrote in *The Times*. *'If he ends now, it will be on a happy note.'* He did not and, with Geoff Arnold struggling for fitness and Bob Willis moving to Edgbaston, the county declined to twelfth place in his final season.

"I spent hours trying to persuade Bob to stay," Geoffrey recalls. "He was so obstinate. He'd been called out to Australia and played some Tests in 1970/71, and he was still an uncapped Surrey player. Stuart Surridge said playing for England had nothing to do with it, he had to earn his Surrey cap. 'He's not getting it till he does.' And that was what decided Bob to go.

"Maybe Stuart could have been more diplomatic, but he had such a wonderful record as a leader that Bob should have realised that he'd only got to wait. He just couldn't see it from Stuart's point of view. So he went up to Edgbaston, where I don't think he was ever really at home.

"He was such a difficult person to talk to. The last time I saw him, I asked him, 'Do you ever regret that you left Surrey?' And he said, 'I always regret that I left Surrey.'"

So there was no repeat of the seven championships of the 1950s – and no great improvement in the county's finances. Even the £561 profit of their most successful playing year owed everything to The Who.

*

It fell by tradition to the Surrey secretary to construct the fixture list each summer, and for this task the county received £25 from each of the other counties – "none of it passed on to me, I should add. I used to stay in the office till midnight doing it, as there was never any time in the day."

"It was the only two weeks in the year when you were difficult to talk to," Micky Stewart remembers. "You were ratty and miserable."

"The first thing I had to do was to phone up Lord's for their list of dates. And, when Ronnie Aird was there, the first one on his mind every year was Eton and Harrow. Then Cambridge and Oxford. And it wasn't just Eton and Harrow, there were Clifton and Tonbridge, Rugby and Marlborough, Cheltenham and Haileybury. In the end I said to him, 'Why can't these schools play on their own grounds?'

"One year the Army offered a computer, and I went down to Warminster in Wiltshire to hand everything over. But it was useless. It couldn't cope with all the complications: Kent have to play Sussex at Tunbridge Wells, that sort of detail."

Years later, the Football League's computer proved more effective.

*

Geoffrey's children had grown up, but there were still opportunities for Nora to add those personal touches for which she had been so appreciated at Old Trafford.

"There was a system at The Oval where old England players were provided with a beer-and-sandwich lunch for the five days of the Test match. Nora took it over, and she provided lunches of such quality that a lot of old players came who hadn't come before. She even served grapes that we'd grown on the vine at the back of our house."

*

Soon after his return to The Oval in 1965, Geoffrey turned to his brother Donald, who was a property developer, and he asked him what he would do with the site. "I'd knock the whole lot down and start again," was the reply, and for most of Geoffrey's years as secretary at The Oval there was planning permission granted for a major redevelopment of the whole area. Flats were to overhang the sides of the ground, with the vast playing area reduced at the Vauxhall end to accommodate a luxury hotel. Then, when the hotel trade lost interest and Donald's company was taken over by Costain's, the plan became to relocate the company headquarters there.

"It didn't happen for various reasons. I'm glad it didn't, too. There would have been too much concrete, too much overhang of buildings, too much reduction to the playing area."

They were bold plans, but bolder still was the suggestion that they should abandon the site altogether. They were only tenants of the Duchy of Cornwall, and there was a growing feeling that the Duchy had lost interest in them.

Prince Charles was certainly no great enthusiast for the game. In fact, his first appearance at The Oval was on the occasion that they staged an Australian Rules Football match.

"Sir Patrick Kingsley was the Duchy's representative," Bernie remembers. "Geoffrey had a lovely rapport with him but, once Sir Patrick went, they looked on The Oval as a plot of land that could eventually be sold – because they thought Surrey would go bust."

Sir Patrick's successor met with Maurice Allom, the Surrey president, who reported back to Geoffrey his teasing first remark: "I didn't realise cricket was played by grown-ups."

Micky Stewart sits beside Geoffrey as he tells the story. "Played by grown-ups? It isn't, is it?"

One suggestion that was gaining support was that Surrey should surrender the remaining years of its lease and find a site outside London where it could build a new ground with modern facilities and ample car parking. In 1972 the committee commissioned Cooper Brothers to assess the viability of the proposal, and the report – written by John Timberlake, a Cambridge tennis blue – began with an outline of the county's situation:

> *While most of the first-class counties have to contend with their own individual problems in addition to those of a national nature, Surrey seems particularly unfortunate with its own share of difficulties:*
>
> *(a) The Oval:-*
>
> *(i) is not in the county of Surrey;*
>
> *(ii) is a large, old ground that is expensive to maintain;*
>
> *(iii) is a Test match ground, steeped in tradition and prestige, which adds to the cost of maintenance;*
>
> *(iv) is poorly provided with car parking facilities.*
>
> *(b) the population of the county of Surrey, being cosmopolitan, is less likely to possess a sense of loyalty to its county than does a more in-bred population, such as that of Yorkshire, and is therefore less likely voluntarily to rally to its support when financial help is needed;*
>
> *(c) the Club is short of capital and a sound asset-backing to its financial position – even The Oval is not freehold occupied.*

In the end, the report accepted the view that insufficient funds would be available to develop a new ground to Test match standards and that the county could not withstand the loss of its Test match revenues. Surrey should stay at The Oval and seek to develop the site.

"My personal view at the time," Geoffrey says, "was that it was extremely doubtful that the cricket-watching public in London needed two grounds. Lord's was better equipped, and its Test match revenues were far superior to those at The Oval. I thought the time would come when Surrey would move into the county of Surrey, and perhaps Middlesex would move to The Oval and play as London."

"Years after you left, Geoffrey," Bernie says, "we had the chance to move to a new site in Tolworth, near where they were constructing the M25. I still think we made a mistake not going there."

*

They were difficult years for cricket – and it did not help when the game was plunged into an international crisis by South Africa.

In the autumn of 1967 Geoffrey and Nora Howard went there for the first time. They stayed with Nora's oldest schoolfriend and her husband, an opthalmic surgeon, and they looked up Tom Reddick, who had been coach at Old Trafford in Geoffrey's last years.

"I played my last cricket match out there – at the age of 58. It was against a school side. I borrowed the gear to play and kept wicket. Jack Plimsoll, the left-armer, was bowling; he was quite pacy. At the end of the day we all went for a meal, upstairs in a restaurant, and, when it was time to go, I could hardly move. I had to go downstairs backwards, holding on with both hands. I've never been so stiff in all my life."

The stiffness soon cleared – unlike the unease he felt when confronted with the apartheid way of life.

"We stayed in one of the most exclusive areas of Cape Town, yet our hosts didn't feel that they could go out for a walk alone. I remember going into this toilet in a park and not realising that it was for Blacks Only. And on the buses there were seats reserved for the whites; when the blacks got on, they would sit as close to the white seats as they could. I felt so uncomfortable all the time.

"The whites had little respect for the blacks. They quite liked them when they had them as domestic servants – 'kaffirs' – but that was all."

As a cricket administrator he was used to hearing attitudes that were not his own, but nothing in his life had prepared him for what he encountered in Apartheid South Africa – as his daughter Ursula confirms.

"I was living at home at the time, and I'll never forget how he was when he came back. I know he'd voted Labour after the war, but I'm not sure he did after 1951. He was a member of the cricket establishment.

"When he got home, he took to his bed for the best part of a week. He's always been an emotional man, but he was deeply shocked, traumatised even, by the dreadfulness of what he'd witnessed. We all saw the difference in him after that. It was quite a turning point in his life."

While he was in South Africa, he took the opportunity to discuss with leading figures in the cricket world the M.C.C. tour scheduled for the following winter. Basil d'Oliveira, the Cape Coloured, had become a leading member of the England side – with a Test batting average over 50 – and Geoffrey was anxious to find out how his selection would be received.

"I remember asking somebody, 'What will happen if, at some function, Basil d'Oliveira is dancing with a white girl and somebody protests? Because that's not allowed under the rules of apartheid.' But they were determined that somehow they would get over that. They'd have a black man booking into white hotels, but they were going to work it out.

"The President of the Western Province Cricket Association said to me that they didn't want him but that they realised they'd got to have him."

By the Oval Test the following summer, the whole position had changed.

Basil d'Oliveira had not had a good tour of the West Indies and, despite being England's leading run-maker in the first Test against Australia at Old Trafford, he had been dropped from the side. *'England had needed him as an all-rounder,'* *Wisden* concluded rather harshly, *'and he had failed as a first change bowler.'*

In the following ten weeks he found no form with the bat, scoring fewer than 400 runs at an average below 20, and his chance to play for England in his native homeland appeared to have passed. The relief in South Africa must have been immense.

Then, by a set of coincidences beyond prediction, he found himself not only playing in the final Test at The Oval but scoring a magnificent 158 and taking a crucial wicket in the final thrilling session.

The first chance event was that Colin Cowdrey was playing at The Oval a week earlier and noticed that the pitch favoured the medium-paced, rather than the fast, bowlers. So, when his fellow selectors opted for a pace attack of Snow and Brown, he asked them if they would mind his recruiting a medium-pacer if conditions closer to the start of the match warranted it. Tom Cartwright was first choice, then Barry Knight, then d'Oliveira. In fifteen Tests d'Oliveira had taken only 17 wickets, but he was high in the national bowling averages that summer.

The second chance event was that Roger Prideaux declared himself unfit. "He was ducking the match," Geoffrey thinks. "He fancied his chances of being selected for South Africa, and he didn't want to fail at The Oval."

A third twist of fate then occurred. Both Cartwright and Knight were unsure of their fitness for a five-day match, and by a process that must have seemed incomprehensible to the casual observer d'Oliveira was summoned from Worcester. He had been dropped after making 87 not out at Old Trafford, now he was back with just two fifties to show for ten weeks of county batting.

"If it hadn't been for Colin Cowdrey, he'd never have been picked."

By Friday afternoon d'Oliveira was the hero of all England. Faced with the greatest challenge of his life, *'he batted until five o'clock,'* John Woodcock reported, *'with the minimum of effort, never a hair or a nerve out of place. He was impassive and assured; his best shots were powerful but seldom physical.'*

"Basil d'Oliveira in form was a wonderful player, and in that innings he showed everybody his real ability."

*'On this form,'* John Woodcock added, *'he should go back to South Africa, as a member of the M.C.C. team.'*

The Surrey secretary knew differently. His telephone rang, and the caller was on the line from the Prime Minister's Office in Pretoria. "A fellow called Teeni Oosthuizen. He was a director of Rothmans, based in South Africa, and he'd been trying to contact Billy Griffith. 'I can't get hold of the M.C.C. secretary, so will you take a message to the selectors. Tell them that, if today's centurion is picked, the tour will be off.'"

Geoffrey has told me the story several times, and the words of the telephone message are always the same when he repeats them. "Tell them that, if today's centurion is picked, the tour will be off." He duly passed the message to Doug Insole, the chairman of selectors.

At lunchtime on Tuesday a storm broke. Rain lashed down over The Oval, and great puddles seemed to have destroyed England's chance of squaring the series against Australia. "Jim Swanton came in and said, 'That's it for the day.' But Colin Cowdrey was a great optimist. 'Oh, I'm not so sure,' he said. 'I think we might get back out.'"

There followed an extraordinary afternoon as members of the public, armed with forks by the ground staff, prodded holes and created the drainage that allowed play to resume at 4.45. For half an hour the Australian batsmen seemed secure, then d'Oliveira bowled the vital ball that cut in and clipped Jarman's off stump. The sun beat down on the damp pitch, and Colin Cowdrey promptly recalled Derek Underwood to test the incoming batsmen. With four wickets in 27 balls, he *'seized his opportunity on this unforgettable day'*, and the series was squared at one match all.

The next day another storm broke – as the selectors announced a tour party that did not contain Basil d'Oliveira. They preferred the batting of Roger Prideaux and the bowling of Tom Cartwright.

Ten of the best men in English cricket had been present in the room when the decision was made, men whom Geoffrey admired and trusted: men like Les Ames and Peter May, Colin Cowdrey and Donald Carr, Billy Griffith and Doug Insole. The omission of d'Oliveira from the tour party was, in many ways, no stranger a decision than his belated selection for the Oval Test. But was it really possible for each and every one of them, in his unspoken thoughts, to put out of his mind the implications of the message that Geoffrey had passed on to them?

The selectors deliberated till two in the morning, and they decided that Basil d'Oliveira would be their first reserve if anybody dropped out. But this was not announced and, when Tom Cartwright – a bowler – withdrew and was replaced by d'Oliveira, seemingly a batsman, it looked as if the selectors had bowed to the wave of protest that had greeted their original decision.

The South African government cancelled the tour, claiming that political influences had been brought to bear on the selectors, but Geoffrey knew differently: that the greatest political influence that had been brought to bear had not come from the protests in the United Kingdom but from the Prime Minister's office in South Africa, and that the decision to cancel the tour because of d'Oliveira's inclusion would have occurred if he had been selected in the first place.

"Poor Colin," he says. "He couldn't see how badly it had all been handled. He really thought the tour could have been saved. I remember him saying that he was going to consult a bench of bishops."

*

The South Africans were scheduled to tour England in 1970 and, like all his fellow administrators, the Surrey secretary was busy making the necessary arrangements. As the compiler of fixtures, he was required to draw up a revised list in February, for a truncated tour that would visit only Swansea of the non-Test match grounds. The Oval would host two fixtures: Surrey in July and the final Test in August.

Forces were moving fast against these efforts. A young South African exile, Peter Hain, had organised large demonstrations against the Springboks rugby tour during the winter, and his campaign to Stop the 70 Tour was attracting influential support.

The Reverend David Sheppard, by this time the Bishop of Woolwich, was one who wanted the tour cancelled, though he did not endorse the methods being suggested at some of the meetings: running onto the pitch and flashing mirrors into the eyes of the batsmen. Instead, he became chairman of the Fair Cricket Campaign, with vice-chairmen Edward Boyle, the former Conservative Education Minister, and Labour MP Reg Prentice. The secretary was Betty Boothroyd. One of their tactics was to target leading figures in the world of cricket whom they felt might be persuaded.

"A person would be named," he recalls. "The discussion would get as far as, 'Well they wouldn't listen to anyone from the Labour Party; and of course it mustn't be anyone from the Church.' Edward Boyle would then put his hand up and say, 'I'll go.'"

The Surrey secretary was identified as somebody worth a visit.

"We asked the Head Teacher of Kennington School to take some black sixth-formers to see him. The boys told him how they loved coming to The Oval but would not feel able to enter the ground if an All-White team called South Africa was playing. Instead, they would be on the street outside, protesting."

Geoffrey Howard's first instincts were to ensure that the game of cricket went on, that it ran smoothly and fostered good relations. The previous summer there had been demonstrations when Wilfred Isaacs' XI, a South African side, had played at The Oval. "A group of protestors ran onto the pitch and stopped the game. After they'd gone, we discovered that they'd left all these little stones everywhere. I remember getting quite a round of applause from the members after I'd picked them all up."

Surrey had already purchased rolls of barbed wire – but, confronted with these sixth-formers, the secretary remembered again the trauma of his trip to Cape Town, the unyielding tone of that telephone call from Pretoria, even perhaps his grandfather's concern to improve the world for all its people.

"Geoffrey told me afterwards," David Sheppard says, "that the meeting changed his position about the tour."

The Metropolitan Commissioner of Police added further pressure: "I wonder if you've considered two things, Mr Howard," he said. "How much it will cost to police and how long you think it will last. My own estimate is that the tour could not possibly continue for more than two or three weeks."

Geoffrey attended a private meeting at the house of David Sheppard, where he was joined by actor Peter Howell, whose brother had played for Surrey as an amateur in the 1920s, and Jim Swanton. "We were discussing what we could do about the situation," he says, "but I can't recall anything we decided." However, he does remember Jim Swanton at a lunch at The Oval.

"Peter Lindsay-Renton was there. He lived in South Africa and was very pro-apartheid. 'I do congratulate you,' he said to Jim, 'on the stance your paper has taken on this tour.' And Jim replied, 'I hope you don't associate me with the politics of the paper I write for.' There was a good deal of the liberal in Jim, though you might not think it. He was a very Christian chap."

The pressures grew on the Cricket Council. According to *Wisden*, those opposed to the tour included the Archbishop of Canterbury, the Chief Rabbi, the Sports Council, even the Queen herself. Countries were threatening to boycott the Commonwealth Games in Edinburgh, and the International Olympic Committee, angered by the rejection not only of Basil d'Oliveira but also of the American tennis player Arthur Ashe, expelled South Africa.

On May the 18th the Cricket Council met at Lord's for a long and difficult discussion, but *'by a substantial majority'* it decided to honour its invitation to the South Africans.

*'It has always believed that cricket in South Africa should be given the longest possible time to bring about conditions in which all cricketers in their own country, regardless of their origin, are able to play and be selected on equal terms.'*

Three days later the Home Secretary James Callaghan invited the Council's officers to a three-hour meeting, at which he requested that the tour be cancelled *'on the grounds of broad public policy.'*

They acceded. In place of the South Africans they raised a Rest of the World eleven to play the five Tests, but the bitterness lingered in the world of cricket. There were some at The Oval who attributed their secretary's position to the influence of his family. "Hallo, Nora," one member greeted his wife. "How are your friends in the Red Brigades?"

"I don't think we were gauging public opinion adequately," Geoffrey says now. "It would have been a fine series. South Africa had some very entertaining cricketers. But there was such a strong anti-apartheid movement by then; it wasn't really anything to do with cricket anymore. I think that, if the tour had gone ahead, it would have done the game a great disservice."

But did the cancellation have any effect? "Oh yes. I think it was a great shock to the South African government. I don't think that they realised till then the strength of anti-apartheid feeling worldwide."

In mid-June the British general election returned to power a Conservative government, but the controversies over the South African tour had clearly left Geoffrey more irritated with the prevailing politics of cricket than he had previously been.

"The committee was drawing up the guest list for the Oval Test, and somebody said, 'What about the new Prime Minister?' And everybody said, 'Oh, yes, Ted Heath, we must invite him.' Well, they'd never invited Harold Wilson, and he was much more interested in cricket. I was so angry that I went back to my office and wrote Harold Wilson a letter, inviting him as my personal guest."

"And did he come?" I ask as we sit around the table in the Surrey Committee Room.

Geoffrey is between Micky Stewart and Bernie Coleman, three past presidents looking back on their long involvements with the club.

"No. He wrote me a nice letter back, thanking me. I wonder what would have happened if he had come. I don't suppose I'd be sitting here now."

The current president, John Major, smiles benignly from his portrait on the wall.

*

In February 1974, Geoffrey Howard reached retirement age, but his successor, Warren Sillitoe, was an army officer completing a tour of duty in Northern Ireland and unable to start till the autumn. So Geoffrey completed one last summer, and in late August The Oval entertained the Pakistanis, whom he had seen develop over the years into a formidable Test-playing country. The young Zaheer Abbas made a brilliant 240, and Jim Swanton included in his match report a paragraph, 'HOWARD'S LAST TEST'.

His ten summers back at The Oval had been crisis years for English cricket, but Surrey County Cricket Club had got through them – and soon there would be fresh sources of income.

"Geoffrey's whole experience is possibly irrelevant to the game today," Derek Newton says. "The problem now is how to manage the money coming in from television. In Geoffrey's day it was, How do we survive?"

"Rupert Murdoch runs my life," Micky Stewart adds.

"I was talking to the chief executive a couple of years ago," Geoffrey says. "He said to me, 'I see my job as to keep expenditure within seven million pounds.' Well, I tried to do that with one hundred thousand.

"It's all money now, isn't it? What they charge members for lunch and tea during the Test match, I could feed myself for a fortnight on that."

# CHAPTER THIRTEEN

# BUSIER THAN EVER

# RETIREMENT

# 1974 –

The retirement greetings offered plenty of advice: 'Don't get too fond of your armchair', 'Avoid mid-day pub sessions' and the one Geoffrey remembers best, from his daughter Joy, 'Keep in the mainstream of life'.

Soon the comments were coming from the other direction. "I remember Nora saying to me, 'You haven't forgotten you've retired, have you?'

He had been a cricket administrator for 27 years and, as we complete this book, he has been retired for another 27. "And I've worked as hard as I did when I was in cricket. I've never stopped working. In the opinion of my family, I never will."

The house near The Oval was tied to his post as secretary so he and Nora prepared for retirement by renovating a derelict farmer's house in the Cotswolds, to which they moved in September 1974. "I was determined to keep out of the way of my successor. I didn't want to be like Rupert Howard at Old Trafford."

He restored a canal boat up in Tewkesbury, registered for an Open University degree and started to experiment with gliding. He and Nora took a party of Surrey members to watch England in Australia, and he returned to India for the Calcutta Cricket Club's Golden Jubilee. At the same time he planned the writing of several books: a biography of Len Hutton, a history of professionalism in English cricket and, for his family, the story of his own life.

The canal boat restoration took many happy hours, but some of the other projects were shelved when he found himself converting the adjoining cow barn into a small house.

Initially he had only bought it – for £150 – because he did not want its demolition to leave his house and garden exposed to general view. He had thought only of making it watertight and using it as a workshop. But his chequered working life had left him with an inadequate pension, and he set to turning the barn into a holiday cottage to let.

It took five years – years of hard physical labour with occasional help from three local workers – but, just after the letting agency had surveyed it, Nora had a stroke, and they decided to give up the larger house and see out their days in the newly converted barn.

"She recovered wonderfully, though she never really walked properly again. Within a fortnight she was sitting up in bed, embroidering. I've still got two pyjama jackets where she sewed my initials on the pockets. The first one is very shaky, but the next is perfect."

By this time, Geoffrey was back in the world of cricket – as Honorary Treasurer of the Minor Counties Cricket Association.

"I was travelling back from my last ever meeting at Lord's, in 1975, with Reggie Forrester, the Minor Counties chairman, and I was just making conversation. 'Who is your treasurer?' I asked him, and he said, 'We haven't got one. Would you like to do it?'"

For eight years, unpaid, he held the office – and not just as a time-server but, as in his previous posts, wanting to take things forward. "There were nineteen counties," he recalls, "each of them parochial and reluctant to move with the times." With a little persuasion, the changes came: the championship was divided into two regional sections to create a proper all-play-all contest, a knockout competition was introduced, and commercial sponsors were found for both.

In 1977 the Minor Counties side beat the touring Australians in a two-day match at Sunderland and, amid the euphoria, Geoffrey proposed that they built on the success with an overseas tour that winter. Using contacts he had established on holiday, he persuaded the counties – "in some cases reluctantly" – to put up £200 each for a representative side to visit Kenya for three weeks.

The captain was Cheshire's David Bailey, who had played for Lancashire in the late 1960s. The vice-captain was Devon's Doug Yeabsley, "a very fine bowler. Several first-class counties were interested in him, but he was dedicated to schoolmastering." North and south rarely met on the Minor County circuit, but Doug remembers how Geoffrey created a great team spirit among the party. "He was a wonderful organiser, and he was so respected everywhere we went. It all ran like clockwork."

Geoffrey was nearing seventy, but his enthusiasm was undimmed. "It helped build our confidence as Minor County cricketers," Doug recalls, "but we were also helping to develop the cricket out there. I know we took a lot of equipment out for the Africans."

He managed two more tours there, the final one in 1986. By this time Geoffrey was 77, but he was clearly in better shape than the 69-year-old Len Hutton.

"Donald Carr approached me at Lord's," Geoffrey recalls. "He asked if I could arrange for Len to come out with us. 'He's feeling the cold and would like some time in the sun.' I got the East Africans to pay all his expenses and to provide free accommodation for Dorothy and, in return, Len was going to coach, talk and umpire.

"In the event, it wasn't what Len thought it was going to be. We arrived at Nairobi, altitude 5000 feet, and of course it does hit you when you get out of the pressurised aircraft and you haven't got any breath. I remember, I had to carry his bags for him.

"He was different the next day when he went down to see the boys practising. He was amazed how good they were. I think he thought that, because they were Minor Counties cricketers, they wouldn't be able to play. But I'm afraid he lost interest. He didn't stay till the end."

Geoffrey's years as Treasurer were over and, when a projected tour of Bangladesh fell through, it seemed that he had finally retired from cricket. He was nearing eighty, and he looked forward to some quiet years with Nora and another go at his autobiography.

It was not to be. The Surrey chairman, Derek Newton, arrived one day and, over dinner, asked him if he would become the next president of the club. "It was one of the most delightful moments of my life," Derek says. "I shall never forget the beam on his face. 'I can't do that,' he said. 'I've only been the secretary.'"

He succeeded Sir Michael Sandberg, chairman of the Hong Kong and Shanghai Bank, and he still recalls his first meeting as president. "I was very nervous. I was so out of date. Nora and I had been living in each other's pockets. I didn't even speak the language of 1989: 'top lines' and 'bottom lines', 'pro-active' and 're-active'. I was very, very shaky, and at the end of the meeting I heard somebody saying, 'It doesn't look to me as if the new president is going to get through the year.'"

Derek has a different view. "He was an admirable president, so conscientious it wasn't true."

Back home, his daughter Rosalind bought him a flight in a hot air balloon for his eightieth birthday. Born in the year Blériot crossed the Channel, he had trained as a pilot's navigator in World War Two and several times had flown the plane on his tour of India. He had taken lessons in gliding after retirement, now he could enjoy the countryside to the south of Bristol from the comfort of a basket.

"We probably shouldn't have gone up. The wind was quite strong, and we were flying rather close to the flight path of Bristol Airport. I said to the chap, 'Are you looking for somewhere to land?' And he said, 'I'm always looking for somewhere to land.' 'Where are you making for then?' 'I'm making for that field over there.' And I watched as the field went away in the other direction.

"We finished up with the balloon hanging off some telegraph wires and us in the basket in a ditch. It was a rough old landing. My last balloon flight."

*

The years passed.

In 1995 Nora died, after sixty years of marriage.

Six years later, there are still times when he struggles with his feelings of loss, as I discovered one morning when he greeted me with a quotation from Tennyson.

*O for the touch of a vanished hand*
*And the sound of a voice that is still.*

But he stays busy – in the house and the garden and attending public functions. In 1998 he flew with a cousin to Cornell University, for a symposium to mark the centenary of his grandfather's book.

In 1999 Surrey celebrated his ninetieth birthday with a lunch, at which he wore the same yellow shirt he had shown the committee in the early 1970s.

Then at the start of 2001 we began work on this book. There were several batches of manuscript in a file marked Autobiography. There was the transcript of four meetings with Peter West. But we decided to start again.

"The clock is ticking," he said. "We need to get a move on."

Every Tuesday morning I drove from Bath, travelled past the farmfields that surround the A46 and turned left in Nailsworth, threading my way up a succession of ever-narrower lanes till I reached his barn. "Come in, Stephen," he would say. "The kettle's on." And we would sit on opposite sides of his table, a tape recorder between our two cups of coffee.

He told me of the sudden move to Letchworth and to boarding school after his mother died. "Father was so upset, he couldn't face the task of telling us – so it fell to Grandfather."

There were the years of Private Banks cricket. "Nobody ever told me that the most important thing in batting is staying in. When your game of cricket is once a week, starting at two o'clock and finishing at eight, you don't want to play maiden overs."

The century for Number 2 Balloon Centre at Lord's. "I think the main feeling I had was that I shouldn't have been playing, not with a war on."

The decision to leave Martins Bank. "It would have been so different, had I not joined the Air Force in 1939. By the time I was halfway through the war, I began to think that I wouldn't go on banking all my life."

The chance appointment as Surrey's assistant secretary. "I've always been interested in people, and cricket has given me such a wonderful outlet for that interest."

The weeks have passed, and the people of this book have come alive for me through his memories.

Brian Castor in his swivel chair at The Oval. Idris Begh, full of his own importance. Tommy Higson talking his way into the F.A. Cup Final. And Len Hutton, struggling with the responsibility of the M.C.C. captaincy.

The voices have become a part of my life.

"Did you give Hammond these tickets? Well, you shouldn't have done. I've taken them away." … "Well, good luck, old boy. Rather you than me." … "You must understand, Mr Howard, that a lot of the crowd come to watch me umpire." … "If today's centurion is picked, the tour will be off." … "Nobody knows me better than you, Geoffrey." … "Mr Howard, he is my father. I must speak to him."

Cricket was like a second family to him.

*

I arrived one morning to find him singing *'Green Grow The Rushes O'*.

"We were on the coach in New Zealand. We were off to see the hot springs at Rotorua, and we sat and sang it all the way through – with some gusto. Bill Edrich, Keith Andrew, Frank Tyson and me. Led by Frank Tyson, I think. I wonder if anybody still sings it like that."

*Three, three the rivals*
*Two, two the lilywhite boys, clothèd all in green ho ho*
*One is one and all alone*
*And ever more shall be so.*

"I've been through it right up to twelve, but I can't remember eight and nine."

Each week we have journeyed backwards, but the world still moves on. Cricket has money now that it never dreamt of when Geoffrey was a county secretary, and Old Trafford and The Oval have developed far beyond the improvements he struggled to make.

India, Pakistan and Sri Lanka are now in the front rank of Test-playing countries, with luxury hotels and large cricket stadiums. The England tour managers take out assistants to help with finance, travel, press relations, injuries, coaching and more.

Yet, for all the improvement, there nags in him a disappointment that the spirit in which games used to be played has not been preserved.

"It isn't dignified to throw yourself on the floor when you've just beaten your opponent in a final at Wimbledon, is it? The manners have changed, and bad manners are accepted.

"I said to Jack Simmons at Old Trafford, 'If I were in your position, I would say to the players that, when a wicket falls, they should stay in their positions in the field, not rush up and hug each other.' 'Oh,' he said, 'I couldn't possibly do that.' Well, why couldn't he? He's their employer, isn't he?"

Then, on the day after the Old Trafford Test, his copy of *The Times* was covered with photographs of Pakistani bowlers over-stepping the popping crease on deliveries that had claimed England wickets. "I would make it a condition of television broadcasts that they did not show replays questioning the umpire's decision. It's not very sporting to publish all this when you've just lost a game, is it?

"The worst development in my opinion is the decline in influence of the Marylebone Cricket Club. Its importance is not accepted in this country as it once was."

*

"Looking back, perhaps I've been overactive. I'm at the stage when I've started to enjoy sitting and philosophising. I wish I had had that tendency earlier."

Chapter by chapter the book has emerged, and on my travels I have not met anybody in the world of cricket who does not have the highest regard for him.

A lovely man ... The best tour manager I had ... He commanded such respect ... So unfussed ... You could always go to him if you had a problem ... Always so straight ... The best administrator in the history of the game.

"I can't recognise myself," he says. "Do people really think of me in that way?"

I pause for a while before asking the question that I hope will give me an ending for this book.

"And if you look back on it at all, Geoffrey, what are you most proud of?"

He sits in his armchair, in the house that he made from a cow barn.

The manuscript of this book sits on the table between us. The product of eight months of hard remembering. It is another achievement in a long and happy life.

"Most proud of?" he repeats, blowing gently through his lips. "Wife and family, really. The rest was just a means of looking after them."

*

I ring him when I reach home.

"It's nine for the nine bright shiners, eight for the April rainers."

"Ah yes, the April rainers." There is a comfort in recovering the detail. "I've just been going over the names of all the staff at Old Trafford. Harry Dyderski, Alf Wilkinson, Edna Bownass, Bill Berry and Tom Mound." His list goes on. "They're as real today as they were then. What could I have done without them? Nothing. It was a real privilege to have worked with them."

*

It was his turn to ring me the next morning.

"I slept like a log when I got into bed last night. Then I woke up, and I started thinking about that question you asked me. What was I most proud of? And I tried to think which people in the book would have given the same answer as I did. Jack Hobbs, Ebenezer Howard, Leonard Hutton, Peter May, Rupert Howard, Brian Close, Alf Gover, Brian Statham. All eminent men, they would all have said what I did."

*

One day, when the book was still in its infancy, we went into his back room in search of photographs. He pulled out the album of his India tour and some snaps of his family when they were young. Then he found a box in the corner, pulled it out and opened it.

There were the letters he had written home every day from his three tours. All carefully folded in chronological order and preserved in this long unopened box.

Here were his innermost thoughts, shared with his family at the time. The uncertainties and frustrations, the excitements and triumphs, the daily routine and the homesickness.

"Fancy Nora keeping them all those years."

I stood quietly by as the feelings welled up inside him.

"What would I have done without Nora?"

## ACKNOWLEDGEMENTS

I wrote this book as a result of many visits to Geoffrey Howard, and I would like to express my thanks to him for making me so welcome each time. I would also like to thank both him and his daughter Frances for all the sustenance they provided on these visits.

Geoffrey and I made four visits to meet people, and I would like to thank each of them for entertaining us and giving us so much of their time: Donald and Stella Carr, Rose FitzGibbon and Sheila Delve, John Woodcock, and Derek Newton, Bernie Coleman and Micky Stewart.

I would especially like to thank Scyld Berry, both for recommending the idea of the book to me and for encouraging me at every stage, and Derek Newton, Bernie Coleman and Raman Subba Row, whose support has been invaluable.

I have made use of the transcript of four conversations between Peter West and Geoffrey Howard, the fourth of which also includes Tom Graveney, and I would like to thank both Peter and Tom for setting down so much valuable material. I would also like to thank Doug Yeabsley, for discussing with me the first Minor Counties tour of Kenya, and the Rt Rev Lord Sheppard of Liverpool for showing me an extract from his forthcoming memoirs.

I visited Old Trafford, where I would like to thank the Reverend Malcolm Lorimer for providing me with access to the old minute books, and the Surrey History Centre in Woking, which houses that county's records.

I would like to thank David Smith of Corsham, Humphrey Keenlyside of London and Peter Rear of Lichfield for their meticulous and perceptive readings of the manuscript.

I have made regular use of the following reference books:

*Wisden Cricketers' Almanack*
Bailey, Thorn & Wynne-Thomas, *Who's Who of Cricketers* (Newnes Books, 1984)
Robert Brooke, *A History of the County Cricket Championship* (Guinness, 1991)
Jim Ledbetter & Peter Wynne-Thomas, *First-Class Cricket, 1931-39* (Limlow Books, 9 volumes, 1991-9)
Swanton, Plumptre & Woodcock, *Barclays World of Cricket* (Collins, 1986)

I have also read and occasionally quoted from the following books:

Trevor Bailey, *Wickets, Catches and the Odd Run* (Collins Willow, 1986)
Scyld Berry, *Cricket Odyssey* (Pavilion, 1988)
Mihir Bose, *A History of Indian Cricket* (Andre Deutsch, 1990)
Brian Close, *I Don't Bruise Easily* (Macdonald & Jane's, 1978)
Denis Compton, *The End of an Innings* (Oldbourne Book Co Ltd, 1958)
Colin Cowdrey, *M.C.C. – The Autobiography of a Cricketer* (Hodder & Stoughton, 1976)

A.E.R. Gilligan, *The Urn Returns* (Andre Deutsch, 1955)
Alfred Gover, *The Long Run* (Pelham Books, 1991)
Tom Graveney, *Cricket Through The Covers* (Frederick Muller, 1958)
Gerald Howat, *Len Hutton* (Heinemann Kingswood, 1988)
Len Hutton, *Fifty Years In Cricket* (Stanley Paul, 1984)
Len Hutton, *Just My Story* (Hutchinson, 1956)
Sir Henry Leveson Gower, *Off and On the Field* (Stanley Paul, 1953)
Tony Lock, *For Surrey And England* (Hodder and Stoughton, 1957)
Michael Marshall, *Gentlemen and Players* (Grafton Books, 1987)
Peter May, *A Game Enjoyed* (Stanley Paul, 1985)
Patrick Murphy, *The Centurions* (J.M. Dent & Sons, 1983)
John Oslow et al, *Garden Cities and New Towns (Hertfordshire, 1990)*
Jim Parks, *Runs in the Sun* (Stanley Paul, 1961)
Ian Peebles, *The Ashes 1954-1955* (Hodder & Stoughton, 1955)
Pat Pocock, *Percy* (Clifford Frost Publications, 1987)
Alan Ross, *Australia 55* (Michael Joseph, 1955)
Henry Sayen, *A Yankee Looks At Cricket* (Putnam, 1956)
Brian Statham, *A Spell At The Top* (Souvenir Press, 1969)
E.W. Swanton, *Victory in Australia* (The Daily Telegraph, 1955)
Fred Titmus, *Talk of the Double* (Stanley Paul, 1964)
Donald Trelford, *Len Hutton Remembered* (H.F. & G. Witherby, 1992)
Frank Tyson, *A Typhoon Called Tyson* (William Heinemann, 1961)
Cyril Washbrook, *Cricket - The Silver Lining* (Sportsguide Publications, 1950)
Johnny Wardle, *Happy Go Johnny* (Robert Hale, 1957)

also from the following newspapers:
The Times, Daily Telegraph, Manchester Guardian, News Chronicle, Daily Mirror and Daily Herald

from the following cricket magazines:
The Cricketer and Wisden Cricket Monthly

and from the year books of Surrey and Lancashire County Cricket Clubs.

As always, I would like to thank Sue and Martha Kendall for putting up with me while I wrote the book, especially Sue who made many helpful suggestions about the text as well as contributing some delightful illustrations.

I learnt much while writing the book and I had a great deal of fun. I hope that my writing has communicated this.

Stephen Chalke
Bath, October 2001

# INDEX

**Also available from Fairfield Books**

# FRAGMENTS OF IDOLATRY

## FROM 'CRUSOE' TO KID BERG

### by David Foot

Character studies of twelve sportsmen and writers whom the award-winning author has admired in his life: Raymond Robertson-Glasgow, Carwyn James, Patsy Hendren, Alan Gibson, Tom Cartwright, Reg Sinfield, Jack 'Kid' Berg, Maurice Tremlett, Walter Robins, Alec Stock, Alf Dipper, Horace Hazell.

*Sports writing on another plane.* **Ian Wooldridge**, Daily Mail

*Irresistible. He is the most felicitous of cricket's current authors.*
**Robin Marlar**, The Cricketer

*David Foot's first collection of portraits* Beyond Bat and Ball *is the best book about cricketers I have ever read. His new collection is a splendid successor.*
**Stephen Fay**, Wisden Cricket Monthly

# RUNS IN THE MEMORY -

## COUNTY CRICKET IN THE 1950s

### by Stephen Chalke

**with illustrations by Ken Taylor**

**and a foreword by Tom Cartwright**

Twelve county cricket matches brought back to life by the memories of the participants – including Arthur Milton, Harold Rhodes, Don Shepherd, Tom Cartwright, Martin Horton, Dickie Dodds, Dennis Brookes, Bryan Stott, Jim Parks, Malcolm Heath, John Pretlove, Terry Spencer, Ken Biddulph and Merv Winfield.

*Cameos of recall are two-a-penny, ten-a-page in this quite riveting book. Right up my street - any romantic's street, in fact. Unquestionably the book of the year.* **Frank Keating**, The Guardian

*Here is a fresh pen. Chalke extracts from the players of the 1950s pearls of reminiscence and frank thoughts on the present.*
**E.W. Swanton**, The Week, naming it as one of his six best cricket books